WRITING
BROADCAST NEWS

WRITING
BROADCAST NEWS—
Shorter, Sharper, Stronger

REVISED AND EXPANDED

Mervin Block

Bonus Books, Inc., Chicago

Library of Congress Cataloging-in-Publication Data

Block, Mervin.
 Writing broadcast news : shorter, sharper, stronger / Mervin Block. —
Rev. and expanded ed.
  p. cm.
 Includes bibliographical references and index.
 ISBN 1-56625-084-6 (alk. paper)
 1. Broadcast journalism—Authorship. 2. Broadcast journalism—Style
manuals. 3. Report writing. I. Title.
PN4784.B75B56 1997
808′.06607—dc21   97-6266

Bonus Books, Inc.
160 East Illinois Street
Chicago, IL 60611

01 00   5 4 3 2

Printed in the United States of America

To the memory of my parents

CONTENTS

Acknowledgment   ix

1 | Dozen Deadly Don'ts   1

2 | Venial Sins   19

3 | Top Tips of the Trade   32

4 | Lead-ins, Lead-outs, Voice-overs   51

5 | Style: Clarity begins at Home—and Office   59

6 | My Least Worst   72

7 | Your Turn   97

8 | Reams of Rules   128

9 | Who Says?   141

10 | Leading Questions (and other problems)   160

11 | Bad News   178

12 | A "Guilty Conviction" (and other offenses)   198

13 | The *Ing* Thing (and other wrong things)   221

14 | Noosepapers (and when they eat their words)   242

15 | After Math   259

16 | All Else   284

Appendix A: Further Reading and Reference   291
Appendix B: Grammar Hotline Directory   297
Index   305

ACKNOWLEDGMENT

My deepest thanks to my superb editor, Julia Hall. My original manuscript for this revision was much longer; she helped make it shorter, sharper, stronger. But if anything's wronger, blame me.

1

DOZEN DEADLY DON'TS

Any writer who knows a lot knows there's a lot to know. And every writer should know that what counts most is what you learn after you know it all.

As a working writer, you know that writing is work. But what you may not realize is that you do a lot of work before you write—as well as after. *Before* is when you grasp the ins and outs of writing. *After* is when you spot any flaws, see what you can improve, and figure out how to make your scripts more speakable, understandable and commendable. So our goal is to get all three steps—*before, after* and the crucial *during*—down cold.

The best way to approach your scripts is to apply the rules that govern broadcast newswriting. Some, you already know. Some, you don't know you don't know. And some, you may not like at all. Yet, just as rules govern broadcasting, rules also govern newswriting. So let's look at rules. Not that this is a rule book. No, it's a professional writer's handbook, a guide to making scripts shorter, sharper, stronger.

You may think rules are for use when brains run out. Or that rules are made only by rulers. But I'm going to rule out any *ukase, diktat* or *fiat*—no European imports. And no *bull*. I'm going to call these rules *tips*—even though my mental computer has programmed them as rules. They weren't handed down to me at Mount Sinai; I've never even been in that hospital. But I absorbed these rules while writing in network newsrooms and refined them while teaching in college classrooms.

Whether you call them tips or rules, put them to work. They do work. And as the ads for kitchen gadgets claim, they're simple, reliable and fully tested. No matter how experienced you are, if you apply these rules, you are bound to write better.

When I began to write broadcast news, I had mastered three basic rules: 1) write on only one side of the paper, 2) don't write more than one story on a page and 3) keep the keys clean. But over the years, I've digested some other valuable rules while working for old pros in broadcast newsrooms; I've recalled some rules from classes in broadcast newswriting; and I've devised some rules from insights gained through writing day after day after day. Also, I've assimilated rules laid down by various writing experts, especially Strunk and White—and *they* call them rules. And I've learned a lot from my mistakes. As you probably know, mistakes can be our best teachers. So the sooner we make our first thousand mistakes, the sooner we can correct them.

Often, the right thing to do is not to do the wrong thing. The Ten Commandments tell us mostly what *not* to do. According to the Talmud, the Old Testament sets forth 365 negative commandments and 248 positive commandments. Not that I want to turn a script into Scripture. But if the Good Book sees the positive purpose of the negative, so should we.

In a burst of originality, I've labeled the most important no-no's the Dozen Deadly Don'ts. Then I discuss the Venial Sins. Next, pivoting from Don'ts to Do's, I've listed what I call the Top Tips of the Trade.

You already know some of these how-to techniques. But though we're taught once, we must be reminded many times. These reminders and tips—or rules—are omnidirectional: They cover radio and television, AM and FM, a.m. and p.m. And they apply to all kinds of scripts: from 20-second stories to two-hour specials, from anchors' "readers" to reporters' "wraps."

A writer who understands the Don'ts can see why they may be even more important than the Do's. Walter Cronkite was so impressed by the ability of Maine lobstermen to find their way through thick fog, he once asked a laconic local, "How do you know where the rocks are?" "Don't," the man replied. "I know where they ain't."

Just as a jazz musician performs his magic by knowing which notes not to play, the careful writer knows what *not* to write.

Here are the Dozen Deadly Don'ts—not necessarily in order of sinfulness. Remember: Our scripts will suffer from—if not die for—our sins. So don't commit any of them:

1. Don't scare listeners. And don't scare them away. A prime—but not prime-time—example is this first sentence of a broadcast script:

This is a very complicated and confusing financial story.

Why start with a turn-off? No matter how complex or confusing the story, our job is to simplify and clarify, not scarify. We're often faced with stories that seem impenetrable. But we need to get a grip on ourselves—and on our notes or source copy—and plow ahead. And not tell our listeners that we're baffled or buffaloed (even if we are). "The world doesn't want to hear about labor pains," the pitcher Johnny Sain said. "It only wants to see the baby."

That scare was probably not intentional; we certainly don't want one that is:

How does the thought of 10 percent ground bones and other meat remnants in hot dogs, sausage or bologna sound to you?

I'd tell the weenie who wrote that, "Don't try to upset me or my stomach. And please don't question me."

Many scripts are scary for another reason: They've been put on the air apparently untouched by human hand—or mind.

2. Don't give orders. Don't tell listeners to do this or do that. Don't tell them to listen, or watch, or stay, or fetch. Just give them the news.

3. Don't bury a strong verb in a noun. Instead of writing a lead about a "bomb *explosion*" write: "A bomb *exploded*." Nouns are the bones that give a sentence body. But verbs are the muscles that make it go. If your first sentence lacks a vigorous verb, your script will lack go-power.

4. Don't start a story with *as expected*. When I hear an anchor say *as expected* at the top, it's usually a story I had *not* expected. Hadn't even *sus*pected. Most listeners tune in to hear the *un*expected. Even seers have no idea of what to expect. *As expected?* By whom? Not by your average listener. When listeners hear a story begin with *as expected* and the story turns out to be something they did *not* expect, they probably feel they don't know what's going on.

Often, when newswriters start with *as expected,* they do so because *they* have been expecting a development. Or their producer has told them to keep an eye peeled for the story a news agency says will be moving shortly. So they've been scanning the wires. And after hours of expectation, the story finally arrives. Without thinking, without considering their listeners—listeners who aren't newshawks, listeners whose reading is limited to the program listings—the writers rush to type the words that have been on *their* mind. And, as expected, they start with that deflating phrase *as expected,* which takes the edge off any story.

Even more of a turn-off than *as expected* is a negative version that I've heard with my own ears—no one else's. It went something like this: "*Not unexpectedly,* Senator Blather said today he's going to run for re-election." Another variation: "The *long-awaited* appointment of Judge Michael Mutton to the State Supreme Court was made today by Governor Grosvenor." It certainly wasn't *long-awaited* by listeners. Probably only by Mutton. (And his Li'l Lamb Chop.)

4a. Don't start a story with *In a surprise move.* A network also broadcast this lead (all scripts that were broadcast are boldface):

In a surprise move, the Interstate Commerce Commission rejected the proposal to merge the Santa Fe and Southern Pacific railroads.

I had long forgotten about the proposal. The ICC had been considering it for two and a half years, so how could I be surprised about the decision when I wasn't aware it was pending? For whom was the rejection a surprise? People in the transportation industry, perhaps. But for the rest of us, news is full of surprises.

4b. Don't start a story by saying, *A new development tonight in the....* Every item in a newscast is supposed to be fairly new, based on something newly developed. Some writers try to go beyond that wasteful opening with "A *major* new development tonight...." What's to be gained by telling people, "I've got news for you"? Friends may say that on the phone, but professionals don't proclaim it on the air.

And don't start a newscast by saying, "We begin with...." As soon as you open your mouth, listeners know you've begun. Equally useless: "Our top story tonight is...." If it's the first story, it should be the top story. Top stories run at the top. So skip that needless opener and go straight to the news. And don't write, "Topping our news tonight...." Sounds like Reddi-wip.

4c. Don't start a story by saying someone *is news, is in the news, is making news, or is dominating the news.* Without ado or adornment, go ahead and tell the news. That's what a newscast is for. That's why they call it a newscast. Everyone who's mentioned in a newscast is "making" news. So when writers say someone "is making news" or "making headlines," they're wasting time, time better spent reporting news.

Another waste of time is the lead that says someone "made history today." Or "entered history books today." Only historians will decide what was historic. And it won't be today.

Equally pointless is this lead: "They're rewriting the record books today in. . . ." That script is what needs rewriting. Just tell the news. And if someone has broken a record worth reporting, say so—simply.

5. Don't characterize news as *good, bad, interesting* or *shocking*. Just report the news. Let the listener decide whether it's good, bad, interesting or shocking. What's good for some is bad for others. What seems, at first glance, to be good, can turn out to be bad. What's good for a city-dweller may be bad for a farmer. What's good for Luke Skywalker may be bad for Lucy Streetwalker. Good news for Wall Street may be bad news for Main Street. A steep fall in oil prices seems like good news. But in many places in this country, it turns out to be bad news. So the best course is: just tell the news.

Also undesirable for newswriters is the good news–bad news combo: "Governor Gibson had good news and bad news today. He said he's going to push for a tax cut—but not this year." What's objectionable is that the phrase "good news and bad news" is worn out—like old news.

But it's not wrong to use the "good news" approach when the news is indisputably good for a *specific* group or person: "The I-R-S had good news today for taxpayers." Or "Governor Boodle received good news and bad news today. His good news: He was put on probation. His bad news: He has to make restitution." Otherwise, the time-consuming, subjective "good news" label is bad news. And please don't call a story "unusual." We don't report the usual, do we? Not usually.

5a. Don't start with a participial phrase or a dependent clause. It's not the way we talk. It's not the way anyone talks. And it's not the way to help listeners latch onto a story.

Would you say to a friend, "Needing new shoes, I'm going downtown tomorrow to buy a pair"? No. You'd say, "I need new shoes, so tomorrow I'm going downtown to buy some." Yet, some newscasters do use the type of participial phrase we see in the first sentence of that paragraph.

A lead that backs into a story with a participle is weak and murky. It requires too much of listeners. The participial phrase with secondary information that listeners hear at the start means nothing—not till they hear the next cluster of words and discover what the subject of the sentence is. Then they have to rearrange the word clusters to make sense of what they just heard. How many listeners have the time, energy and aptitude to do that while the wordathon rolls on and on?

Try making sense of this lead, reprinted just as written for a local broadcast:

Saying their project could never be compatible with the river which bears its name, the Regional Planning Council denied approval of the massive 1800-acre Wekiva Falls Complex in North Orange and Lake County.

If you were listening to that, could you tell what the subject of the sentence is—or is going to be? After such a clumsy approach, would you care?

Once you've established the subject in the first sentence, it's all right to start your second sentence with a participial phrase. But when you do start with a participial phrase or dependent clause, the subject should be the same as in the previous sentence. Otherwise, you're creating the same sort of puzzle for listeners.

Also, if you put a subordinate clause *after* the subject, you're separating the subject from the verb. So try to avoid subordinate clauses that separate subject and verb. The greater the distance between subject and verb, the greater the difficulty for the listener. Listeners hear only one word at a time. By the time they hear the verb, they have to rewind mentally and figure out who's doing what. While listeners are puzzling over it, they can lose their train of thought. And if they do lose it, they probably won't be able to get back on board.

To make the subject of the story clear and unmistakable, the best pattern for writing your first sentence is subject-verb-object: Start with the subject, go directly to the verb, and follow with the object. The closer the verb follows the subject, the easier for the listener to follow. So go with S-V-O.

When you go with S-V-O, listeners pick up the subject right away. They don't have to exert themselves to grasp the thread, and they can hang on to it. Listeners aren't supposed to do the work; you are. Listeners have only one chance. One. They can't read your script. They can't ask what you meant. They can't set a story aside and go over it at their leisure. But they *can* turn to another newscast. So as you write, think of your listeners. If you write for *them,* they'll stay with *you.*

5b. Don't start a story with a quotation. Listeners can't see quotation marks. And they can't examine your script. So when an anchor starts with a quotation, listeners assume the words are the anchor's own. It's especially confusing for listeners when the anchor opens with an assertion that's bold, startling or open to question—and then gets around to telling who first spoke those words.

Likewise, if a story needs attribution, the way to proceed—the *broadcast* way—is to put the source, or attribution, first. Remember: Attribution precedes assertion.

When we talk to each other, we automatically put attribution first. We don't stop to think about it. Our conversations follow the S-V-O pattern naturally and spontaneously: "Jim told me, 'Blah, blah.' And Jane replied, 'Hah, hah.'" Is any other word order suitable? Nah, nah.

In the unlikely event your news director rebukes you, you might complain to a friend, "The Boss told me today I have to learn how to park my bike straight." Without thinking twice, you'd put the attribution first. You sure wouldn't blurt out: "'You have to learn how to park your bike straight.' That's what the Boss told me today." Yet, we hear anchors start a story with a quotation—or an indirect quotation or a stunning statement—that sounds as if they're expressing their own views:

"Mayor Filch needs to be taught a lesson. That's the opinion of a retired janitor, Boris Bravo. He told a City Council meeting today. . . ."

A listener could easily take that first sentence as the start of an editorial. But if the anchor provides attribution before assertion, listeners can consider the source: "A critic of Mayor Filch says he ought to be taught a lesson. The critic, Boris Bravo, is a retired janitor. He told a City Council meeting. . . ."

Here's another type of hard-hitting lead we often hear with no preceding attribution:

"Anyone who chews five sticks of gum a day can ensure healthy gums and teeth. That's the finding of a study done by researchers in Asunción, Paraguay, and it shows that. . . ."

All it shows is that some newspeople should work harder at understanding how people speak. And how they listen. (See pp. 141-145.)

5c. Don't start a story with a question. Why not? Opening questions tend to sound like quiz shows or commercials. Questions can be hard to deliver, draw an answer you don't want, and trivialize the news. Also, questions delay delivery of the news. And listeners are looking for answers, not questions.

6. Don't start a story with *There is, There are* or *It is.* They're dead phrases—wordy and wasteful. The power of a sentence lies largely in a muscular verb. A sentence gets its get-up-and-go from an action verb like "smash" or "shoot" or "kill"—or hundreds of other verbs that express action.

Although *is* and *are* are in the active voice, they aren't *action* verbs. And they don't convey action. They—and other forms of *to be*—are *linking* verbs. They link the subject of a sentence with a complement—another noun or adjective, a word that identifies or describes the subject. Other linking verbs include *have, seem, feel* and *become.* Not one of them has the power to drive a sentence. They only keep it idling. So when you start a sentence with *there is,* you're just marking time until you introduce the verb that counts.

A network evening newscast:

> **There is a major power failure in the West affecting perhaps as many as 17 states. Utility company officials say a power grid that delivers electricity from the Pacific Northwest went down today. The cause of the blackout is not yet known, but it happened on a day when power resources were being stretched by record hot temperatures, including 102 degrees in Salt Lake City.**

The *weather* was hot, not the temperatures. So the script should read "record *high* temperatures."

Now let's make that lead read right: "A power failure has blacked out a large part of the West."

Another *there* lead, this on local television, needs corrective surgery:

> **There's a train rolling through town tonight. But this is one you definitely won't mind missing.**

By deleting *there's,* we make the sentence shorter. And by making it shorter, we make it stronger. The story is about a train, not about *there.* After we lop off *there's,* let's write it right: "A train is rolling through town tonight. . . ." There are instances, though—as in this sentence—when *there are* may be appropriate.

6a. Don't write a first sentence in which the main verb is any form of *to be,* like *is, are, was, were* and *will be.* It's not wrong, just weak. Sometimes it's acceptable, even desirable. But it's better to search for an action verb. An exception to avoiding *is* in a first sentence: when *is* serves as an auxiliary or helping verb, as in: "Mayor Glom *is going* to Guam." But *is,* alone, is usually a nerd word.

A sentence we often hear on the air:

"The President is back in the White House."

Factually and grammatically, the sentence passes muster, but it doesn't cut the mustard. The *is* lacks movement. It merely expresses a static condition, not action. The next sentence is better because it has an action verb indicating someone has *done* something: "The President has returned to the White House." Or "The President has arrived back at the White House."

Yet the use of *is* in a first sentence is all right when the sentence is short and the story big. For example: "The teachers' strike is over." Or "Mayor Smiley is dead." The second sentence gets its impact from *dead.* Which leads to another tip: certain one-syllable words that end with a hard consonant—like *dead* (or *drunk*)—gain extra impact when used to end a sentence. (No, I'm not suggesting you write *dead drunk.*)

Let's look at this sentence: "The death toll in the X-Y-Z crash has now risen to 149." That's a big number, but it's not presented in the most effective way. The sentence is all right, but the word "death" doesn't have the impact of "dead," particularly when "dead" is used as the last word. By the time the listener hears "149," he may not remember whether it refers to fatalities or casualties. "Casualties" includes dead *and* injured. So let's rewrite that: "The toll in the X-Y-Z crash has now risen to 149 dead." See the difference? *Hear* the difference?

One of the biggest weaknesses in broadcast news stories is the opening sentence. Too many limp—or just lie there. Every lead can't be a grabber, but what listeners hear first can be crucial as to whether they keep listening. So newswriters should choose action verbs.

This network script shows how *not* to do it:

> **There was another clash in Britain tonight between police and gangs of youths. The latest incident was in the northern London district of Tottenham, where hundreds of youths overturned cars, threw gasoline bombs and set fires. Several policemen were reported injured. The incident followed the unexplained death of a West Indian woman during a police search of her home.**

Let's see where that lead went wrong. The story had plenty of action that could have been reported with vigorous verbs. Instead, the writer began with the flabby *there was.* And then further weakened the sentence with *another.* When *another* is so high up, it often makes a story less newsy. After all, the main point of the story isn't that the two groups clashed *again.* The story is that they *clashed.* And if it weren't a sizeable clash, it probably wouldn't be worth reporting. The writer sapped the strength of a good verb, *clash,* by using it as a noun. Also, *youth* isn't a conversational word, not in school rooms, not in living rooms, not even in newsrooms.

One way to pep up the first sentence of that script: "Hundreds of young people in London *went* on a rampage tonight. They *set* fires, *overturned* cars and *threw* gasoline bombs." Which approach sounds stronger?

7. Don't start a story with the name of an unknown or unfamiliar person. Names make news, but only if they're recognized. An unknown name is a distraction. It can't be the reason you're telling the story; you're telling it because that person figures in something unusual. If the name means nothing to listeners, they're not likely to pay close attention and thus will miss the point of your story. The best way to introduce an unknown is with a title, or a label or a description: "A New York City milkman, Gordon Goldstein [who took that name because it's a blend of Guernsey and Holstein], was awarded five million dollars in damages today for. . . ."

Many stories don't need a name. Without a name, a story flows better and runs shorter. What does an unknown name in a distant city mean to you? Or your listeners? But, if you're writing about a runaway or a fugitive, the name may be essential.

What's in a name? It depends. Before using a name, ask yourself whether the story would be incomplete without it. Would a listener be likely to phone your newsroom and inquire, "What's the name of that Alaskan you just said was arrested in Hawaii for cavorting in a Chicken Man costume?" (And if the listener says "cavort," try to get *his* name.) It is standard, though, to start a story with the names of people who have titles, prominent people who are in the news constantly: President Whoever, Secretary of State Whatever, British Prime Minister Hardly-Ever. And omit their first names. The same style applies to mention of your mayor, police chief, coroner, governor and maybe a few other public officials.

We can also start a story with the name of someone who has star quality, a person whose name is widely known—in almost every nook and cranny, by almost every crook and nanny. But we use that person's first name *and* precede the name with a label: "The actress Emma Thompson," "the painter Pablo Picasso," "the author John Updike."

We don't use anyone's middle name—unless. Unless we're writing about someone who has long been identified with a middle name, like John Paul Jones. Or Martin Luther King, Andrew Lloyd Webber or Mary Tyler Moore.

Skip initials, too—unless the person you're writing about has long been identified with an initial: J. Edgar Hoover, Michael J. Fox, Edward R. Murrow. Another exception: an initial may be desirable if you are trying to avoid a mixup with a widely known person who has the same (or a similar) name.

Broadcast newswriters customarily omit "Junior" and "the Second" after someone's name—unless *not* using them could cause confusion with prominent sound-alikes. But there's no need to include someone's first name *and* a nickname. Go with one *or* the other. But *not* both together. It's not conversational. We don't have time, especially for those silly uses of first names with standard diminutives, like Thomas "Tom" O'Connor. Besides, have you ever heard of a Thomas called Sam?

When you do use names, try to use as few as possible so listeners can keep their eye (or ear) on the ball. Overuse of names—sometimes *any* use—leads to clutter. Don't diffuse the focus of a story; keep the listener's mind out of the clutter.

Also: don't start a story with the name of an unfamiliar organization. And watch out for organizations with ambiguous or misleading names. For example: the imaginary Good Government Group. Listeners can't see those capital letters. They may think those words are your description of a group of dedicated citizens working for good government. Across the country, newsrooms are bombarded with letters and news releases on imposing letterheads—some from phantom organizations. The Good Government Group may be only one man who bought stationery and rented a post office box—to undermine good government.

7a. Don't start a story with a personal pronoun. This script started with a personal pronoun, *he,* and kept *he-he*ing:

> **He walked out of a New York prison today looking a little slimmer and slightly grayer. But one thing has not changed. He's still followed everywhere he goes.**

Who *he?* I want to know from the get-go who or what a story is about. So when I hear a script start with *he,* I wonder whether I missed the first sentence, the one that identified the subject. (That script was broadcast in northern Ohio, so you could say listeners were clueless in Cleveland.) Withholding the identity of the subject stumps listeners. I don't like newscasters to play games with me. And I won't waste time with newscasts that don't present news in a clear, understandable manner. And I'm not alone.

A newspaper feature can start with *he* because a reader can spot who *he* is from a headline or a photo; but we don't open a conversation with a clueless pronoun. If we rely on the best pattern of all, subject-verb-object, we'll avoid premature pronouns.

That script is also flawed by its misuse of *prison.* The subject of that script had been locked up in *jail. Prison* and *jail* shouldn't be used interchangeably. *Prison* is where people convicted of major crimes—felonies like murder, rape, robbery and burglary—serve time. *Jail* is where people are held for trial, or do time after conviction for minor crimes—misdemeanors like petty larceny, disorderly conduct and malicious mischief. Also held in *jail* are people convicted of felonies who are awaiting transportation to *prison.*

One other point: the script says the prisoner walked out looking *slightly grayer.* The man alluded to, Joseph Buttafuoco, known to newswriters as Joey, had spent 77 days in jail. Is it likely that in less than three months he had turned *slightly grayer?* And that a reporter would notice? Or was "slightly grayer" the writer's artificial color?

8. Don't write a first sentence that uses *yesterday* or *continues.* Both words are bad news. Listeners tune in expecting to hear the latest news, the later the better. They want to hear news that has broken since they last heard or read the news. Imagine tuning in to an evening newscast and hearing an anchor start talking about something that happened *yesterday.* Yesterday? I thought yesterday was gone for good. Who cares about yesterday? I want to hear what happened today. *Yesterday* is still common in newspaper leads, but for broadcasting, it's too old, too dated, too rearview-mirrorish.

If you must lead with a story that broke yesterday, update it so you can use a *today.* Or use a present tense verb with no *yesterday* or *today.* Or if you find out, just before tonight's broadcast, that the mayor's wife was kidnapped last night, you can write around *last night* or *yesterday* by making use of the present perfect. The present perfect tense expresses an action carried out before the present and completed at the present, or an action begun in the past and continuing in the present: "Mayor Hudson's wife *has been* kidnapped." In a later sentence, you can slip in that dirty word *yesterday.*

But a script mustn't deceive listeners by substituting *today* for *yesterday,* and it mustn't try to pass off yesterday's news as today's. Use ingenuity in figuring out how to write a first sentence without harking back to yesterday. You don't need to be a historian to know that these days, yesterday is history.

A worse sin than using *yesterday* in a lead is using yesterday's news. Try, whenever you can, to give your story a forward thrust, not a backward glance. And steer clear of *continues* in an opening sentence. In a second or subsequent sentence, *continues* isn't objectionable. But it's meaningless to end a story with "the controversy continues." Or "the investigation continues."

The problem with *continues* is that it doesn't tell a listener anything new. Worse, it tells listeners that nothing's new. *Continues* doesn't drive a sentence or story. It merely says something that has been going on is still going on. It tells the listener this is going to be a story that's not news—just olds.

News is what's new. When you have to write about a long-running story—a siege, a drought, a hunger strike—search for a new peg. If you can't find a new peg, find a different angle of attack, move in from a different direction. Focus on whatever has occurred today or is going on today, something you can report for the first time, something that you didn't know about yesterday. Find a verb with verve, says Merv.

Another word to avoid: *details.* In my book, *details* is a dirty word. And this *is* my book. Certainly, writers should have an eye for detail. And know when and how to present a *telling* detail—yet not tell many details. And not call them *details.*

When I hear the word *details,* I think of the tiny print in a lease or a contract, the specs for a stereo component, or something else where I don't want to get bogged down with details. I assume that most listeners regard *details* with similar lack of interest. Yet anchors often introduce reporters this way: "Sally Golightly has the details." Better: "Sally Golightly has the story." Or a "Sally Golightly reports." Or "Sally Golightly reports that [provide a fact from her script]." Or say it some other way. Just don't bother me with *details.*

8a. Don't start a story with a sentence that has a *no* or *not.* At least, try not to. Rewrite your negative lead to make it positive. Instead of saying, "The President is not going to take his planned trip to Tahiti," you'll have a stronger opening by saying, "The President has canceled his trip to Tahiti." A basic rule of writing or speaking is: Put your sentences in a positive form. In *The Elements of Style,* Strunk and White say that, generally, it's better to express even a negative phrase in a positive way: "did not remember = forgot"; "did not pay any attention to = ignored."

Another argument for avoiding *not:* in some cases, a listener may confuse *not* with *now.* We shouldn't go overboard worrying about listeners' hearing problems, but it's the reason some broadcast newspeople write *"one* million" instead of *"a* million"—lest a listener mistake *a* for *eight.*

A similar concern leads many newsrooms to report that a defendant was found *innocent* rather than *not guilty;* they fear that some listeners might not catch the *not.* Or that the newscaster might inadvertently drop the *not.* But many writers (and I'm one) prefer writing *not guilty*— because it's clear and correct. Juries don't find people *innocent.* How could a jury find someone *innocent,* which means without sin?

8b. Don't start a story with *another, more* or *once again.* With few exceptions, those words are turn-offs. If we start a story with *another,* it sounds as if whatever the story turns out to be, it's bound to be similar to a story told previously, one that's not much different. Perhaps just more of the same.

A broadcast example:

Another jetliner tragedy in Britain today. A chartered airliner caught fire on take-off in Birmingham, and 54 passengers were killed.

The crash is newsworthy on its own merits, not because it was the third airline accident within a month. To punch up that fact, I'd give it a sentence of its own: "A British jetliner caught fire on take-off in Birmingham, England, today, and 54 passengers were killed. It's the third airline disaster in less than a month."

New York City averages about three homicides a day, yet who would think of starting a story, "Another man was shot dead in Manhattan today"? Or "Another tourist was mugged in Central Park today"?

Also, starting a story with *more* signals the listener that what's coming may be more of the same—what some pros call "the same old same old." Usually, it's better to skip *more* and go straight to whatever the new *more* is. One reason many broadcast writers start with *more* is that it's an easy way to go: "More headaches for the President today," "More wrangling in City Hall today," "More arrests in the Acme Power case." Want more?

9. Don't cram too much information into a story. Too many facts, too many names, too many numbers, too many words are just too much for too many listeners. They can't process such a steady flow of facts. Brinkley has said the ear is "the worst, least effective way to absorb information." That's *David* Brinkley, not Christie.

No matter how complex the story, our job is to condense the facts and give the listener not just the essence but, rather, a highly concentrated essence—the quintessence. The architect Ludwig Mies van der Rohe, a minimalist, used to say, "Less is more." When it comes to lead sentences, "More is less." Moreover, more is a bore.

10. Don't use newspaper constructions. Here's an example of a common newspaper construction: "The chairman of the Senate Foreign Relations Committee said today Beijing should stop threatening Washington. Senator John Walton said. . . ."

Newspaper readers would probably see that Walton is the person described in the first sentence, the committee chairman. But in broadcasting, the nature of the medium leads many listeners to assume that the Walton in the second sentence is another person and that Walton is adding *his* voice to the chairman's. In broadcasting, this is better: "The chairman of the Senate Foreign Relations Committee, John Walton, said today. . . ." Or else "The chairman of the Senate Foreign Relations Committee said today. . . . Chairman John Walton told. . . ." That makes Walton's identity unmistakable. P.S. Don't call anyone a chair. Or a couch.

Another common newspaper construction ends a sentence with "according to . . ." or "she said." But that's not *our* style. We in broadcasting never end a sentence with attribution. Or never should. As number 5b points out, our slogan is: Attribution precedes assertion.

And for writers with a newspaper background, a reminder: Don't write in inverted-pyramid style. Leave that to print people. If you don't know what an inverted pyramid is, don't ask. You'll have one less print habit to kick.

In journalism school, a class in *broadcast* newswriting taught me not to use *newspaper* terms. After that instruction sank in, it struck me as sensible. Why should we in broadcasting use the language and style developed over centuries for another medium, a medium that broadcasting tries to distance itself from—and distinguish itself from?

Some newscasters refer to people or stories "in the headlines." What headlines? Why are those newscasters plugging newspapers? And why do they talk about their "front page," their "sports page," their "people page," their "back page," even their "cover story"? "Cover" for TV? Yep. And they aren't referring to dust covers. Another publishing word borrowed by broadcasters is "magazine." Perhaps its use in broadcasting can be justified, because it's also a place of storage and a storehouse of information. But "pages"? The only pages in broadcasting run errands.

Then there's the newspaper ritual some broadcasters follow mechanically: reporting the composition of a jury by sex. How often do we hear a story start, "A jury of seven men and five women convicted a Palookaville man of murder today"? The news is the verdict—not the jurors' sex. The number of men and women has been known from the outset of the trial.

Almost all juries—except a petty jury (6 members) and a grand jury (23 members)—consist of the same number of citizens, 12. No matter how many are men and how many are women, the total is always 12. Listeners who hear that 5 women, or 7, sat on a jury aren't learning anything of consequence. So why take valuable air time to report the composition of the jury? No one reports a decision by "the seven-man, two-woman U-S Supreme Court."

If a rapist is convicted by a jury of 12 women, the makeup of the jury *is* newsworthy. But, except for uncommon circumstances, the makeup of a jury, a committee, or a legislative body is irrelevant. Equally grating: "The seven-man, five-woman jury deliberated for seven hours." Generally, the length of deliberations is not worth mentioning, unless it's unusually long or unusually short. Otherwise, who cares?

Another usually meaningless figure: the number of counts in an indictment. As they say in court, circumstances alter cases. But it's usually better to skip the number of counts and just say a man was indicted for allegedly defrauding investors of 10 million dollars. If he was indicted on 500 counts—one for each complaint—I would use that. Why? Because that would be the highest number of counts under one roof since a Hapsburg ball.

Still another newspaper ritual that wastes listeners' time—and yours as a writer: saying that the person just indicted "faces 765 years in prison." Assuming the indictment is not dismissed, assuming the accused goes to trial, assuming the guy is convicted, assuming a judge imposes the maximum, assuming the conviction is not reversed, assuming the sentence is not commuted, he'll never serve 765 years. Never in a million years.

In addition to avoiding newspaper rituals, broadcast newswriters should avoid newspaper words. Newspapers use them because they're short enough to be shoehorned into headlines. But people don't use newspaper headline words in conversation: *vie, nab, oust, laud, quiz, grill* (unless you're writing about steaks and chops), *foe, woe, fray* (please don't write that someone "was shot in the fracas"), *hike* (as a synonym for *raise* or *increase*), *ink* (as a synonym for the verb *sign*), *pact* (please don't let anyone *ink* a *pact* or ask for a *hike* in her *pact*), *opt, eye* (as a verb), *blast, rap* and *hit* (when they're intended to mean *criticize*) and *up* as a verb: "The workers want to *up* their pay." Which reminds me of a *Reader's Digest* title: "How We Upped Our Income; How You Can Up Yours." All those short words—and others—can be fitted into one-column heads in papers. But they're not words that we use when we talk; even newspaper copy editors don't *speak* them.

Slay is another newspaper word we should kill on sight. *Slay* is a good Anglo-Saxon word, but *slay* is not so strong as *kill* or *murder.* And *slay* isn't conversational. I don't know anyone who says *slay.* Nor do I know anyone who uses the past tense, *slew,* or the past participle, *slain.* So don't use *slay* unless you're talking about dragons. Or Santa.

Also: When writing about a young person, don't call him, her or it a *youth,* as in: "Police are also questioning the youth about several other murders." It's not uncouth to say *youth: youth* has long been used to describe a young person, especially a young man between boyhood and adulthood. But *youth* is a print word, not a broadcast word. Have you ever used it in conversation? Do you ever hear anyone else use it? If so, please report him to the Bureau of Youth Abuse.

Other words commonly used in print that shouldn't be used in broadcast copy: *former, latter, respectively.* Why not? Because few listeners remember names or items mentioned even moments earlier; and they certainly can't look at your script to see what you were referring to.

Another newspaper word that's not a broadcast word: *accord.* Some broadcasters use it because they don't want to repeat *contract* or *agreement.* But have you ever heard anyone outside a newsroom say *accord* (except in a Honda showroom)?

11. Don't lose or fail to reach a listener. The best way to keep a listener is by talking *to* the listener, not *at* the listener. And by working at your job, not forcing him to do your work. He won't, so you must. Writing is hard work; it's easy only for those who haven't learned to write.

Compressing a long, complex story into 20 seconds is a challenge. Telling that story well is even harder. As Confucius should have said, "Easy writing, hard listening. Hard writing, easy listening."

12. Don't make a factual error. That's the deadliest sin of all. It causes you to lose your credibility. And eventually your audience. Perhaps even your job.

When you write your next script, keep the Dozen Deadly Don'ts in mind. Soon, you'll see how avoiding those tempting traps helps make your copy more lively.

But if you want to win a Peabody and not wind up a nobody, here's another important rule: Don't be intimidated by rules. Newswriting isn't an exact science. To improve your scripts, go ahead: bend a rule or break one—if you must. But only when you can improve a script.

First, though, you must *know* the rules and *know* when you're breaking them. As the poet T. S. Eliot said, "It's not wise to violate the rules until you know how to observe them."

2

VENIAL SINS

A notch or two down the scale from the Deadly Don'ts are the Venial Sins. They may not be deadly, but they are wrong:

Don't *start* stories with prefabricated phrases. Among the most trite: "This is the story of," "It's official," "Once upon a time," "Now it can be told," "It shouldn't come as any surprise," "It had to happen eventually," "Mayor Mozzarella made it official today," "The mayor fired the opening shot today in the . . .," "When was the last time you . . .?" "Believe it or not!" "[Lebanon] is no stranger to violence," "Oliver Orville is no stranger to politics," "For City Hall today, it was the best of times, it was the worst of times," "It was business as usual today at . . .," "What we know now is . . .," "It's that time of year again," "Here we go again."

Don't *end* stories with prefabricated phrases. Shun: "Now the ball is in the mayor's court," "Don't count him out yet," "As Yogi Berra put it, 'It's not over till it's over,' " "It'll probably get worse before it gets better," "The full story is yet to be told," "There's no end in sight," "So he's on safe ground—for the foreseeable future" (in contrast to the *un*-foreseeable future?), "Police are investigating" (since when is that news?), "No one knows what the outcome will be," "What happens next is anyone's guess," "The outcome remains to be seen," "Only time will tell," "No one knows for sure," "In the final analysis," "There's no end in sight"—and variations without end.

Don't use prefabs anywhere. Most of these word clusters are the kinds that secretaries can type on a word processor with one keystroke, like "In response to your letter" and "Very truly yours." Lawyers call these word-strips "boilerplate," and they are extruded into deeds, wills and contracts, with little thought or effort. Among pre-fabs used in broadcast news: "At a hastily called news conference," "At a crowded news conference," "In a prepared statement," "In a bloodless, pre-dawn coup," "In an abrupt about-face" and "None the worse for wear."

Don't waste words. Not only do excess words waste time, but they also dilute the impact of what we say. Some words are usually excess baggage. So watch out for:

In order—as in "They went to the White House *in order* to protest the President's action." In most cases, when we delete *in order,* the sentence means the same.

In the process of—as in "The mayor is now *in the process of* deciding whether to run for another term." When you delete *in the process of,* the meaning is the same; and the sentence is improved.

Literally, actually, really—as in "The umpire *literally* walked off the field." Or "The sheriff *actually* saw the crash." Those adverbs don't help. So they hurt. *Really.*

Suddenly, gradually, finally—as in "*Suddenly,* he fell off the roof." No one falls gradually. Remember that scene in Hemingway's *The Sun Also Rises* when Bill asks, "How did you go bankrupt?" And Mike replies: "Two ways. Gradually and then suddenly." *Finally,* those adverbs add nothing to a sentence but bulk. Usually.

Flatly—as in "She *flatly* denied it." and "He *flatly* refused." A denial is a denial. A refusal is a refusal. So *flatly* falls flat. In *The Careful Writer,* Theodore M. Bernstein calls *flatly* "almost always superfluous."

Personally, officially—"The governor *personally* favors taking steps to stop the project." *Unofficially,* those adverbs only delay delivery of the news. Another adverb that's usually unnecessary is *formally. Seriously.*

Miraculously—Leave miracles to ministers. If you get the urge to write "Miraculously, no one was killed," try "Somehow, no one was killed."

Local and nearby—as in "The injured were taken to a *local* hospital." Or to "an *area* hospital." (*Area* is rarely an adjective, except in "area code" and "area rug.") Where else would the injured be taken? To an out-of-town hospital? If someone is taken to a distant hospital, it may be worth reporting. Otherwise, listeners assume the injured were taken to the nearest hospitals. A nearby hospital isn't worth mentioning. But when anyone is taken to a hospital across the street, that may be part of the story. Ambulances *take* people; but scripts shouldn't *rush* them. Ambulances do rush; so do firetrucks. That's their job. But in copy, *rush* sounds breathless. And please don't write that the injured were taken to three *different* hospitals. All hospitals are different. And separate.

We hear anchors say, "The indictment says the defendants met on seven *separate* occasions." *Separate* is superfluous. Of course, the occasions were separate. Otherwise, the defendants would have met only once. Better: "The indictment says the defendants met seven times." "*Separate* occasions" and "*different* hospitals" are common lapses to which a good writer cannot be indifferent.

A total of—as in "A total of 50 people were hurt." A total waste.

Then—as in "After he was arrested and charged, he was *then* freed on bond." When the chronology is obvious, *then* tends to be unneeded: "After he was arrested and charged, he was freed on bond."

The fact that—as in "The marchers were protesting *the fact that* the sheriff refused to release the two prisoners." Better: "The marchers were protesting the sheriff's refusal to release the two prisoners." When you eliminate *the fact that* from a sentence, you almost always improve your script. That's a fact.

Meanwhile—as in "*Meanwhile*, the White House said it's studying the problem." I hesitate to say there's never an occasion to use *meanwhile*. But I've never run across it—except right here. Use of *meanwhile* to tie two items together shows listeners the stitches. By directing attention to itself, *meanwhile* gives away our m.o. Transitions should be unnoticeable. A skillful cabinetmaker joins his panels neatly. Leaving the joints exposed is considered poor craftsmanship, and Ron Meador says bridging them with crude or clumsy devices "is like assembling fine furniture with roofing nails."

Another reason a careful writer avoids *meanwhile:* other careful writers have told him to. Also, it evokes facetious undertones, as in the pornographer's "Meanwhile, back at the raunch."

The BBC stylebook calls *meanwhile* "a lazy link word that is almost always redundant." *Meanwhile* means "at the same time" or "in the intervening time"; even more meaningless is *in the meanwhile.* Also avoid *meantime,* unless you're writing about G.M.T.—Greenwich Mean Time.

When you need a transition from one story to a closely related story, you can start the second item with a dateline: "In Washington, the Administration says it's studying the problem." Or link the second story by starting with a time-element like *tomorrow.* Or *later.* Or find a fact in the second story that makes the two stories related and slip that fact into your first sentence to serve as a bridge. Or link the items with *and* or *but:* "*And* the City Council also voted to turn Main Street into a pedestrian mall." Or "*But* the City Council rejected the mayor's proposal. . . ."

Whatever you decide, don't use *on another front* as a transition, unless you're writing about a war with several fronts—or a weather front. Also, avoid using *closer to home* as a transition. Sometimes we hear that after a foreign story. Yet the new story often turns out to be nowhere near where we are. But don't use *elsewhere;* everywhere is elsewhere.

Don't use *In other news* as a transition. Every story on a newscast is other news. Each story differs from all other stories. If the first five minutes has been devoted to one big story, shift to the next story by going to a commercial. Or pausing. Or changing tone. Or changing camera. Or anchor. Or writer.

According to an able transition team, Arthur Wimer and Dale Brix, the best transitions are word bridges. At least when they seem helpful and logical and the words aren't wasted. "Otherwise," they say in their *Workbook for Radio and TV News Editing and Writing,* "don't use [transitions] if they seem forced, illogical or awkward."

After many a tragedy, we hear this transition: *on a lighter note,* which implies that what we just heard was light and what we're going to hear is even lighter. After a tragedy, anything is lighter, including a lesser tragedy. After a bombing, a local anchor said,

On a much lighter note. . . .

And a network anchor said:

Health officials today raised the number of known Ebola patients in Zaire to 114, with 79 dead. On a much lighter note from the world of micro-bugs, there is word tonight of a remarkable achievement.

On a heavier note: Please weigh your words.

Speaking of strained segues—and that's another type of transition to trash—this was broadcast on a New York City TV station: After an anchor described John Glenn (erroneously) as "the first man to orbit the earth," his co-anchor said,

And speaking of the earth, the earth has weather, and here's our weatherman.

And speaking of weathermen, they, too, can chill me. A weatherman on another New York City station said, we're

sitting under a convective flow.

Huh? What's that? And a Los Angeles meteorologist reported

a split flow in the 500-millibar chart,

whatever that is. Made me think of splitting for Malabar. Or Malibu. But let's not use as a transition that old Monty Python line: "And now for something completely different."

Don't use non-broadcast words. A non-broadcast word is one not readily understood by most listeners. A listener who's baffled by a word on a newscast isn't going to reach for a dictionary. How many listeners understand *infrastructure?* Or *draconian?* Or *byzantine?* How many *writers* do?

I remember a network anchor's asking me the meaning of *evanescent.* I knew. But I didn't know whether he knew and was testing me or just was avoiding a trip to the dictionary. Maybe he figured that if I knew, everyone knew. So he went ahead and used *evanescent* in his newscast. What we write is indeed evanescent, *fleeting.* But *evanescent* is a non-broadcast word. So is *vagaries.* How many listeners know what they are? Or confuse them with vagrants?

I don't have a complete list of non-broadcast words, but here are some warning signs: If you suspect that a word you're considering is a non-broadcast word, you're probably right. If you've never run into the word before, never used it and never heard anyone else use it, or if you have to look it up in the dictionary, it's a good word *not* to use. Some newswriters think that by slipping in a big word or an off-beat word they'll make a big impression. On whom? Their boss? Their audience? Well, they do make an impression—and it's unfavorable.

We hear *gubernatorial* on the air during political campaigns, but it's a word that deserves retirement. I doubt that anyone outside newsrooms ever uses it. Not even gubernators. And don't dare use obscure or sesquipedalian words. The best policy: Save big, fancy words for Scrabble.

Don't use hollow words. Hollow words are often combined with words that do matter. But the hollow words just take up time, space and energy. In a word, they're nothing but padding. These extraneous words, when used in certain combinations, include *incident, activity, condition* and *situation.* Newscasters talk about "the shooting *incident*" when all they should say is "the shooting." (Incidentally, a shooting is hardly an incident. An incident is usually a minor event, such as a jostling on the bus.) Also, don't write about "the famine *situation*." A famine is a famine. And everything is a situation. We're in one right now.

Some weathercasters refer to "thunderstorm *activity*" when they should say only "thunderstorms." They may say "the storm *condition*" will last several hours. That sentence, too, would be stronger if it were un*conditional;* just say "the storm." We hear weathercasters talk about the temperature's reaching "the 45-degree *mark.*" By itself, *45 degrees* is enough. And "the temperature's falling to zero *degrees.*" Zero is on the thermometer, but zero is not a degree. Zero is zero.

Newscasters also talk about a trial that has been "one month *long.*" Better: "The trial has lasted a month." We hear about an attorney who needs *one month's time.* But we have no time for *time.* Some newscasters may say: "The test will run for a three-month *period.*" Better: "The test will run three months." Period!

Don't use vague words. One of the most popular is *involved.* When I hear that someone was involved in a crime, I don't know whether he committed the crime or was a victim. Or a witness. Whenever possible, be specific.

Don't use vogue words. Several of these buzzwords and fad words that shouldn't find their way into your copy: *accessorize, arguable, high profile, icon, interactive, interface, meaningful, methodology, parameters, parenting, prioritize, pro-active, scenario, supportive, viable.*

Don't use weary words. A weary word has been used up through overuse. The first one that comes to mind, and it comes to many minds, is *controversy.* That's why so many newscasters refer to a *new contro-versy,* or to a *controversial* candidate, a *controversial* bill, a *controversial* plan, a *controversial* move, a *controversial* movie, a *controversial* action, a *controversial* faction. Almost everything is controversial. Even Santa Claus. Some people object to him because they regard Christmas as a sacred day, not to be mocked by Santa and his commercial ties.

So who or what is *not* controversial? Congress debates bills, people argue over candidates, objectors circulate petitions, and pickets protest. Broadcast newswriters who want a strong word for a lead promptly may reach for *controversy* or *controversial* because they think it's the best and fastest way to go. But they don't realize that the more they use *contro-versy* and *controversial,* the less they mean (See p. 184-186.)

Don't use weasel words. You may think you're being more solemn and respectful by saying someone *passed away.* Or *passed.* Or *passed on.* Or *succumbed.* No. Those euphemisms may be well intended, but they're wordy and indirect. So hereafter, when dealing with the hereafter, just let people *die.* And if you're tempted to use *expired,* perish the thought. Save *expired* for contracts and subscriptions.

Don't use windy words. Some newswriters use windy words either to inflate their stories or because they're not aware of simple synonyms. They use *commence* when they could say *start*. Maybe they think *start* is too common and that they ought to give their copy a touch of class. But there's no point in putting on airs. Windy words just slow down listeners' comprehension, add length to a story and dilute its impact.

Other highfalutin words that we hear too often: *utilize* instead of *use; implement* (verb) instead of *carry out* or *put into effect; implement* (noun) instead of *tool.* And please don't use *initiate,* unless you're writing about a fraternity. We have no need to say *approximately* when all we need is *about.* Mark Twain said, "I never write 'metropolis' for seven cents when I can get the same . . . for 'city.'"

Don't use wrong words. Make sure you know what a word means before you use it. The best way to make sure is to check a dictionary. One of the most frequently misused words in scripts is *dilemma.* It doesn't mean *problem, plight* or *predicament.* A *dilemma* is two alternatives that are equally undesirable.

The ten other most misused words, according to a *Los Angeles Times* survey: *egregious, enormity, fortuitous, hopefully, ironically, penultimate, portentous, presently, quintessential, unique.* Another word that's often misused is *heroics.* Dictionaries define *heroics* as "talk or behavior that is excessively dramatic and intended to seem heroic." So *heroics* shouldn't be confused with *heroism.*

Words we should steer clear of include *pled,* misused as the past tense of *plead.* The preferred form is *pleaded* (consult your *Associated Press Stylebook and Libel Manual*). And use the preferred past tense of *sink (sank), shrink (shrank), fit (fitted), broadcast (broadcast), dive (dived)* and dozens of other verbs. Watch out for regular *and* irregular verbs—and other irregularities.

And keep an eye out for words with contrary meanings, like *sanctions.* When newscasters say the United Nations "imposed sanctions," they mean "penalties." But in most dictionaries, the first definition of the noun *sanction* is permission or approval. The fourth or fifth definition, depending on your dictionary, is "a penalty." The verb *sanction* means "allow." So the use of *sanctions* in a script can leave listeners in a quandary.

Another word to watch out for is *depose,* which means "to remove from office or power." But *depose* also means "to take a deposition from." So if you write that an official was deposed, your sentence may be ambiguous; and an editor who sanctions ambiguity should be deposed.

Also watch out for sound-alikes, words that sound the same but have contrary meanings, like *raze.* To raze a building is to tear it down. But a listener hears *raise* and thinks a building is going up, not coming down. And "to *halve* pollution" is far different from "to *have* pollution."

Don't use foreign words and phrases. Many listeners have all they can do to understand basic English. Surveys estimate the number of illiterates in this country at more than 20 million. And not everyone classified as literate is a prospective Ph.D. So writers should stick to English, the only language we expect listeners to know. Most listeners don't read the *New Yorker* and don't work the *New York Times's* crossword puzzles. And, except for immigrants, most of us don't use or hear foreign words in conversation. The people we're writing for are people who understand only one language, English. Plain English. So let's stick to everyday words. Every day. (See p. 175.)

I don't want to seem persnickety, but we should also avoid *per.* No, that's not a peremptory command. As with other tips, rules, principles or whatever you call them, I'm not saying, "Never, ever, under any circumstances whatsoever." All I'm saying is, whenever possible, avoid *per.*

Most experts oppose the use of *per* where *a* or other familiar English words will do. For example, instead of writing "55 miles per hour," write "55 miles an hour." Instead of *per week, per pound,* write *a week, a pound.* And avoid *per se, per annum, per capita, per diem* and *per deum*—unless you write with divine inspiration. Also avoid *amicus curiae, caveat emptor, en route, gratis, ipso facto, quid pro quo, status quo, via, vis-à-vis,* etc., especially *et cetera.* Avoid almost all other Latin words and terms. I say *almost* all because a few are so deeply rooted in our common speech that they are acceptable, such as *percent.* It comes from the Latin *per centum,* meaning "by the hundred." But use *percent* only *after* a number. Not "A large *percent* of cooks were out of work." But "A large *percentage* of cooks were out of work."

A few Latin words may be acceptable *in extremis* when no English equivalent is available or when the Latin can be readily understood. The Latin term *in absentia* may be acceptable to report the case of a defendant who was sentenced when not present. At least, *absentia* sounds like *absence.* But I think it would be better to say "He was sentenced although [he was] not present." Or "although he didn't show up." Another acceptable Latin term is *persona non grata,* the diplomatic term for someone declared unwelcome—not to be confused with *persona au gratin,* a diplomatic big cheese. Otherwise, foreign words are just not *à propos.*

The columnist Mike Royko once took a swipe at Americans who use foreign words: "Just as irritating as restaurants are books and magazines that slip French words in and expect us to understand them. That's why I gave up reading the *New Yorker,* which is one of the worst offenders. I don't know why that magazine does it. Half of all New Yorkers I've known can't speak understandable English, much less the language of the bwah and fwah."

Not only should newswriters avoid foreign words, but we should also avoid words with roots in Latin or Greek. Instead, we should, whenever possible, use words of Anglo-Saxon origin. So let's not use the verbs *exonerate* (clear), *extinguish* (put out), *facilitate* (help, ease), *endeavor* or *attempt* (try) and *triumph* (win). And let's not use the nouns *insurgent* (rebel), *conflagration* (fire), *altercation* (fight), *lacerations, abrasions* and *contusions* (cuts, scrapes and bruises). Exception: though it's a blend of Greek (from the word for "at a distance") *and* Latin (from the word for "see"), our listeners should have no trouble understanding the word "television."

Another language to steer clear of is the language of lawyers, exemplified by *therefore* and *nevertheless.* No need for a newswriter to use any of them. Here are the basic English equivalents: *therefore* = so; *nevertheless* = even so; *notwithstanding* = despite. Also, skip *however.* Instead, use *though, yet, still* or, most often, *but.*

Don't use clichés. One cliché is not worth ten thousand pictures. The usual picture a cliché brings to mind is that of a lazy or weary writer. So much copy is clotted with clichés it curdles the mind. A Los Angeles TV newswoman reported that an executive was confident that the movie industry, stung by an investigation, would get a

clean bill of health.

I'd like to see one of those bills of health, clean or soiled. Or one of those "bargaining tables" I hear about so much. Or a "bargaining chip." Or even a bargain.

A New York City TV reporter, covering a double murder, said,

The police have their work cut out for them.

Made me wonder whether the victims had been dismembered. Another reporter said three fugitives had everyone on

pins and needles.

(That script should have been spiked.)

Often, when a blackout, blizzard, flood or shutdown hits a community, a newscaster says residents are "taking it in stride." I've never heard that anyone is *not* taking it in stride.

A network newsman keeps calling gold "the yellow metal" and silver "the gray metal." But I haven't heard him call copper "the red metal" or U.S. currency "the green paper." Yet.

Another cliché: *met behind closed doors.* As in: "The President and his national security adviser *met behind closed doors.*" Where else would they meet? On a bench in Lafayette Park? Some writers even have people *huddling behind closed doors.* If the secrecy of a meeting is unusual or significant and worth mentioning, you can say, "The committee met in closed session." Or "met in secret." Or "met privately." But don't let people *huddle* unless there are eleven of them and one is a quarterback.

Also objectionable in news scripts are catchphrases lifted from commercials: "As for your umbrella, don't leave home without it." My advice: Don't reach out and touch any of them. And avoid—almost all the time—song titles and lyrics. How many times have you heard this lead-in to a voice-over, "It rained on the city's parade...."? How many times have you written that? Promise not to do it again?

The most cliché-clotted copy I've ever heard on the air: "[A candidate] *dropped the other shoe* today and *threw his hat into the ring* for President, and now it's *a whole new ballgame.*" As Shakespeare put it, and he *was* tuned in: "They have been at a great feast of languages, and stolen the scraps."

When it comes to scrapping clichés, experts disagree. Several experts say some clichés have *a saving grace.* In *The Careful Writer,* Theodore M. Bernstein of the *New York Times* said: "Use a cliché only with discrimination and sophistication and . . . shun it when it is a substitute for precise thinking."

But many other writing experts say clichés cause air pollution. For them, all clichés are *dead as a doornail.* The columnist Colman McCarthy told how, as a college English major, his required reading list was crushing. So he adopted a method suggested by the writer John Ciardi: "Read a writer's essay, poem, story or column until the first cliché. At that collision, stop. Then drop."

The grampa of good grammar, Henry W. Fowler, also condemned clichés. But he said writers would be needlessly handicapped if they were *never* allowed to use, among others, *white elephant, feathering his nest, had his tongue in his cheek.* In *Modern English Usage,* he observed, "What is new is not necessarily better than what is old; the original felicity that has made a phrase a cliché may not be beyond recapture." (As George Burns put it, "If you stay around long enough, you become new.")

Don't substitute synonyms for words that are easily understood. Many writers dread using the same word twice in a 20-second story, not to mention twice in one sentence. Perhaps they fear that someone in charge might think that using *said* twice in a story indicates an anemic vocabulary. So they figure the best way to dispel any such notion is to find a different word for *said*. But in writing broadcast news, the best verb to express oral communication usually is *said* (or *says*).

Says—along with *said*—is part of natural speech. You tell a friend, "Jim says he's going to lunch early." You don't say, "Jim stated—or commented, or observed, or announced, or related, or remarked, or any of dozens of other verbs of utterance—that he's going to lunch early." The word *says* has been compared to a skillful stagehand: he does his work well, moves the show along and stays out of sight.

Some synonyms for *said* cause copy to be either stilted or tilted. Copy that sidesteps *said* is stilted when it uses *state* or *declare*. Those two verbs are best reserved for formal statements or declarations. And copy may be tilted when, as a synonym for *said*, the writer uses a verb that might reflect on the person who was doing the saying, or calls into question his veracity: *admit* ("He admitted having a car"), *claim* ("He claims he wrote the book himself"), *insist, maintain, complain, concede.*

Several other verbs are often used as the equivalent of *say*, but they don't have the same meaning. One is *explain*, as in: "He explained that the Bulls won." That's hardly an explanation. *Explain* should be reserved for explanations. *Explain* is not to be used as Ring Lardner did in *You Know Me, Al:* " 'Shut up,' he explained."

Point out is another verb not to be substituted for *say*. Save *point out* for pointing to facts, not assertions that may or may not be true. It's wrong to write: "He pointed out that his contract is still valid." He says it is. But maybe it isn't. A correct use for *point out:* "He pointed out that the largest state is Alaska."

Laugh is also used incorrectly as a synonym for *say*. "She *laughed* that losing isn't everything." People do laugh, but they don't laugh words. Better: "She said with a laugh that she would try again" or "She laughed and said she'd try again." And don't let anyone *chirp* even if you're quoting a jailbird who has turned canary.

Another problem crops up when a writer uses *said* <u>before</u> mentioning the person who's doing the saying: "Said one official: 'The mayor is disheartened by the outcome. . . .' " The writer might have been trying for a change of pace or for what he thought was streamlining. But in placing *said* before the subject, he's transgressing against the fixed word order of the normal sentence and violating conversational style. People don't talk like that. They don't tell a friend, "Said the magazine renewal letter: '*Time* is running out.' " It's unnatural. Says who? Says me.

But don't just take it on my say-so; listen carefully to what people say and how they say it. Wolcott Gibbs of the *New Yorker* once wrote a profile of *Time*'s co-founder, Henry Luce, and parodied *Time*-style of yore, which often ran counter to standard English: "Backward ran sentences until reeled the mind . . . Sitting pretty are the boys . . . Where it will all end, knows God!"

Enough *said?*

Some writers who shy away from short words or avoid using a simple word more than once in a story look for what's called an elegant variation. If they were writing about bananas, they would, on second reference, talk about "elongated yellow fruit." It's easier for a listener if we use "banana" twice in 20 seconds. Or even three times. Just don't slip on an appealing variation.

Don't hotrod. Hotrodding is high-powered writing. Hotrodders pepper their copy with words like *special, major, important, extra, crisis, unique, unprecedented.* In certain stories, those words may be apt. But everything can't be special. "Where everybody is somebody," William S. Gilbert wrote, "nobody is anybody."

Hotrodders ratchet up a spat between two public officials into a *clash.* And they *lash out* at each other. When the two officials meet, it's at a *summit.* Or it becomes a *confrontation* or *showdown.* When an official announces a drive or a campaign against almost anything, it becomes a *war.* So we have a *war* against crime, a *war* against drugs, a *war* against illiteracy, a *war* against pornography, a *war* against scofflaws. After being bombarded by all these *wars,* listeners lose their understanding of war. So far I haven't heard of a *war* against potholes. Or crabgrass. But at this very moment a newscaster in West Overshoe may be preparing to launch another such war.

When hotrodders write about experts, the experts are described as *respected.* Awards are *prestigious.* Fads or trends become *revolutions,* disclosures *shockers,* increased costs *astronomical* (because they've *skyrocketed*). Two other popular words in the lexicon of hotrodders: *mystery* and *mysterious.* When I was a newspaper cub (an *ink*ling), I learned that rewritemen used those words when they were short on facts and long on fancy.

No discussion of hotrodding can ignore *spectacular.* Broadcasters often apply it to fires or to fire footage (and they're not all fire buffs—or firebugs). Hotrodding sportscasters apply *spectacular* to a baseball player's catch, a football player's run, a tennis player's serve or a golfer's drive, not to mention the Amalfi drive. In fact, *spectacular* seems to be an all-purpose adjective, one that some writers use whenever they can't think of anything else to hold their audience.

One way to avoid hotrodding is not to write on a hypewriter. We want our copy to be calm, clean, clear and crisp, true and trustworthy. And free from sin.

3

TOP TIPS OF THE TRADE

Now that we've looked at the Don'ts, let's look at the Do's. Even among the Do's are a few tips that reinforce the Don'ts. But I call all of them the Top Tips of the Trade. And no matter what you call them—tips, reminders, principles, guidelines or rules—they'll help you do a better job. Also, they'll help your listeners. Now let's examine these tips:

1. Start strong. Well begun is half done. The most important words you'll write in a story are those that come first, what Mitchell Stephens calls (in *Broadcast News*) "the lead's lead." So bear down on your first sentence. "Start strong" doesn't mean to make the story stronger than the facts warrant; and it doesn't mean to exaggerate or misrepresent. But it does mean to put all your mental power into the start. Your first words are very likely to determine whether your listeners keep listening. So focus on your first words and your first sentence. If you set sail with even a small compass error and if it's uncorrected, you can wind up way off course, even on the rocks, or at the bottom. As Euripides once told me, a bad beginning makes a bad ending.

2. Read—and understand—your source copy. Read it to the end. Carefully. Don't write a script after reading only two or three paragraphs of the source copy. If you don't understand something, don't use it. Because, if *you* don't understand it, how can you write it so that your listeners understand? Too many writers lift words and phrases from source copy and transplant them into their own copy without knowing what they mean. When an editor or producer asks what something in the script means, many a writer replies, "Well, that's what the wire copy says." Don't be a copycat.

3. Mark key facts. By marking your source copy—preferably with a red or orange pen—you'll see instantly what's important and what you should consider including in your script. This can be a big help in boiling down the important and interesting to the essential. Your markings will also help when you check those facts in your completed script against your source material. You can make your mark by circling, underlining or highlighting.

As you develop your news judgment, you'll do a better job deciding which facts to use and in which order. And which facts to omit. The more you learn about what makes news, the better you'll be able to write news. So it helps to ponder the question "What is news?" One of the best answers is provided by an authority on journalism, Melvin Mencher. He says: "Most news stories are about events that (1) have an **impact** on many people, (2) describe **unusual** or exceptional situations or events, or (3) are about widely known or **prominent** people." In *Basic News Writing,* 5th ed., he goes on to say that other elements heighten the news value of an event, including **conflict, proximity** and **timeliness.** "Boiled down to its essentials," Mencher says, "every story is about either a **person** who has said or done something important or interesting or a **person** to whom something important or interesting has happened." Or the story is about "an **event** of importance or interest to many people."

4. Think. Don't write yet. Think. Don't just do something; sit there! Allow time for incubation and meditation. Even if you're fighting the clock, you may be able to take as much as 30 *seconds.* And if you're working on a script for tomorrow, you can afford more than that.

I had a producer who'd snap: "Write. Don't think." Wrong message. Unless you're up against a deadline, with no time to spare, please take time to think. Even if it's for only 30 seconds, think. Think what the story is all about; think what the heart of the news is; think of the best way to tell it. Think.

5. Write the way you talk. If you don't talk the way a good writer should, perhaps you should become a Trappist (and shut your trap).

No one writes exactly the way he talks or talks the way he writes. So writing for broadcast is a compromise. But keep in mind that you're writing for people who can't read your script. They only hear it. And they hear it only once. One way to make sure they get it the first time around—and they get only one crack at it—is to use workaday words and phrasing.

No need to stoop to the style of Dick and Jane. But you should write in a straightforward, linear fashion—without detours or zigzags—so that ordinary listeners can grasp your script word by word, word for word, word after word. It is unswerving directness—and adherence to rules— that enables listeners to follow the thread of your story.

When you're writing, don't think about telling *all* those people out there. Don't write your script for legions of listeners. Write as if you're telling *one* listener. Think of a friend sitting in your den (if you have a den *and* a friend). Or think of a friend on the phone. Or tell it the way you'd like to have someone tell it to you. The skills you bring into play at this point are selecting, summarizing and story-telling. Always remember that you're writing for the ear, not the eye.

6. Apply the tips and rules in this list. Our source copy doesn't play by these rules. Wire copy for newspapers generally crams the Five W's—*who, what, when, where* and *why*—and *how* into the first paragraph or two. And for good reason: When a newspaper sets a story into type and it's too long for the allotted space on the page layout, an editor is most likely to trim from the bottom, often lopping off entire paragraphs. Because many, if not most, wire service reporters come from newspapers, they stick with that form of writing.

Another reason newspaper people put the best first is that if they're writing against a deadline, they don't know whether they'll be able to get more than a few paragraphs into the next edition. So they figure they'd better jam their best material into the lead. They set down facts in descending order of importance, writing in a pattern known as the inverted pyramid. So newspaper reporters develop the habit of front-loading, putting all the best material at the top. And they write the most expendable material last.

But we broadcast writers don't usually have room for the Five W's and How. And how we don't! So we ignore the inverted pyramid. But we can't ignore the flaws of some wire copy written in wirese or journalese. Journalese is defined in *Webster's Unabridged Dictionary,* 2d ed., as "writing marked by triteness, oversimplification, verbal distortion, unwarranted exaggeration, and coloring for persuasive or sensational effect."

Journalese is a quaint tongue we have to translate into basic English while we write. As newspaper style developed over the centuries, it deviated further and further from the way people speak. Read a newspaper or wire service lead aloud and you'll be reminded how different they are from us, how print style doesn't suit our broadcast needs. That's why we've developed our own broadcast style, a style geared to a receiver far different from the eye: the ear.

People who read newspapers can give them their full attention. They read whatever they wish and at their own speed. And they can reread and mull over whatever interests them. Listeners can't do that with broadcast stories, so we must adjust our language to allow for the peculiarities of their hearing apparatus, which processes information relatively slowly. That's why we must make our copy simple and direct.

An approach for this kind of lean, clean, clear writing is sketched by Strunk and White: "Vigorous writing is concise. A sentence should contain no unnecessary words, a paragraph no unnecessary sentences, for the same reason that a drawing should have no unnecessary lines and a machine no unnecessary parts. This requires not that the writer make all his sentences short, or that he avoid all detail and treat his subjects only in outline, but that every word tell."

Set your mental processor to adjust every sentence until it conforms with broadcast rules. Writers who have mastered the rules know that rules help make their writing work. Yet, the ultimate test for any kind of writing isn't whether it follows the rules but whether it works.

7. Develop the courage—and the competence and the confidence —to write simply. How simply? Don't worry, we're not writing for simpletons. But we are writing for a general audience, comprising listeners at all levels of interest, knowledge and brainpower. Which means we would do well to heed Edward R. Murrow's advice to his European staff: "Imagine yourself at a dinner table back in the United States, with a local editor, a banker, and a professor, talking over the coffee. You try to tell what it was like, while the maid's boyfriend, a truck driver, listens from the kitchen. Talk to be understood by the truck driver while not insulting the professor's intelligence."

8. Refrain from wordy warmups. Get to the point. But what if you don't get the point or don't even see the point? If you've read the source copy, marked it, thought it through and are still stumped, put your source copy face down and tell the story to your keyboard in your own words. If you do that without glancing at the source copy, you'll probably confine yourself to the highlights, which is just what you're supposed to do. Don't fret about producing perfect copy; just get it down in rough form. You may not be sure what you want to say until you see what you've said.

Read your script and reread it. Delete any unnecessary words. If you don't need to keep them in, you do need to keep them out.

If that approach doesn't work, pretend you're telling the story to a friend by phone. Let's say your friend is out of town and you're out of pocket. You wouldn't rattle on. You wouldn't digress or say any more than it takes for your friend to get the gist. You'd tell your story hurriedly, and you'd hit only the high points. You wouldn't talk in the curt style of a nine-word telegram (isn't the tenth word usually Love?). You'd speak in a conversational style. So once you delete the unnecessary words, you'll have your lead. Or at least a good framework for your script.

If you find that that doesn't do the trick, try to visualize tomorrow morning's newspaper and its front page: how would the banner stretching across the top of the page capsulize the story? Which few words would a headline writer choose to condense a complex event? When you put your mind to it, you can often get a handle on a story that way.

If a gas tank blows up and kills 50 people, a newspaper headline might read, "50 DIE IN BLAST" But for us, in broadcast news, even after filling in that scanty line with verbs, articles and a few facts—"Fifty people are dead in the explosion of a gas tank in Hackville"—the result is unsuitable. As soon as you say 50 people *are* dead, the story starts sliding downhill. It's best to set the scene first and tell what happened. *Are* is weak, as is any form of *to be; explosion* obscures *explodes;* and the place-name is mentioned last, so the listener doesn't have the slightest idea where the explosion happened until the end of the sentence.

The newspaper banner offers only the bare bones. You need to take that skeleton and flesh it out to get a sentence in broadcast style: "A gas tank in Hackville blew up today and killed 50 people." Why didn't I write "blew up today, *killing* 50 people"? Because a finite verb, one with a tense *(killed),* is stronger than a participle *(killing)* with its *ing* ending. (See Freeman's rules on p. 138.) *Died* is best used for people who died of natural causes.

The second sentence of a script usually answers questions raised by the first: How many people were hurt? What caused the explosion? Did the victims work at the gas storage depot? Any homes damaged? What is the impact on Hackville?

Too many questions to be answered in one sentence. So the third sentence answers questions raised by the second sentence as well as any other unanswered questions. And the fourth sentence, if your story runs that long, answers questions not answered by the third sentence. Ideally, your sentences hold hands: they flow smoothly and seamlessly. And listeners aren't aware of your hard work and careful construction.

When I'm stumped in deciding what a story is all about, I use the technique I just laid out: I try to picture the front page of tomorrow morning's newspaper. Some newswriters begin by shutting their eyes; some stare into space, as if they expect to see cue cards; some hop right to it and bat out a story one, two, three. Some imagine the event in their mind's eye. The mind's eye can see plenty: from a nuclear explosion to a sunset in Sarasota. The best way is the one that works for you. If you haven't found your way, keep at it anyway.

9. Put attribution before assertion. This is one hard-and-fast rule a writer mustn't play fast and loose with. If you're sure your information is factual, you may be able to go ahead without using attribution. Or at least you may defer identifying the source. But if you're writing a story that seems iffy, or at least not solid, let your listeners know who's behind those assertions at the outset. We don't usually attribute stories to wire services because, in a sense, they work for our news department.

If a wire service moves a big story that seems improbable, a network will try to pin it down. If a networker cannot verify it and the story is too big to ignore, a newscaster may start the story this way: "The Associated Press says the Chief Justice of the United States is going to undergo a sex change." (The title is not "Chief Justice of the U.S. Supreme Court.") If the story were less startling, or less unlikely, the broadcaster might delay identifying the source but would make it clear that the information is not in the realm of established fact: "The Chief Justice of the United States *reportedly* plans to retire soon." The next sentence would justify *reportedly* by linking it to the people doing the reporting: "The Associated Press also reports he's going to move to Hawaii. The A-P says the chief justice has told associates he wants to. . . ."

That's the same way we handle big stories broken by newspapers: "The Chief Justice of the United States reportedly is going to enter a monastery. The New York Times also reports he plans to. . . ." No responsible news organization wants to say, on its own authority, with no confirmation: "The Chief Justice of the United States is entering a monastery." Nor is it good enough to start by telling about the Chief's impending departure and then saying, "That's what the New York Times reports today." Not good enough because you've presented the departure as fact, then told the listener it may not be a fact.

An offense against good judgment occurs when the newscaster presents a shocking assertion in a way that implies it represents the newscaster's fact-finding or thinking: "Good evening. The United States should bomb Moscow back to the Stone Age." The second sentence then pulls the rug out from under the opening: "That's the opinion of Councilman Tom Troy." The opinion of a councilman? Listeners should know up front who's doing the saying so that they know how much weight to give the opinion. And so they don't assume the anchor himself is sounding off. All of which underlies an immutable—and oft-repeated—basic of broadcast newswriting: Attribution precedes assertion. (See p. 141-145.)

10. Go with S-V-O: subject-verb-object. Start sentences with the subject, go straight to the verb, then the object. That's the standard pattern of sentences for people who speak English. The closer the verb follows the subject, the easier for the listener to follow. Yes, I've said that before (See p. 6.), and I reserve the right to say it again.

Avoid subordinate clauses. In rereading your script, if you find a subordinate clause that contains essential information, give it a sentence of its own. Or parcel out that information in other sentences.

11. Limit a sentence to one idea. This makes it easier for listeners to understand a story they can't read, let alone reread. By limiting a sentence to one idea, the writer serves listeners by uncomplicating stories, by simplifying (but not over-simplifying) them, by reducing difficult, complex stories to their crux.

12. Think small. Use short words and short sentences. The words that people use most frequently tend to be short. We don't want to use baby-talk, but we do want to make ourselves understood by people who may be only half-listening, people who may be listening amid distractions, people on the go, people who have a lot on their minds, people who have no opportunity to check your script, people who can't rip out your story and go over it at their leisure—or ask you what you mean. People are accustomed to hearing words the same way they absorb them in an ordinary conversation, in a linear fashion, and they are best able to understand them that way: short words in short sentences. People are more comfortable with short words. That's why some big words have been bobbed: "telephone" *(phone),* "airplane" *(plane),* "parachute" *(chute),* "automobile" *(auto* or *car),* "refrigerator" *(fridge),* "television" *(t-v),* "air-conditioning" *(a-c* or *air).*

13. Use familiar words in familiar combinations. Using familiar words is not enough. You have to use them in ways that listeners are accustomed to hearing. A broadcaster said,

The economy shows growth signs.

All good, plain words—but. But we don't talk that way. And, I hope, we don't write that way. We'd say straight out, "The economy shows signs of growth."

14. Humanize your copy. Write about *people,* not about *personnel.* Whoever wrote this wire service story should be reported to the Missing People's Bureau:

Tribal factions angered over a beer hall dispute fought with sticks and iron bars Sunday at Kloof gold mine west of Johannesburg, killing seven black miners and badly injuring 39, police said.

For use on the air, this wire story needs major surgery. *Faction* is an abstraction. Listeners can't see factions; but they can see people. So we should talk about people: blacks, or black miners, or black tribesmen— but not about factions.

Another type of story that often needs humanizing is a statistical release. Instead of writing about "a decline in births," we should, when possible, write about "fewer babies." Instead of writing about "unemployment," we should, when time and context permit, talk about "people out of work." Instead of talking about "deaths," we should, where appropriate, write about *"people killed"* or *"people who died."* People want to hear about *people.* Abstractions don't breathe—or bleed.

Besides humanizing stories, we should also be on the alert to localize them, to bring a national story down to a local level. And report its local effects.

15. Activate your copy: Use action verbs and active voice. If your copy lies there limply, give it some get-up-and-go with verbs that move. When you write in the active voice, the subject of the sentence acts. The passive voice is weak because the subject of the sentence doesn't act but is acted upon. Use of the passive conceals the actor: "Mistakes were made." Or "A cherry tree was chopped down."

Another fault: Besides concealing the actor (also known as the doer or agent), the passive voice is wordy. And dull. In some cases, though, the passive may be better: "Mayor Byrd was hit by an egg. . . ." You sure wouldn't write, "An egg hit Mayor Byrd" or "A protester threw an egg that hit Mayor Byrd."

I won't say, as a passivist would, "The passive is to be avoided." Nor will I say passively, "Action must be taken." But as an activist, I do say, "Join the action faction. Avoid the passive." Act now.

16. Avoid a first sentence whose main verb is any form of *to be: is, are, was, were, will be*. They are all linking verbs and merely link a subject with a predicate, which identifies or modifies it. Other linking verbs include *become, feel, has.* They can link, but they don't *do* anything. They don't express action.

Verbs that do express action are called transitive or intransitive verbs. A transitive verb transmits an action of the subject to an object: "A truck *hit* a school bus. . . ." There, the subject, *truck,* acts on the object, *bus.* An intransitive verb expresses an action without reference to an object: "A truck *blew up* outside City Hall today." But *is* transmits no action. Even so, *is* performs a necessary function when it serves as an auxiliary verb in the formation of tenses: "Mayor Holmes *is searching* for a new. . . ." So there, *is* becomes a helping verb, not a linking verb.

Far stronger than a verb form that ends with an "ing" is a finite verb, one with a tense: "Mayor Holmes has started to search for a new. . . ." *Is* without a participle simply says someone or something exists or else describes someone or something: "Mayor Holmes *is* a man with a plan." *Is* lacks energy. It doesn't move, it doesn't express action, it doesn't tell us something happened; it just is. *Is* has a place in writing, but not in a lead.

Despite all those objections, *is* may be all right in a few leads: "Senator Hooper is dead." Or "The war is over." Those sentences get their punch from their brevity and their gravity. That first example also benefits from its strong last word, *dead.* "Dead" gains extra impact from being a one-syllable word ending in one of the consonants that can close a sentence with a thud. Or thwack.

But valid uses of *is* in leads are few. The great strength of the English language, the educator Ernest Fenollosa wrote, "lies in its splendid array of transitive verbs. . . . Their power lies in their recognition of nature as a vast storehouse of forces. . . . I had to discover for myself why Shakespeare's English was so immeasurably superior to all others. I found that it was his persistent, natural, and magnificent use of hundreds of transitive verbs. Rarely will you find an 'is' in his sentences. . . ." And, as the poet Robert Graves said, "The remarkable thing about Shakespeare is that he really is very good—in spite of all the people who say he is very good."

17. Avoid *may, might, could, should, seems.* They, too, are linking verbs, but they're even wimpier than *is:* they wobble. And they waffle. They don't say anything for sure. Whenever possible, make a definite statement, not one that has the ring of *maybe yes, maybe no.* Can you imagine a strong script that starts with a sentence riding on *seems?* That's even weaker than *is.* At least, *is* says something is. *Seems* says only that it *may* be. So another word to avoid in a lead is *may.* Even softer is the verb *might,* which in the present tense *(might* is also the past tense of *may)* indicates a possibility that is even less likely than *may.*

If the facts of the story suggest that something *may* occur, think through the lead carefully to find a way to say something definite. Instead of "The space shuttle Pegasus may finally get off the ground today," I'd say, "The space shuttle Pegasus will try again today to get off the ground." The second lead may be only marginally better, but it has more strength than *may,* which carries the burden of an implicit *may not.*

18. Put your sentences in a positive form. Try to avoid *not* and *no.* That old song says it best: "Accentuate the positive, eliminate the negative, latch on to the affirmative, don't mess with Mister In-Between."

19. Use present tense verbs where possible. The verb that can be used most often in the present tense is *say.* You may even be able to use the present tense throughout your story. In the second or third sentence, you can shift to the past tense. Example: "Governor Smiley says he's going to visit China. His goal, he says, is to push for business for the state's farms and factories. The governor told a dinner audience in Middletown tonight that he plans to leave next month." Note: In the second sentence, the attribution is delayed. That's all right because the first sentence led with attribution. It is allowable to defer attribution until after the first few words; but it's definitely a no-no to defer attribution until the end of any sentence. (See pp. 138-141.)

A newspaper or wire service reporter might end a sentence with "the governor said" or "according to the governor." People don't talk like that, and we broadcasters don't write like that. The second sentence in that example does need attribution because we don't really know what his true goal is; it may be no more than a free vacation.

20. Don't start with a question or a quotation. Some writers do that occasionally for a simple reason: Going with a question or a quotation is an easy way to start. But, in the case of quotations, it's wrong; and you can quote me. They're wrong on several counts. Listeners can't see quotation marks. So they assume the opening words are the anchor's own. Worst of all, when listeners hear a story start with a quotation, they're apt to accept the first sentence as a fact. Not until the second or third sentence do they find out that it's merely an opinion or an allegation of someone other than the anchor.

In conversation, people don't begin with a quotation—or a strong statement—and then back into attribution: "The trouble with Doctor Proctor is that he mocked her. So says Sue. . . ." Or "That's what Sue says. . . ." Or "That's Sue's opinion." People just don't talk that way. Besides, a quotation is rarely the most important part of a story. So boil down the quotation and say it better. In your own words.

As for question leads, I wouldn't rule them out absolutely, though I think you should limit yourself to one every six months. But don't ask a question that might elicit a "No." Or a "Who cares?" Our job is to answer questions, not to ask them. At least not on the air. (See pp. 160-163.)

21. Use *and, also, but, so, because*—to link sentences. Connectives join sentences and allow listeners to see how they're tied together in one fabric. Using connectives makes it easier to follow the thread.

No matter what your sixth-grade teacher might have told you, feel free to start a sentence with a connective. Example: "Mayor Collins was indicted today. A grand jury charged him with grand larceny—stealing more than 10-thousand dollars from petty cash. *Because* of the indictment, the mayor said, he's taking indefinite leave." *Because* connects that sentence to the one before. And *indictment* also helps the listener even though *indicted* was used in the first sentence.

Use possessives—*his, her, its, their*—to tie sentences and facts together. Instead of talking about "*the* car," make it "*her* car." If you think listeners could have any doubt about who *he, she* or *it* refers to, don't hesitate to repeat the noun itself. Problem: "The car crashed into a home, and *its* roof caved in." The antecedent of *its* is *home,* but some listeners might take it to mean that it was the *car* whose roof caved in. To remove all doubt, delete *its* and substitute *the home's.* Although we have to be frugal in using words, don't hesitate to repeat a word to make sure a sentence is clear. You must write not only so that you can be understood but also so that you can't be misunderstood.

22. Try to put the word or words you want to emphasize at the end of your sentence. Try to construct periodic sentences. A periodic sentence creates tension, interest and emphasis as it goes along by placing the most important word or words at the end. So don't take the edge off by ending a sentence with weak, incidental or irrelevant words.

One expert says books about writing have not given the element of emphasis enough emphasis. According to Theodore A. Rees Cheney in *Getting the Words Right,* "A word or idea gains emphasis (and is therefore remembered) if it is positioned right before the period that ends the sentence. . . ." The type of sentence suggested by Cheney builds tension and suspense by saving its impact or meaning until the end. F. L. Lucas writes in *Style,* "The most emphatic place in clause or sentence is the end. This is the climax; and during the momentary pause that follows, that last word continues, as it were, to reverberate. . . . It has, in fact, the last word."

In *The Elements of Style,* Strunk and White also tell us how to deal with emphasis: "The proper place in the sentence for the word or group of words that the writer desires to make most prominent is usually the end."

And David Lambuth says in *The Golden Book on Writing:* "Unless you have good reason for doing otherwise, put your most important word or phrase at the end of the sentence. The most important word is usually a substantive [a word or group of words having the same function as a noun] or verb. Don't sacrifice the strategic final position to a preposition or even to an adverb, unless it really is the most significant word—which it sometimes is. The well-known advice against ending a sentence with a preposition is valid only [with] unimportant prepositions. In certain cases, a preposition is the most emphatic word to end a sentence with."

In contrast to the periodic sentence, the cumulative (or loose) sentence makes a statement and keeps on going, adding subordinate elements, like modifiers, clauses and phrases, as it rolls all over the place, which is what this sentence is doing before your very eyes, accumulating more add-ons. It could have ended after any of the last few commas.

"There is a slackness to a loose sentence, a lack of tension," Thomas Whissen says in *A Way With Words.* He calls it comfortable and easy to write. But he observes, "There is no real build-up, no anticipation, no excitement."

A contemporary expert, Bryan A. Garner, writes in *The Elements of Legal Style:* "It is only a slight exaggeration to say that a 'sentence must be so written that the punch word comes at the end.' That the end is emphatic explains why periodic sentences work."

One of the benefits of the periodic sentence is that it builds up to the main point. Unlike the loose sentence, it doesn't make its point and then run downhill. As Lambuth writes, "Build *up* to your big idea, not *down* from it."

Most sentences in newspapers and wire copy are loose. And most of us, when chatting, use loose sentences. If we had time to think through our thoughts thoroughly, we'd use far more periodic sentences. They carry the most impact and are the most rememberable.

Bell Labs has found that people remember best what they hear last, so if you want your words to sink in and to be remembered, use periodic sentences. Not exclusively, but frequently.

Let's see how to transform leads that rely on loose sentences to leads that put the emphasis at the end of the sentence, where it usually belongs. Here's a lead from a network newscast:

> **Matters went from bad to worse between the United States and Libya today.**

The point of the story is the slide from bad to worse. But the point lies in the middle of that excerpt, which means it's buried. That's the worst place to put the most important fact. Better: "Relations between this country and Libya have gone from bad to worse."

Here's another network example that needs restructuring:

> **Union Carbide said today that *equipment trouble and workers who didn't know what they were doing* were to blame for this month's chemical leak at the company's Institute, West Virginia, plant that sent more than a hundred people to the hospital.**

That's some sentence! Not a good one, but a long, busy and confusing one. Imagine trying to read that on air. Imagine listening to it. Imagine trying to understand it.

I've italicized the key fact—the cause of the leak. Or, at least, what the owner says is the cause. And that key fact shouldn't be submerged in the middle of that marsh. As it's written, the most memorable part of the sentence focuses on the people hospitalized, a fact reported previously—

many times. Now let's apply the principles of emphasis to improve that sentence: "Union Carbide says the leak at its plant in Institute, West Virginia, was caused by equipment trouble and workers who didn't know what they were doing." The original sentence was 41 words; the rewrite, 26 words. Shorter, sharper, stronger.

23. Use contractions—but cautiously. Although contractions are conversational and time-savers, some contractions can cause confusion. The most common hazard is *can't.* Even careful listeners—and careful listeners are not plentiful—can miss the final *'t;* so they think they heard *can,* which is contrary to what the script is trying to stress: can*not.* We risk misleading listeners when we use a negative contraction, if loss of the final letter(s) leaves the positive form of the verb reverberating.

Some contractions are safe to use: among them, *don't* and *won't.* If a listener misses the final *'t,* he's not going to mistake *don't* for *do.*

24. Pep up your copy with words like *new, now, but, says.* Not only does *new* signal listeners that they're hearing news, it can also compress a mouthful into one short word. Instead of writing, "The government issued a report today that says . . .," we can start speedily, "A *new* government report says. . . ."

Now has two good uses: it can show that an event is going on at this very moment, or it can indicate a reversal in course. For example: "Sheriff Gooch is now on his way to the district attorney's office." The *now* makes the sentence more vivid, more current, more newsy. And now is also effective in pointing up a change: "Sheriff Gooch has denied he knew of. . . . But *now* he says. . . ."

25. Watch out for *I, we, our, here, out, up, down.* When *I* is used in a direct quotation in a story, it's open to misunderstanding: "The mayor said, 'I need to take off weight.' " The listener has good reason to believe the mayor is referring to the anchor. So paraphrase: "The mayor said he needs to take off weight."

And I'm also puzzled when a newscaster uses *we.* Is the newscaster using *we* to avoid *I*? When she says *we,* is she referring to her newsroom, her community, or what? *Our* is too possessive unless you're writing about something that is yours, something that belongs to you or your station. Avoid "*our* troops" unless your station maintains its own militia. As newspeople, we report from the sidelines, not as partisans or participants.

Here should almost always be deleted from copy. *Here* causes the listener to wonder whether the speaker means "here in our newsroom" or "here in our town." Newscasters also start stories like this: "*Here* in Hicksville. . . ." Hicksvilleans know they're in Hicksville. They don't need to be reminded.

Up and *down,* as directions, are objectionable for similar reasons. In conversation, when talking about the town to our north, we'd say "*up* in Hangtown." When writing for broadcast, don't say "*up* in Hangtown." For folks north of Hangtown, Hangtown is *down.* Another adverb to watch for is *out,* as in "*Out* in Far Corners." People out there regard themselves as insiders. In their worldview, every place else is *out.*

26. Omit needless words. (Thank you, Strunk and White.) Rid your copy of *that*s, *which*es, *who is*es, *of*s and other space-eaters. As you read your script, you may spot a few of them sneaking in. In most cases, they can be deleted with no loss of meaning—and with a gain in clarity. Needless words lengthen your sentences and force your listeners to work to extract the substance. The fewer (but well chosen) words you use to tell a story, the clearer and more forceful the story.

The importance of examining the need for every word is pointed up by Harold Evans in *Newsman's English:* A London fishmonger had a sign that said: FRESH FISH SOLD HERE. A friend persuaded him to rub out the word FRESH; he wasn't expected to sell fish that wasn't fresh. Then the friend persuaded him to rub out HERE; he's selling the fish, naturally, in his shop. Then the friend urged him to rub out SOLD; he isn't expected to give it away. Finally, the friend persuaded him to rub out FISH; you can smell it a mile off.

27. Hit only the main points; trash the trivia. Just because the wires carry something doesn't mean we should use it. Some wire service reporters write long because they haven't learned to write short. Some write long because newspaper clients have plenty of space to fill. And some papers with news holes shovel in wire copy by the yard.

But we broadcast newswriters must be highly selective. The minutiae that a newspaper might print are, for us, useless. Be sure every word you use is essential and nothing is superfluous.Whatever you say, say it only once. Life's too short for repetition—except for my suggestions.

28. Don't parrot source copy. When a wire story has a clever play on words, or an unusual combination of words, avoid borrowing that language. Why? Because if we do borrow, a listener who recalls hearing the same words on an earlier newscast on another station may say, "So that's where that jerk gets his news!"

Even though broadcast wires are supposed to be written for the ear to accommodate subscribers, the quality of the copy is uneven. Not all of it is written by people who are adept or experienced. Why parrot what *any* writer has said? Aren't you a better writer? Or trying to be one? We should rewrite wire stories using our own words and phrasing.

29. Place the time element, if you need one, *after* the verb. The listener who turns on your newscast tonight has every reason to believe that all your stories are today's news, not yesterday's. What will catch the listener's ear and prompt him to keep listening is an action verb, not a "today."

30. When in doubt, leave it out. Go with what you know. Just before airtime, when we handle so much copy, we probably can't find answers to all our questions about the source material, or resolve ambiguities, or reconcile discrepancies. Yet we can't assume. Or speculate. We deal only in facts, not in conjecture. The wires are not infallible. Far from it. Their stories are gathered, written and edited not by superhumans but by imperfect humans like us. (Isn't *that* a scary thought!)

You must be even more careful if your source copy is a press release. Wire service stories are written by newspeople who work for news agencies; in effect, they work for us. They're hired for journalistic skills. And they're trained to report objectively. But press agents aren't journalists. They're not disinterested parties. And they don't work for us. They work for someone else. Their silent slogan is, "Whose bread I eat, his song I sing."

Whether they call themselves press agents, press information officers or public relations counselors, they still work for private parties. And, as the adage has it, "Who pays the piper calls the tune." With few exceptions, they are not paid for their objectivity, devotion to the public weal and dedication to Truth. The press releases they write, which they often label *news* releases, are written for the benefit of their private interests, not our public interests. Sometimes their interests and ours intersect, and we find a release worth using. But that release may or may not be accurate. It may or may not be complete. It may or may not be fair.

If you decide to use a press release or a part of one, rewrite it. But first, make sure that the person named as the sender did in fact send it, that it's not a hoax. Even if it's not a hoax, remember that the release comes from someone who is, in effect, a salesman, trying to "sell" you a story, one written to advance his interests, not necessarily yours.

If you doubt any key points in the release, pick up your phone and verify them on your own. If you can't verify them but decide to go ahead anyway, be sure to attribute them to someone named in the release. Many press agents are honorable people, and they write releases that are reliable. But some press agents slip in a few curves. It's your job to detect them—and reject them. "The most essential gift for a good writer," as Hemingway put it so elegantly, "is a built-in shockproof shit-detector."

Another source of problems—and opportunities—is telephone tips. People phone newsrooms with all sorts of motives: some callers are looking for kicks, some for rewards, some for vengeance. Any caller can identify himself as just about anyone else. Listen carefully, ask questions and treat each call as potentially newsworthy. But when you hang up, don't go straight to your keyboard. Verify everything you want to use. But don't try to verify a tip simply by phoning the tipster and talking to him again.

Some pranksters delight in phoning in obituaries. Never use an obit before first checking with the undertaker. And watch out for mischief-makers. I remember a cub reporter who was refused service by a Chicago nightclub because he wasn't wearing a tie. So he walked across the street to a saloon, where a TV set was carrying a telethon. In a twinkling, he got an inspiration. He phoned the telethon and said he was the manager of the nightclub that had denied him service and wanted to make a contribution to fight some dreaded disease: $5. The TV host's on-air announcement of the measly gift made the famous club look like a den of scrooges, and the reporter got his revenge. Yes, I did. (Thinking about it makes me want to hum "Pranks for the Memories.")

Yet, you shouldn't take my cautionary words as advice to hang up on unfamiliar or anonymous callers. Or to ignore them. Or to make prank calls of your own. Another Chicago reporter, Martin J. O'Connor, used to say he didn't care if a tip came from Judas Iscariot. If Marty could confirm it, he'd run with it. Once you have confirmed a story, it's yours.

31. Don't raise questions you don't answer. Don't insert a fact that cries out for clarification. A local script about a fire in a trailer park said a man was killed in a trailer, "where he lived with a companion." But the script didn't tell listeners whether the companion survived, nor whether the companion was a colleen or a collie.

32. Read your copy aloud. If it sounds like writing, rewrite it. What counts is not how it looks but how it sounds. If it sounds un-conversational (as if written for the eye), rewrite it. When you read it aloud, you can also catch any unfortunate combination of words. For example: a BBC news reader (as the Beeb calls anchors) said—so the story goes—that, in a golf match, Lord Hampton "had been playing a round" with Lady Fairfax. If the writer had read his script aloud, he might have caught that double meaning. I'm not saying a writer should have a dirty mind, but it helps. It also helps to have a mind that's nimble enough to catch a single word that seems safe on paper but can cause trouble. For example: *query.* You may never be tempted to use *dastard,* but be careful of *duck, shift, finger, morass, Uranus* and *horticulture.*

The network broadcaster who wrote the following news item also should have listened to his script:

> **An Interior Department report on Teton Dam is still**
> **pending. So are Congressional studies of the Bureau of**
> **Reclamation and other dam-building agencies.**

The writer should have caught *dam-building agencies.* The listener can't see the hyphen, so the phrase sounds like a curse. If you read your script aloud to yourself before turning it in, you'll catch innocent combinations of words that sound damning.

33. Rewrite. The art of writing lies in rewriting what you've already rewritten. Check all names, dates, amounts and facts with the source copy. Take time—and make time—to give your script a good going-over. Is every word necessary? The rule: If it's not necessary to put it in, it *is* necessary to keep it out.

After you get rid of any clutter and trim the flab, ask yourself: Are the words right? And in the right order? And does it read right? Also: Is every bit of information right? Accuracy is imperative. As one news agency used to say, "Get it first, but first get it right." (The agency had trouble getting it either way—and went the way of all flash.)

Spare time is scarce in newsrooms, particularly as air time approaches. When you get to work, go to work. If you skip the chitchat and bear down on writing, maybe you can save enough time to rewrite your copy. And then re-rewrite it. The importance of rewriting is illustrated in George Plimpton's interview with Hemingway for the *Paris Review:*

> P. How much rewriting do you do?

> H. It depends. I rewrote the ending of *Farewell to Arms,* the
> last page of it, 39 times before I was satisfied.

P. Was there some technical problem there? What was it that had stumped you?

H. Getting the words right.

Getting the words right!

Broadcast newswriters don't have the time Hemingway had. We write in haste and can't revise at leisure. But if we're working on a piece that doesn't have to go on today's next newscast, we can let our script sit overnight and cool off. The next day, having forgotten the precise wording, we can read our script as if it's new and written by someone else. We can go over the script energetically and enthusiastically. With fresh eyes. And refreshed mind. Maybe this time, after another rewrite or two, we'll get the words right.

But the perfect is the enemy of the good. The writing coach Don Fry sees it like this: Listeners don't need a perfect lead, or even a great lead. Just a good lead.

After you read a wire story or other source copy, you need to apply all of those top tips instinctively. You can't take time to review each one step by step, like an airline pilot going down his checklist for takeoff. You should absorb those tips so they become second nature and you're able to apply them on autopilot. Then your scripts will be all set for air.

Murphy's Law is right: "Whatever can go wrong will." But Mervy's Law says: "Whatever *can't* go wrong, will." So reread, recheck, reflect, relax. Then pray. And polish your résumé.

4

LEAD-INS, LEAD-OUTS, VOICE-OVERS

N ow that we've seen how stories can take off, let's see how we can make some other things fly: lead-ins, lead-outs, voice-overs, tease(r)s and one-minute newscasts. The tips and rules that guide us to writing better stories also serve in writing these other elements of a newscast. But each of them has its own peculiar needs.

Lead-in

An anchor reads it to lead into a reporter's narrative or a natural sound cut, perhaps of a shouting match. The lead-in sets the scene and identifies the reporter—or the people who are the loud speakers.

The lead-in's job is to alert listeners and prepare them for what's coming—the important, fascinating, exciting, horrifying or amusing story that's about to unfold—but without using any of those adjectives. Yet the lead-in is more than a billboard for the coming attraction. It sets up what follows so it makes sense to a listener. And it supplies a crucial fact or two that may be missing from what follows. Generally, a lead-in should supply the "where." On the other hand, if the reporter immediately says where he is, a lead-in needn't include the "where."

Lead-ins must do more than just lead in. They should keep listeners listening, either through the impact of hard facts told well or through the engaging grace of a light touch. A lead-in should grab a listener by the throat, or by the ears—but gently, politely. Not an easy assignment, especially if the reporter's story is a 97-second weakling. And not if we comply with the truth-in-advertising laws, never promising more in the lead-in than the piece delivers. All we need are the same skills we use in writing "readers" (or "tell" stories)—scripts unaccompanied by footage.

Lead-ins come in many varieties, but, in general, they can be classified as hard or soft. A hard lead-in is usually used to introduce a hard-news story. Ideally, the reporter writes his script as if he were telling the whole story. Then, before the newscast, he gives his first sentence (or two) to the anchor to use as her lead-in. After the anchor goes on the air and delivers that lead-in—or a rewrite that retains the essence of the original—the reporter picks up the narrative with the second (or third) sentence of his script. That way, the story flows seamlessly. No maddening repetition, no gaps, no flaps, no traps.

When an anchor doesn't have the benefit of a proposed lead-in from the reporter, the anchor (or writer) should write a lead-in that sets up the story—almost like a newspaper headline. But with sentences that don't sound like headlines or use headline words. If the writer has the opportunity to read the reporter's script in advance, he can include any *essential* facts missing from the script. Or he can give one or two of those facts to the anchor for a tag at the end of the reporter's piece.

A soft lead-in is one usually reserved for soft news. (One kind of lead-in that you don't want to write is *squishy* soft.) Soft lead-ins intro features, human interest and semi-soft stories. Good soft-news lead-ins are hard to write. But, by writing and writing and writing, you can learn to get it right.

As with the Deadly Don'ts recited at the outset of this book, the Don'ts are especially important in writing lead-ins:

1. Don't use the same key words the reporter uses. Don't introduce him or any speaker with the same words he starts with. Violation of that rule produces "the echo-chamber effect." It sounds—and resounds—like this, with the anchor speaking first: "Governor Goober warned today he's fed up with state employees who loaf on the job." Then we hear Goober say: "I'm fed up with state employees who loaf on the job." Or instead, we hear the reporter say, "Goober said he's fed up with state employees who loaf on the job." Listener: "Haven't I heard that somewhere before?"

Or the anchor leads in with something like this: "Old MacDonald said today he's going back to his farm. Steve Simpson reports he's pining for his pigs, ducks and cows." Then he begins, "MacDonald is pining for his pigs, ducks and cows." This leaves the listener higgledy-piggledy, and the duplication wastes time, and crowds out other material.

Instead of starting the second sentence with the reporter's name and stepping on the reporter's lines, the anchor could say, "He [MacDonald] has been working as a bricklayer, but now he has decided to throw in the trowel. Steve Simpson has the story." By saying Steve has the story, the anchor is suggesting that the best is yet to come.

If possible, a writer should prepare a lead-in only after reading the text of the cut or the reporter's script. Or at least talking with the reporter so the writer knows what the reporter is going to say. Or so the reporter knows what the lead-in is going to say.

2. Don't steal the reporter's thunder. Although the lead-in for a hard-news story should hit one or two highlights, the anchor shouldn't skim off all the good material. Otherwise, the reporter's account will be anticlimactic. It will sound as if the reporter got his news from the anchor. Or, as they say so delicately in the barnyard, the reporter will be left sucking hind teat.

3. Don't write a soft lead-in for a hard-news story. A soft lead-in may work for a feature story, but a hard-news story calls for a hard-news lead-in. A lead-in is like a store's display window. A dime store doesn't dress a window with diamonds. And a diamond merchant doesn't display dimes. Hard news, like diamonds, deserves an appropriate showcase.

4. Don't write a lead-in that conflicts with the reporter's script. This may seem abecedarian (no kin to ABC's Sid Darion), but every so often we hear a reporter say something that contradicts what the anchor's lead-in has said. That's a mislead-in.

5. Don't overstate or oversell. The lead-in shouldn't promise—or suggest—more than the reporter can deliver. It should adhere to standards of journalism, not descend to hucksterism.

6. Don't be vague. Sometimes, because of the way newscasts are put together, we don't know exactly what the reporter in the field is going to be saying, or which segment of a speech is going to be used. So we have to write "blind"—without saying anything specific. And we put down only enough words to allow the control room to roll tape: "The new chairman of the city transit agency, Lionel Train, spoke out today on the agency's problems." But that's flat. Writing blind—like flying blind— can be risky. Whenever possible, say something substantive: "The new chairman of the city transit agency, Lionel Train, said today that he'll clean up the agency's problems within six months."

7. Don't use a faulty "throw line" at the end of the lead-in to introduce a reporter. You confuse a listener by saying, "Jerry Jarvis has the story," if the next voice we're going to hear is not that of the reporter but of a woman taking an oath of office. One way to handle that "throw line" is to say, "Jerry Jarvis looked on as Mary Barton took the oath."

Most lead-ins run less than 20 seconds, and a few run barely 5 seconds. No matter what it takes to do the job, no matter what the length, every word counts. And the shorter the lead-in, the greater the need for every word to carry its weight.

Voice-overs

If you're in radio, you don't have to worry about V/O's, the scripts that are read over silent videotape. And if you're in TV, you don't have to worry either, as long as you observe these tips:

1. View the footage before writing. If that seems obvious, think of all the V/O's you've heard on the air that didn't fit the picture. If previewing the videotape is out of the question, try to get a shot list (a.k.a. shot sheet, shot card, spot sheet and breakdown sheet). That list itemizes the scenes in chronological order, describes the contents in a few words and provides the running time of each shot as well as the cumulative time. If you do preview the footage, make your own shot list. Without such a list, by the time you get back to your keyboard, you may forget whether the third scene shows injured people or overturned trailer homes, and you may need to know for certain.

Your words don't need to match the picture every step of the way. But they should add to what viewers see—and, if necessary, help them understand what they're seeing. If need be, start to identify the setting and the main characters an instant or two before each new scene comes up. In some pieces, "spotting" a new character—by name or description—is imperative. We call this "keying," "writing to picture," or "cuing words to picture." If we want to write about something the camera didn't shoot or the tape doesn't show but that's pertinent, we "write away from picture."

To help establish what it's all about at the start of a V/O, it's usually best for the script to match the picture. After the viewer is told what it's all about, it may be all right to write away from picture. But don't get carried away. Don't describe in detail what viewers can't see for themselves.

2. Don't state the obvious. For too many writers, this is not so obvious. That's why we hear lines like "This is the man," "this is the lake," "this is the man jumping into the lake." Viewers can see that. We serve them by supplementing what they see by putting the picture into perspective. We inform them that the water temperature was 35 degrees, that the man weighed 250 pounds and that he didn't know how to swim.

Avoid "Here we see," "shown here" and "seen here." If we're seeing an overturned mobile home, the script needn't whack viewers over the head with a "here." If something needs to be explained or spelled out, do it unobtrusively and without fanfare.

3. Don't tell viewers to "watch this." If you wish to direct your viewers' attention to something that's about to occur in a long shot, do it subtly. Let's say that in a few seconds a man in the crowd is going to pull a gun and fire. Unless viewers know in advance, they might not be focusing on that part of the screen and could miss the critical part of the action. We can tip them off without issuing orders: "A man on the far right, the man in a khaki jacket, pulls out his gun and prepares to fire at a policeman."

4. Don't fight picture. Our words shouldn't be at odds with the picture. We shouldn't say zookeepers recaptured two monkeys at the moment viewers see someone holding two children.

5. Don't use the newspaper phrase "left to right." If several people are on the screen and you need to direct the viewers' attention to someone, you can refer to "the man in the ten-gallon hat" or "the woman with the parasol."

6. Don't overwrite. Don't squeeze too much copy into the script, making the V/O run longer than the footage. If you have a feature or a soft-news story and don't have to "hit" any scenes, write loose. That way, the words don't overwhelm or drown out the picture.

7. Don't overload your listeners with facts. Viewers are busy viewing. They're not giving their undivided attention to the words. And too many facts—or words—can cause a sensory overload.

8. Make use of natural sound and silence. Don't feel obliged to cram words into every single second. If the footage has natural sound, like a gurgling brook, let the picture and sound carry the scene. Even when the footage is silent, you can sometimes skip the narrative. Pause.

A few seconds of silence can be eloquent. And, depending on the scene, the anchor's (or reporter's) silence can underline the drama. What kinds of scenes? Perhaps a fireman breathing life into a baby, a lottery winner exploding with joy, a pole vaulter flinging himself over the crossbar.

9. Be sure the "where" precedes or is at the top of the V/O. If the anchor's lead-in doesn't identify the place, be sure it's identified at the outset in the V/O. Sometimes, though, it's acceptable to identify the place with only a super—the superimposition of characters that spell out the name. Viewers should know right away what they're looking at, where it was shot and when (if it's not fresh).

10. Read your V/O against the footage while an editor or desk-mate watches and listens. This is the best way to catch mistakes and weaknesses. If you time each segment of your copy as you write it, the final run-through should be all right. But don't take any chances: Read your V/O aloud against the footage.

The most frequent weakness in voice-overs written by newcomers, according to Charles F. Cremer, Phillip O. Keirstead and Richard D. Yoakam in *ENG: Television News,* 3d ed., is overwriting. They say the problem is not only that the text exceeds the running time of the video but also that viewers drown in the words and don't get a chance to mesh words and pictures in their minds.

Tag

This is the sentence or two that sometimes follow a story or V/O. It's called a tag, cap, button, lead-out or write-out. The tag is supposed to add a bit of information, perhaps an important fact that couldn't be fitted into the lead-in. Or perhaps it's an updated casualty figure. Or late news that should accompany the story just reported. It can be a P.S. that rounds out the story. Or a correction of something that the correspondent had recorded but wasn't edited. Or it might be an anchor's comment or aside. Whatever you call it or whatever you put into it, keep it short and to the point.

Some anchors begin their tags by saying "Incidentally" or "By the way." But it's best to refrain from those transparent efforts to be casual. If an item is indeed incidental, it doesn't deserve valuable air time. And if the item is not incidental, it shouldn't be minimized by being called incidental.

Tease(r)

A tease is terse. It's designed to inform viewers what lies ahead, to pique their curiosity and tempt them into staying tuned. A tease needs more than compression; it needs crushing. Or squashing. What you might call minimalism to the max. With only several seconds to work in, a writer needs a big vocabulary of short words. Also: creativity, imagination and a discriminating disdain for the rules. Often, there's not enough room for a complete sentence, so she needs to write her line like a headline: "Murder at the Waldorf." Good tease. Lacks a verb but packs a punch.

Yet one of the dangers in condensing a story into a headline is that by reducing and rounding it off, we can easily warp it. And warping can lead to slanting. And distorting. So no matter how catchy the tease you've written, no matter how clever, ask yourself: Is it misleading? Or deceptive? Does it hint of more than the newscast is going to offer? If your answers are no, no, no, then go, go, go.

How often are you annoyed to find that a newspaper headline isn't supported by the story? Often we see that kind of headline in tabloids at supermarket checkout counters. But the headlines are beyond checking out: **Siamese Twin Girls Born Pregnant** and **Man Gives Birth to Test-Tube Twins.** Although I haven't heard anything quite that phony in broadcast tease(r)s, I have heard some that flirt with fraud. The kind of tease that brings teases into disrepute is exemplified by "California's on Fire." But California was not on fire. A few hundred acres were on fire. Lesson: Don't get carried away—or *you*'ll get burned.

Apply the same standards to teases that you apply to news stories. We can't always follow writing rules in writing teases, but we must pursue the paramount goal to be fair and factual. We mustn't overstate or over-promise. (Unless we don't mind being the target of a comedy sketch, we shouldn't write a tease that's a parody of itself: "TV teases taken to task. Tape at ten.")

One-minute newscasts

Excluding commercials, one-minute 'casts usually run less than a minute. Whatever their length or brevity, they represent a challenge that's anything but minute. Jamming four or five stories into 40 seconds or so is like trying to stuff six pounds of suet into a five-pound sack. It's tough. I know. I've written one-minute newscasts (at three networks), and I've even stuffed seven stories into 50 seconds—a series of short bursts.

Writers who do these 'casts frequently develop a knack for ultra-compression. Whoops; that *frequently* is a squinting modifier. It seems to be looking in two directions at the same time: it might modify *do* or *develop*. I edit myself as I go along, almost unconsciously, so I'll re-do that sentence to read, "Writers who frequently do these 'casts develop a knack for ultra-compression." And that's what it takes to develop the knack: frequency.

As with any kind of writing or performing, improvement comes through doing it. And doing it. And doing it. And then reviewing it.

5

STYLE
Clarity Begins at Home—and Office

Style is not like fast food. You can't walk in and say, "I want a style. To go."

Sorry, it's no go. Style is intangible. You can't pick it up or buy it. And you can't borrow a writing style, one that stamps your copy as something special. Although style is not yours for the asking, style *is* gettable. But first, you have to get a handle on it.

When I say "style," I mean *what* you say and *how* you say it, the words you choose, how you use them, the way you construct your sentences. That's *writing* style. It's not the kind of style that style manuals deal with, the basic work rules for a newsroom, designed mainly for uniformity.

Most writers are individualists. They want personal styles. They want their scripts to differ from other people's scripts. And most of those other people want a distinctive style to make *their* scripts stand out. *And* themselves. Many new writers who yearn for a style shoot for the stars; they try to pattern their writing after that of star newscasters widely known for their style. Some newscasters do have fine writing styles. But some establish their reputation for style through a combination of elements that have nothing to do with writing: presence, personality, performance and presentation. If you want to develop *those* qualities, you'll have to read another chapter. In another book. By another writer.

Style is more than an unusual, or unique, way to say something. Trying to define style, a Frenchman said, is like trying to put a sack of flour in a thimble. But if you can't put your finger on style, how can you get your hands on it? Put thimbly: from reading, from listening and from learning. And from writing, writing, writing.

A dictionary defines style as "distinction, excellence, originality and character in any form of artistic or literary expression."

Distinction. Excellence. Originality. That's a lot to aim for. Sure, we write about momentous events, but we spend more time writing about crashes, crimes and coroner's cases. It's hard to make copy about the commonplace interesting, let alone distinctive, excellent and original. And if we all write about the same things, follow the same rules and use the same basic language, how in the world can we develop a style that's noticeable? And recognizable? And admirable?

The answer: Don't worry about developing your own style. Don't even think about it. Work on your craft; hone your skills, and your style will come to you. The development of style may be a process of decortication, a stripping or peeling away. As a writer learns to get rid of nonessentials, he discovers that what's left is style. But a writer shouldn't work too hard at attaining a style or the excessive effort will show.

The attainment of style mustn't be our main goal. Our most important goal is to communicate clearly, to tell a story well, so well that a listener understands it instantly and easily. To do that, we must write simply. We must not stretch and strain to strut our stuff—and that's the sort of sentence to scrap, a succession of hissing sibilants. Alliteration and other devices of rhetoric do work on occasion, but they must be used with care. Anyone searching for a personal style should keep in mind that style is no substitute for substance, and a writer should not sacrifice substance for style. According to my publisher, Aaron Cohodes, the best way for a writer to be different is to be better.

We shouldn't labor to draw attention to our scripts. And we shouldn't draw attention to ourselves. Our focus should be on our listeners. They are the people we should direct our attention to. Those people out there. Them.

Still, you might say, there must be more to style than that platter of platitudes. Right you are when you are right. There's far more. And the more we learn about writing, and the more we write, the more we realize that style is not easy to come by.

To say that style is elusive is not to say what it is. Perhaps some of the world's best stylists can tell us—and tell us how to find it. They've said it far better than I can. So let's turn to these guest lecturers, who clearly prize clarity above all else:

"First, clarity; then again clarity; and, finally, clarity."
ANATOLE FRANCE

"A good style must, first of all, be clear."

ARISTOTLE

"Words, like eyeglasses, blur everything that they do not make more clear."

JOSEPH JOUBERT

"If any man wishes to write in a clear style, let him first be clear in his thoughts."

JOHANN WOLFGANG VON GOETHE

"Clear writers, like clear fountains, do not seem so deep as they are; the turbid looks most profound."

WALTER SAVAGE LANDOR

"In language, clearness is everything."

CONFUCIUS

"Clearness is the most important matter in the use of words."

QUINTILIAN

"Whatever we conceive well we express clearly, and words flow with ease."

NICHOLAS BOILEAU

"People think I can teach them style. What stuff it is. Have something to say and say it as clearly as you can. That is the only secret to style."

MATTHEW ARNOLD

"When you can with difficulty say anything clearly, simply and emphatically, then, provided the difficulty is not apparent to the reader, that is style. When you can do that easily, it is genius."

LORD DUNSANY

"Nothing is so difficult as the apparent ease of a clear and flowing style. . . . Those graces which, from their presumed facility, encourage all to attempt to imitate them, are usually the most inimitable."

CHARLES CALEB COLTON

"Lucidity is the soul of style."

HILAIRE BELLOC

"The indispensable characteristic of a good writer is a style marked by lucidity."

ERNEST HEMINGWAY

"Style is the dress of thought; a modest dress,
Neat, but not gaudy, will true critics please."

REV. SAMUEL WESLEY

"Style is not something applied. It is something that permeates. It is of the nature of that in which it is found, whether the poem, the manner of a god, the bearing of a man. It is not a dress."

WALLACE STEVENS

"Style is organic, not the clothes a man wears, but the flesh, bone, and blood of his body. Therefore it is really impossible to consider styles apart from the system of perceptions and feelings and thoughts that animate them."

J. MIDDLETON MURRY

"Style is the dress of thoughts; and let them be ever so just, if your style is homely, coarse, and vulgar, they will appear to as much disadvantage, and be as ill received, as your person, though ever so well-proportioned, would if dressed in rags, dirt, and tatters."

LORD CHESTERFIELD

"I am well aware that an addiction to silk underwear does not imply that one's feet are dirty. None the less, style, like sheer silk, too often hides eczema."

ALBERT CAMUS

"Style is neither an involuntary matter nor something you add to the text to 'dress it up.' Style should not be thought of as an end unto itself. It is a series of choices—of voice, tone, diction, structure, grammar and usage—that depend on purpose and appropriateness. Putting style in almost always clutters writing up; removing clutter gives writing style."

MITCHELL IVES

"Those most likely to talk about it [style] are least likely to have it. Style in writing compares to intonation in speaking. It may be harsh; shrill; nasal; affected; a soft Southern timbre, or a cockney vivacity. It is as personal as clothes or complexion. It can be controlled and educated, but beneath control it must partly remain instinctive, unconscious and organic. As in clothes so in literature it is most admirable when least obtruded.

"Its very plainness implies high cost; the cost of thinking and study."

CHRISTOPHER MORLEY

"Style is a sort of melody that comes into my sentences by itself. If a writer says what he has to say as accurately and effectively as he can, his style will take care of itself."

GEORGE BERNARD SHAW

"True ease in writing comes from art, not chance,
As those move easiest who have learned to dance."

ALEXANDER POPE

"He that will write well . . . must follow this counsel of Aristotle, to speak as the common people do, to think as wise men do."

ROGER ASCHAM

"When you doubt between words, use the plainest, the commonest, the most idiomatic. . . . Eschew fine words as you would rouge, and love simple ones as you would native roses on your cheek."

AUGUST W. HARE

"Crisp writing usually has a good deal of shortening in it."

ANON.

"Only great minds can afford a simple style."

STENDHAL

"To write simply is as difficult as to be good."

W. SOMERSET MAUGHAM

"The chief aim of the writer is to be understood."

JOHN DRYDEN

"I am unlikely to trust a sentence that comes easily."

WILLIAM GASS

"There is no way of writing well and also of writing easily."

ANTHONY TROLLOPE

"What is written without effort is in general read without pleasure."

SAMUEL JOHNSON

"Ready writing makes not good writing; but good writing brings on ready writing."

BEN JONSON

"You write with ease to show your breeding,
But easy writing's curst hard reading."

RICHARD BRIMSLEY SHERIDAN

"In what he leaves unsaid I discover a master of style."

FRIEDRICH VON SCHILLER

"Style is what gets left out."

BERTHOLT BRECHT

"There is but one art, to omit."

ROBERT LOUIS STEVENSON

"Proper words in proper places, make the true definition of style."

JONATHAN SWIFT

"A man's style is his mind's voice. Wooden minds, wooden voices."

RALPH WALDO EMERSON

"A pen may be just as usefully employed in crossing out as in writing."

QUINTILIAN

"In composing, as a general rule, run your pen through every other word you have written; you have no idea what vigor it will give to your style."

SYDNEY SMITH

"No style is good that is not fit to be spoken or read aloud with effect."

WILLIAM HAZLITT

"Writing, when properly managed, is but a different name for conversation."

LAURENCE STERNE

"The style is the man himself."

GEORGES DE BUFFON

"Montesquieu had the style of a genius; Buffon, the genius of style."

BARON GRIMM

"Words are like leaves; and where they most abound,
Much fruit of sense beneath is rarely found."

ALEXANDER POPE

"A good style must have an air of novelty, at the same time concealing its art."

ARISTOTLE

"Intense study of the Bible will keep any man from being vulgar in point of style."

SAMUEL TAYLOR COLERIDGE

"There is such an animal as a nonstylist, only they're not writers—they're typists."

TRUMAN CAPOTE

"Simple style is like white light. It is complex but its complexity is not obvious."

ANATOLE FRANCE

"A pure style in writing results from the rejection of everything superfluous."

ALBERTINE ADRIENNE NECKER DE SAUSSURE

"A good style should show no sign of effort. What is written should seem a happy accident."

W. SOMERSET MAUGHAM

"Everyone recognizes it, everyone describes it, but no two people agree as to its exact nature."

HENRY SEIDEL CANBY

"Without style there cannot possibly be a single work of value in any branch of eloquence or poetry."

VOLTAIRE

"There is nothing more dangerous to the formation of a prose style than the endeavour to make it poetic."

J. MIDDLETON MURRY

"The greatest possible merit of style is, of course, to make the words absolutely disappear into the thought."

NATHANIEL HAWTHORNE

"There is no such thing as good style or bad style. The question is, does it accomplish its intention?"

CHRISTOPHER MORLEY

"The secret of the style of the great Greek and Roman authors is that it is the perfection of good sense."

JOHN STUART MILL

"A man's style is nearly as much a part of himself as his face, or figure, or the throbbing of his pulse. . . ."

FRANÇOIS FÉNELON

"One should not aim at being possible to understand, but at being impossible to misunderstand."

QUINTILIAN

"You do not create a style. You work, and develop yourself; your style is an emanation from your own being."

KATHERINE ANNE PORTER

"The first rule of style is to have something to say. The second rule of style is to control yourself when, by chance, you have two things to say; say first one, then the other, not both at the same time."

GEORGE POLYA

"To achieve style, begin by affecting none—that is, place yourself in the background. A careful and honest writer does not need to worry about style. As he becomes proficient in the use of the language, his style will emerge, because he himself will emerge, and when this happens he will find it increasingly easy to break through the barriers that separate him from other minds, other hearts—which is, of course, the purpose of writing, as well as its principal reward."

WILLIAM STRUNK JR. AND E.B. WHITE

"We are surprised and delighted when we come upon a natural style, for instead of an author we find a man."

BLAISE PASCAL

"I've been called a stylist until I really could tear my hair out. And I simply don't believe in style. The style is you."

KATHERINE ANNE PORTER

"A strict and succinct style is that, where you can take away nothing without loss, and that loss to be manifest."

BEN JONSON

"As for style of writing, if one has anything to say, it drops from him simply and directly, as a stone falls to the ground."

HENRY DAVID THOREAU

"The style of an author should be the image of his mind, but the choice and command of language is the fruit of exercise."

EDWARD GIBBON

"Whatever is translatable in other and simpler words of the same language, without loss of sense or dignity, is bad."

SAMUEL TAYLOR COLERIDGE

"The virtues of good style are more negative than positive. The man who knows what to avoid is already the owner of style."

HENRY W. FOWLER

"The first and most important thing of all, at least for writers today, is to strip language clean, to lay it bare down to the bone."

ERNEST HEMINGWAY

"I notice that you use plain, simple language, short words and brief sentences. This is the way to write English—it is the modern way and the best way. Stick to it; don't let fluff and flowers and verbosity creep in."

MARK TWAIN

"Obscurity in writing is commonly a proof of darkness in the mind; the greatest learning is to be seen in the greatest plainness."

JOHN WILKINS

"Our taste in style matches our taste in corned beef: Lean is keen."

WILLIAM SAFIRE

"Carefully examined, a good—an interesting—style will be found to consist in a constant succession of tiny, unobservable surprises."

FORD MADOX FORD

"The fundamental rule of style is to keep solely in view the thought one wants to convey. One must therefore have a thought to start with."

JACQUES BARZUN *(quoting an unidentified French stylist)*

"Your writing style is yourself in the process of thought and the act of writing, and you cannot buy that in a bookstore or fix it up in a seminar."

WILLIAM SAFIRE

"For a man to write well, there are required three necessaries: to read the best authors, observe the best speakers, and much exercise of his own style."

BEN JONSON

"A good narrative style does not attract attention to itself. Its job is to keep the reader's mind on the story, on what's happening, the event, and not the writer."

LEON SURMELIAN

"To me style is just the outside of content, and content the inside of style, like the outside and the inside of the human body—both go together, they can't be separated."

JEAN-LUC GODARD

"It is by the use of familiar words that style affects the reader. People feel that using them is the mark of a man who knows life and its daily concerns, and maintains contact with them."

JOSEPH JOUBERT

"Words in prose ought to express the intended meaning; if they attract attention to themselves, it is a fault; in the very best styles you read page after page without noticing the medium."

SAMUEL TAYLOR COLERIDGE

"[The beginner should shun] all devices that are popularly believed to indicate style—all mannerisms, tricks, adornments. The approach to style is by way of plainness, simplicity, orderliness, sincerity."

E. B. WHITE

"A style, representing the sum total of choices made in daily speech and writing, expresses our individual connection with that vast and confusing body of knowledge known as language."

CHARLES W. FERGUSON

"To write in a genuine familiar or truly English style is to
write as any one would speak in common conversation, who
had a thorough command and choice of words, or who could
discourse with ease, force and perspicuity, setting aside all
pedantic and oratorical flourishes."

WILLIAM HAZLITT

"Obscurity and affectation are the two great faults of style.
Obscurity of expression generally springs from confusion of
ideas; and the same wish to dazzle, at any cost, which produces
affectation in the manner of a writer, is likely to produce
sophistry in his reasoning."

THOMAS BABINGTON MACAULAY

"The way of speaking that I love is natural and plain, as well
in writing as speaking, and a sinewy and significant way of
expressing one's self, short and pithy, and not so elegant and
artificial as prompt and vehement. Rather hard than harsh, free
from affectation . . . not like a pedant, a preacher or a pleader,
but rather a soldier-like style. . . ."

MICHEL DE MONTAIGNE

"The first rule of all writing—that rule to which every other is
subordinate—is that the words used by the writer shall be such
as most fully and precisely convey his meaning to the great
body of his readers. All considerations about the purity and
dignity of style ought to bend to this consideration."

THOMAS BABINGTON MACAULAY

"You want to fix up your writing, parse your sentences, use the
right words? Fine, pick up the little books, learn to avoid
mistakes, revere taut prose and revile tautology. But do not
flatter yourself that you have significantly changed your style.
First, straighten out yourself so that you can then think straight
and soon afterward write straight."

WILLIAM SAFIRE

"He who thinks much says but little in proportion to his
thoughts. He selects that language which will convey his ideas
in the most explicit and direct manner. He tries to compress
as much thought as possible into a few words. On the contrary,
the man who talks everlastingly and promiscuously, who seems
to have an exhaustless magazine of sound, crowds so many
words into his thoughts that he always obscures, and very
frequently conceals them."

WASHINGTON IRVING

"To eliminate the vice of wordiness is to ensure the virtue of emphasis, which depends more on conciseness than on any other factor. Wherever we can make 25 words do the work of 50, we halve the area in which looseness and disorganization can flourish, and by reducing the span of attention required we increase the force of the thought. To make sure our words count for as much as possible is surely the simplest as well as the hardest secret of style."

WILSON FOLLETT

"Style is hard to pin down. The difficulty recalls Justice Stewart's remark about obscenity; he couldn't define it, but he knew when he saw it. Whatever it is, style provides the individual hallmark that writers stamp upon their work—but that metaphor is inapt, for it suggests that style is something you put onto a piece after you've finished it, as if it were ketchup on chili, or lemon on fish. Style doesn't work that way. It's more of a marinade, permeating the whole composition."

JAMES J. KILPATRICK

"While one should always study the method of a great artist, one should never imitate his manner. The manner of an artist is essentially individual, the method of an artist is absolutely universal. The first is personality, which no one should copy; the second is perfection, which all should aim at."

OSCAR WILDE

"Style is everything and nothing. It is not that, as is commonly supposed, you get your content and soup it up with style; style is absolutely embedded in the way you perceive."

MARTIN AMIS

"Style is the hallmark of a temperament stamped upon the material at hand."

ANDRÉ MAUROIS

"Style is the image of character."

EDWARD GIBBON

"Style is effectiveness of assertion."

GEORGE BERNARD SHAW

"Style is the essence of thinking."

ROBERT LOUIS STEVENSON

"Style is the physiognomy of the mind."
ARTHUR SCHOPENHAUER

"Style is what gives value and currency to thought."
HENRI FRÉDÉRIC AMIEL

"An honest tale speeds best being plainly told."
WILLIAM SHAKESPEARE

"Be plain and simple, and lay down the thing as it was."
JOHN BUNYAN

"Get your facts right first; that is the foundation of all style."
GEORGE BERNARD SHAW

"Style comes only after long, hard practice and writing."
WILLIAM STYRON

"Now do it—with style."
MERVIN BLOCK

6

MY LEAST WORST

If broadcast news is written on the wind, news scripts are written on tissues. As soon as they've done the job, they're tossed out.

Many newsrooms do hang on to scripts for reference—by insiders. But nowhere that I know of are news script files open to outsiders. When it came time for me to get examples for this chapter, I wanted to find a newswriter willing to share his scripts with strangers and also willing to put up with their criticism—and mine. Eventually, I found one: me.

Over the years, I've written tens of thousands of scripts for broadcast. And once in a while, I saved a page or two, for no obvious reason—perhaps in the belief that one day I'd find something to do with them. Reprinting my own scripts offers several advantages: With access to the writer's mind, I can probe his mental processes and get his frank comments on what he thinks went wrong. Also, I'm able to get his ideas on how the scripts can be improved. And if I have a question, he's always on hand. I don't have to write him, phone him, visit him or humor him.

Some of these scripts aren't so bad. Some aren't so good. Some were written under pressure with only minutes to air, and they show it. Some were written with ample time for writing and rewriting—but don't show it. And some, well, see for yourself.

Please read the first script first. Then read my comment next to it. Next, the second script, then my comment. And so forth. So go forth. Here they are, a fistful of scripts that might be called my least worst:

mb		
OSGOOD	The New York City marathon was won today by an Italian. He ran the 26 miles in two hours, 14 minutes, 53 seconds. He got a good run for his money and good money for his run. Steve Young has the story:	
VTR	TRACK UP:	

My lead-in would have worked just as well without the third sentence. But it has a nice lilt to it and didn't do any harm.

I skipped the name of the marathon winner because the reporter used it. I specified the winner's time because the reporter did not. The reporter did note the amount of the prize, so I didn't have to.

I used the passive voice—*was won*—to set the scene at the outset with the combined "where" and "what" and built up to the "who." If I had used the active voice—"An Italian won the. . . ."—I'd be giving away the key point of the story in the first breath. And when listeners hear that a foreigner has done something, they're probably less interested than when they first hear mention of a widely known sports staple at home.

For similar reasons, I try to use the same approach when I write most stories about someone's winning a prize: "The Nobel Prize in Chemistry was awarded today to a researcher in Ruritania." After you hear "was awarded today to," aren't you eager to hear who won? Don't you enjoy suspense?

mb		
PLANTE	Runner Mary Decker fell short of her goal in the Los Angeles Olympics last summer, but, as Bob McNamara reports from Eugene, Oregon, she's back on track:	
VTR	TRACK UP:	

It runs nine seconds. No wasted words. All one sentence: short, straight, swift.

```
mb
OSGOOD    Two Irish boys ran away
          from home in Dublin three
          days ago, hitchhiked to
          London and took an Air
          India flight to this
          country—all without a
          ticket or passport. A
          policeman at New York
          City's Kennedy airport
          became suspicious of
          them—one 10 years old,
          the other 13—and they
          fessed up. So tonight
          they're going back. If they
```

```
                      could write a book on how
                      they traveled free, it might
                      be a runaway best-seller.
```

You had to read a long distance for a short payoff, so you might call your journey a *pun*itive expedition.

```
mb
OSGOOD    The U-S boycott of the
          19-80 Moscow Olympics
          has now come full circle.
          The United States stayed
          away because of the
          Soviet invasion of
          Afghanistan. Today,
          Afghanistan said it's not
          going to take part in this
          summer's Los Angeles
          Olympics. That makes it
          eight countries, led by the
          Soviet Union, which say
          they do not choose to run.
```

This approach seems preferable to a hard-news lead, which would not be especially exciting: "Afghanistan said today it's not going to take part in this summer's Los Angeles Olympics." Who cares? Sounds like another ho-hummer. My treatment is an exercise in story-telling. A broadcast newswriter's job is not to philosophize or theorize, so I did the best I could with a few facts and a little fancy.

If I could rewrite it today, I'd fix the last sentence: replace *which* with *that* and delete *it*.

Ideally, a network newscast would carry only news that would merit display on page 1 or page 3 of an imaginary national general-interest newspaper. An exception: a newsfeature. The Afghanistan story was printed on sports pages, but I doubt that any paper carried it on page 1, except in Kabul. (And it probably got a good play there on Kabul News Network.)

block CRONKITE	The young woman in the middle of the McGuire sisters' singing act was in the middle again today, this time before a federal grand jury in Chicago. The jury wanted to know about Phyllis McGuire's reputed romance with an underworld overlord, Sam Giancanna. A cameraman for station WBBM-TV filmed the courthouse comings and goings, and

	Stuart Novins reports the doings: OUTCUE:

Until now, no one was aware that I misspelled "Giancana." I'm glad *he* never found out—or I might face a horde of grumblers. In fact, a mob.

mb CRONKITE	Have you ever looked at a can of chili con carne and wondered how much of it is beans? And how much meat? Well, maybe before too long you'll be able to find out. The government said today that it's starting a revision of labeling laws so shoppers can easily tell just what's in a can—and how much of it. Richard Roth has the story in Washington:

A question lead. And a "you" lead. Rarely do I write a question lead. More often, I write a questionable lead. I think this kind of question, one that every listener can answer instantly, is acceptable.

If I had written that story straight, I probably would have started, "The government said today it's revising the law on labeling canned goods so you can easily tell what's inside—and how much of it."

Too many stories, though, start with "the government" or talk about the government. Here was a story that offered an opportunity to get away from the standard governmental yawner. I don't remember whether the wire copy mentioned chili, but as a chili-eater, I'd long wondered how much is carne. Or how little. I figured that if I was curious, a lot of other people were, too. So I decided to spice up the lead by turning it into a question.

"You" grabs listeners by the collar, or by the ear. It's best used when it's almost universally applicable. That's why it sometimes makes sense to write up a postal rate increase this way: "From now on, when you mail a letter, you're going to have to pay two cents more." But it makes no sense to use "you" in restrictive contexts: "You're going to have to pay more for a Rolls-Royce." Ninety-nine percent of our listeners aren't going to be buying Rollses, so they're not going to have to pay anything. Used with discrimination, though, "you" can help you.

mb		
CRONKITE	Great Britain is grim about two crises, one with the pound sterling and now one with a sterling pounder, a pounder of drums, that is, whose percussions have prompted wide repercussions. Alexander Kendrick reports:	
KENDRICK	TRACK UP	
CRONKITE	The latest medical bulletin reports the operation was a success . . . and Ringo	

should be an active Starr again next month. Yeah, yeah, yeah! And that's the way it is, Wednesday, December second, 1964. This is Walter Cronkite reporting from Washington. Good Night.

Signs of strain: *pound sterling* and *sterling pounder.* Not to mention *percussions* and *repercussions.*

No, I don't know why I capitalized *night.* (Who cares?)

If I had the power to recall scripts, this is one of those I'd want brought back to the shop for retooling. No fooling.

```
mb
CRONKITE      When it comes to shops,
              shoppers and shopping,
              there's no time like
              Christmas, no place like
              New York City and no
              observer like Charles
              Osgood:

OSGOOD        TRACK UP:
```

Another nine-second lead-in. This was a hard one to write because it was one of those annual, or biennial, excursions in search of unusual gifts or givers. Writing a lead-in to a frothy feature is hard because the feature itself, as good as it may be, often defies summarizing in several seconds, or summarizing in a way that arrests listeners. And you don't want to give away the best parts of the correspondent's script.

Although that lead-in was hard to write, almost all lead-ins are hard to write. Only someone who doesn't know much about writing finds writing easy.

```
block
REASONER      There's no place like
              nowhere, but Washington
              has a tunnel that goes
              there. Martin Agronsky
              has the story:

VTR
```

Six seconds. They don't make 'em much shorter. Or shallower.

block	
CRONKITE	Humorist Irvin S. Cobb once had some fun with the name of Poet Witter Bynner. Cobb quipped: "'It's been a bitter Winter,' said Witter Bynner." But Winter was no laughing matter today in a large part of the nation. CBS News Correspondent Harry Arouh has the story:
WBBM-RR	OUTCUE:

If it hadn't been for Cobb and Bynner, this lead-in could have been shoved into that tunnel to nowhere.

block	
CRONKITE	Americans may think that the way British play croquet isn't cricket. But despite an ocean of difference between the two groups, they both play with English on the ball and mallets for all. Charles Collingwood reports from London:
VTR	

At least I didn't talk about "no rest for the wicket."

```
mb
CRONKITE      Ronald Reagan's positions
              are seen by some people
              as rigid, so Dan Rather
              compares Reagan's
              rhetoric and record:

RATHER        TRACK UP:
```

1980 Republican convention. That year I was churning out so many lead-ins for videotapes at both conventions, especially for "bank" pieces prepared in advance, I don't remember whether this one was used. So this may be its première.

```
mb
CRONKITE      Our country holds age in
              high regard in coins,
              wines and books—but
              seldom in people.
                So age may be an issue
              in November, and Andy
              Rooney has a new wrinkle:

ROONEY        TRACK UP:
```

This led into a whimsical piece prompted by the Republican Presidential candidate, Ronald Reagan, whose face was well wrinkled.

mb	
CRONKITE	Andy Rooney has taken a look at—or a listen to—convention oratory, and, needless to say, finds most of it needless to say:
ROONEY	TRACK UP:

If this wasn't used at that convention, it can still be used at the next one, needless to say.

block	
RATHER	Good evening. This is the C-B-S Evening News, Dan Rather reporting. As the British fleet advances toward the disputed Falkland Islands, Britain and Argentina may be moving closer militarily. That's because U-S Secretary of State Haig apparently has not brought the two

disputants any closer diplomatically. We have three reports; first,

This lead-in was a hodgepodge because it had to provide an umbrella for reports from three correspondents. *May* is weak, but apparently the shooting hadn't started, we had no reporters with the fleet, and whatever information we had probably was sketchy.

block		
CRONKITE	Two tiny craft managed to meet with pinpoint precision in the infinite depths of space . . . and the United States took another giant step today toward landing a man on the moon. Gemini-six rendezvoused with Gemini-seven high over . the Western Pacific after four hours of maneuvering through light and darkness at 17-thousand, 500 miles	an hour. For Gemini-six's astronauts, the day has been a strenuous one:

Too many numbers in the second sentence.
     "Giant step." Hmm.

block	
con'd. A	
CRONKITE	another "first"—the first American musical message from outer space. He was talked into it, in a sense, by the mission control communicator at Houston—Astronaut James McDivitt:
CRONKITE	You can't blame him if he can't carry a tune; no room up there.

The first page of this script is missing (don't bother looking for it), but the tag may be worth a look—maybe.

block		
REASONER	Good evening.	
	America's two astronauts	
	both took a walk today—	
	on the carrier Wasp as	
	it circled off Jacksonville,	
	Florida. James McDivitt	
	and Edward White	
	reviewed their four-day	
	flight, and the space	
	agency released	
	spectacular film of	
	White's walk in space.	
	The pictures were taken	

		by an automatic camera
		mounted on the spacecraft
		by White himself and by
		another camera held by
		McDivitt. Charles Von
		Fremd reports:
VTR		OUTCUE:

The first sentence made sense to listeners right away if they already knew that one of the astronauts had taken a highly publicized space walk. By that time, the only people who didn't know were isolates and anchorites (not the kinds in newsrooms).

block	
REASONER	Outer space and inner
	grace, star dust and mud.
	Eric Sevareid has a few
	thoughts on these and
	other matters:
VTR	

This lead-in probably ran on an evening when our newscast carried a story about space, the astros' turf.

Writing an introduction to a commentary that skips around without a distinct central theme puts a writer to the test. An anchor's delivery can help him pass.

mb	
RATHER	It may be within the letter of the law, but a letter from a member of the First Family has raised some questions—and eyebrows. Bill Plante has the story at the White House:
PLANTE	TRACK UP:

It's good to avoid starting a story or a lead-in—or a criticism—with an indefinite pronoun, and it's good to avoid *may,* but despite these handicaps, it may work here.

mb	
KURALT	At a time when the President is under fire, and the Presidency, too, it may be helpful to recall a plain-speaking, peppery President, a man who seemed to relish being on the firing line, a man who was quick to fire back or even fire first. And, as Bruce Morton recounts, he also was strong enough to <u>hold</u> his fire— or to <u>light</u> a fire for illumination and warmth:

I suppose I wrote so much because I thought the correspondent's script needed setting up. Whether it needed that much setting up, I don't know. Whoever inserted *his* into my script—third line from the bottom—knew his business. The President was Truman. And the person who deserves credit for *his* probably was the anchor himself.

mb		
OSGOOD	Tornadoes and	
	thunderstorms struck the	
	southeast today and	
	caused at least two	
V/O	deaths. Tornadoes in	
	Laurel county, Kentucky,	
.	in the London area,	
	overturned mobile homes,	
	toppled trees, battered	
	buildings, peeled off	
	roofs, killed cattle and	
	destroyed or damaged a	
	lot of other property. At	

least six people there	
were hurt.	

If Guinness ever lists the record for the most verbs in one sentence, the second sentence would be a contender. It has seven. Seven good ones. The lead refers to the Southeast, but the only place we had any footage from was Kentucky. Right at the top of the V/O, the script makes clear where the footage was shot.

mb	
BRADLEY	Good evening.
	Hurricane Allen is gone
	with the wind—
	downgraded to a tropical
	storm.
	Its winds greatly
	reduced, the storm is now
	moving from the Texas
	coast toward Mexico.
	But when Allen swept
	ashore into Texas from
	the Gulf, it caused
	extensive damage, though
	less than feared.

Gone with the wind? Yes, I was trying for a novel approach.

The last line of the script says damage was less than feared, but between the lines you can read "and less than the producer had hoped for."

mb		
OSGOOD	The weather has been so severe in the Plains states, the temperatures so low, the winds so high and the snows so deep that in some places even highway snowplows have not ventured out.	
V/O	Winds in Minnesota reached 60 miles an hour, temperatures fell to 16-below, and with snow whipped into	whiteouts, visibility shrank to only several feet. Across the Plains states, at least eight people have been killed. The National Guard has rescued hundreds of stranded motorists, but many are still snowbound.

The lead-in bounces around in a sort of singsong, but special delivery drove it home. As you read the V/O, you may be able to "see" the footage.

Ordinarily, eight deaths would make the lead, but I think the deaths occurred over several days. And for all I can remember, on that day there might have been no deaths.

This script was written for a Sunday night newscast, but it has no "today," no "tonight," no "yesterday," no "weekend." With no loss.

mb	
OSGOOD	Capitalism and communism are squaring off in a remote city in China, and it seems that capitalism has got the goods on its rival. David Jackson has the story:
VTR	TRACK UP:

The correspondent told about the emergence of private enterprise and featured busy merchants, which is why I said capitalism *has the goods.* Someone who read the script inserted *got.* If I had ever used *has got* in any English class, I'd never have gotten away with it. But in *The Careful Writer,* Theodore M. Bernstein, a language authority who was an editor of the *New York Times,* wrote: "To see how it adds force, compare *has to meet, must meet,* and *has got to meet.* There cannot be much doubt that *got* in this sense has simply got to win approval."

And that was published in 1968. In 1980, *American Usage and Style: The Consensus* by Roy Copperud said the consensus regards *has got* as standard. For those of us who still think *has got* is redundant, maybe we've got another think coming.

```
mb
SPENCER    A woman in Woodridge,
           Illinois, has won what she
           calls a victory for
           lefthanded people in a
           righthanded world: a
           judgment of 136-thousand
           dollars from a food store
           where she worked as a
           checkout clerk. She's
           lefthanded, but the store
           required her to check out
           groceries with her right
```

```
           hand. So now the store's
           left holding the bag.
```

Although a wire service had moved the story that day, the news was several days old: not fresh, but not yet stale. I did the best I could.

```
mb
OSGOOD     Only a few years ago, oil
           was in such short supply
           that Washington pushed a
           policy of trying to squeeze
           oil out of rock. But, as
           Bob McNamara reports
           from Grand Junction,
           Colorado, some
           companies seem to have
           dug themselves into
           a hole:

MCNAMARA   TRACK UP:
```

To contrast the past and the present, I now think I'd insert "now" after "companies."

```
mb
SPENCER        One of the most enduring
               figures of the Old West
               is the cowboy. But many of
               the pioneer cowboys have
               been largely ignored—
               because they were black.
               Their descendents,
               though, have kept the
               campfires burning and
               their memories glowing.
               Sam Ford has the story in
               Boley, Oklahoma:

VTR            TRACK UP:
```

To save time, I could have skipped the first sentence and started with *many* (and deleted *of the*).

```
mb
OSGOOD         A new study says children
               who become hooked on
               television at an early age
               often become teenagers
               who are overweight. And
               the study by two Boston
               doctors reports that the
               more time these teens
               spend watching T-V, the
               more weight they put
               on—making them truly
               heavy viewers.
```

Satisfactory.

Although the first line, *A new study says* is unoriginal and unexciting, it usually does the job. Can you imagine any listener who wouldn't keep listening?

mb			mb	
OSGOOD	Former President Carter arrived in New York City today to lend a hand—in fact, both of them—to help rebuild a burned-out apartment building.		V/O	building on Manhattan's Lower East Side, Mister Carter, an expert woodworker, is going to use hammer and saw to try to make the place fit again.
V/O	He came by bus with other volunteers from his hometown Baptist church in Plains, Georgia. On arrival, they talked over their one-week project, sponsored by a religious group. At the abandoned			

If you've seen enough TV news, you can almost see the videotape covered by the voice-over: the woodworker himself getting off the bus, people chatting, the abandoned building. It all fits.

mb	
RATHER	Good evening. The greatest threat to economic recovery, the President said today, is high interest rates. But most of the interest during his news conference seemed to be in what was unsaid. Lesley Stahl has the story at the White House:
STAHL	TRACK UP:

Rereading this lead-in reminds me that often a lead-in is merely a stall, playing for time, like preliminary boxing bouts holding the gathering crowd and building expectation until the main event.

mb	
CRONKITE	Although this is the main season for charitable giving, investigators have found that some so-called charities are more intent on taking. John Sheahan has the story:
SHEAHAN	TRACK UP:

The contrast between *giving* and *taking* and the emphasis on *taking* (as the last word) give this lead-in its sting.

mb	
OSGOOD	This country has about 26-million military veterans, but as the two world wars fade away, more old-timers are answering their final roll call. So the largest veterans' organization, the American Legion, is using new tactics to recruit members for posts whose numbers are no longer legion. Bill Whitaker has the story:

This is the kind of story that needs context and perspective, as one newscaster puts it. So the first sentence sets the scene and the tone. And the last may cause a groan.

```
block
CRONKITE      There's a new look in art,
              and there's more to it
              than meets the eye.
              Robert Trout reports:


CRONKITE      I suppose you could
              say, Op goes the easel.
```

The new look in art was Op Art. Op, short for "optical," created the illusion of movement. Op Art was preceded by Pop Art. But there's no such thing as Mom Art.

```
block
CRONKITE      A flip that can launch a
              thousand faces: that's the
              ability of an amazing new
              machine. Nelson Benton
              has the story in Chicago:


VTR


CRONKITE      Nelson, that man looks
              like my Walter ego.
```

The tag is better than the lead-in. But to appreciate the tag, you need to know that while a witness or victim was describing a culprit, a police technician was cranking in features to produce a face on the screen. In this make-believe case, the "witness" (the reporter) carefully described the subject, including his mustache. And the face on the technician's screen turned out to be that of Walter Cronkite.

I started the script the wrong way. The start may be catchy, but it's wrong to start a story by making an assertion and then adding awkwardly, "That's the ability of. . . ." Or "That's what so-and-so says." Or "That according to. . . ." Or "That's what happened when. . . ." Or "That's the opinion of. . . ." Or "Dead. That's what Theophilus Thackeray is."

This lead-in might be better: "A remarkable new machine can provide a sketch of someone police are looking for. A technician can flip a lever and launch a thousand faces." Or something like that. But the script, the scripter, the reporter and the anchor are all beyond recall.

block	
CRONKITE	France long has been a haven for the strange from many lands— heretics, neurotics, the erratic and the erotic. But now France says, "Don't give me your befuddled masses." Bernard Kalb has the story:

With apologies to Emma Lazarus and the Statute of Liberty. Profound apologies.

block		
REASONER	During last Sunday's inaugural demonstration of the Earlybird communications satellite, a Royal Canadian Mounted Policeman broadcast—to the U-S and Europe—a description of a wanted man.	an unidentified viewer in Fort Lauderdale, Florida, tipped police that he recognized LeMay's face as that of a man he knew. LeMay, wanted for bank robbery, was arrested there today aboard his yacht. And once again the Royal Canadian Mounties got their man, this time with the help of Earlybird— and a birdwatcher.
VTR		
REASONER	After seeing the international broadcast,	

My editor, Ed Bliss, taught me to spell out "U.S.," except when using it as an adjective, as in "the U-S Navy." I don't know why I slipped up here and how it slipped through.

In the tease before the preceding commercial, I wrote, "Earlybird catches its first worm."

mb

PAULEY The outlook for wine in California is again—you might say—rosé. After a 17-day strike, winery workers there have approved a new contract, and they'll start going back to work today—just in time for the peak of the grape harvest. They'll get a 13 percent pay increase in the first year, with smaller increases in the next two.

"Today Show," Sept. 22, 1980. The editor crossed out the last sentence, apparently because he thought it would tell our viewers more than they cared to know about winery wages—and what the strike was all about.

mb

BROKAW The Shah of Iran has been flown to New York City for medical treatment. The nature of the Shah's illness has not been made public. But a U-S State Department spokesman says the Shah is "quite" sick. He was taken to New York Hospital-Cornell Medical Center. The Shah arrived in New York City on a chartered jet from

Cuernavaca, Mexico. He moved to Mexico after he lost his throne in Iran 10 months ago.

"Today Show," Oct. 23, 1979. No "today" in this story. The shah landed the previous day or night, so I used the present perfect tense for this warmed-over news.

The first sentence of the script could have been shortened: "The Shah of Iran has arrived in New York City for medical treatment."

```
mb
GUIDA        Some people making news
             today:
             Actress Linda Blair: fined
             five-thousand dollars,
             sentenced to three years'
             probation and ordered
             to make 12 public
             appearances warning
             youngsters about the
             dangers of drugs. Miss
             Blair, who starred in "The
             Exorcist," had pleaded
             guilty to conspiracy to
```

```
                              possess cocaine. No, she
                              didn't say the devil made
                              her do it.
```

Some people making news today was a standing head on the "Today Show" for a short package about prominent people for whom we had a still photo, new or old. The personalities we featured seldom had made anything definable as news and seldom that day, but the justification (if one's needed) was that a wire service had moved an item that the producer considered serviceable. After all, the show must go on.

Someone deleted that last sentence in the script, maybe in fear of being dispossessed.

```
mb
GUIDA        Some people making
             news today: Vladimir
             Horowitz plugs his ears to
             muffle the loud sound at
             a New York City disco.
             Apparently the pianist
             prefers pianissimo.
```

Whoever chose that item must have been at his wits' end, but when it comes to filling a two-hour hole, every whit helps.

As Falstaff said about his ragtag band of soldiers: They'll fill a pit as well as better men.

```
mb
GUIDA        Four Secretaries of State
             do not make a secretarial
             pool. But they do make
             an unusual group at a
             Washington dinner party.
                The current
             secretary, Cyrus Vance,
             chats with former
             Secretaries Henry
             Kissinger, William Rogers
             and Dean Rusk.
             Diplomatically, of course.
```

When newswriters have to think in the middle of the night, they should be forgiven their trespasses and not stripped of their press passes.

```
mb
GUIDA        Athlete O-J Simpson, the
             long-running star of those
             rent-a-car commercials,
             is not going to have the
             driver's seat to himself
             anymore. He's going to
             share the chores with
             Nancy Lopez.
             Miss Lopez—a golfer—
             has been chosen to
             perform by herself and
             with him in the rent-a-car
             spots—and not just
```

```
                     because golfer Lopez is a
                     long driver.
```

Another Golden Oldie. I had to write *something*. But what ever became of Nancy Lopez?

mb
GUIDA

British pop star Elton
John displays his new
thatch of hair. John had
been almost bald until he
started undergoing hair
transplants. He says he's
going to have two more
transplants to thicken his
thatch—although the
head of Britain is already
Thatcher.

Someone crossed out the last phrase, starting with *although*. And if anyone reading this knows who, please phone, fax or FedEx me.

mb
GUIDA

Seven persons in
Wilmington, Delaware,
have pointed to a man in
court and identified him as
the bandit who held them
up, a Roman Catholic
priest. But now another
man has come forward,
saying that <u>he</u> committed
the armed robberies, <u>not</u>
the priest. The judge will
decide how to proceed
after conferring today with
the prosecutor, the priest
and the penitent.

Once in a great while, the segment called "Some people making news" presented something worthy of being called news.

block
Good morning.
Oregon police are searching for a prison escapee who was on board the United Airlines DC-8 that crashlanded in Portland last night. The escapee was being returned by two guards to the Oregon state prison. 185 persons were on board the plane. In the crash, at least 10 were killed and 45 hurt, five critically. And the escapee apparently escaped again.

"NBC News Update." This is a second-day lead. I don't put "yesterday" in a lead, but *last night* was necessary here. In the second line, *who was* can be deleted.

Why would a TV script be written across the full width of the page like a radio script? Simple. That's the way the anchor wanted it. The only thing that matters to me is the writing. Did I select the right facts, did I put them in the right order, did I use the right words, did I tell it right? I hope so.

If you think I should have written "185 *people*" instead of *persons,* you're right. Because of my roots in print, I was accustomed to using "people" for large groups or round numbers, and "persons" for exact numbers. When talking, I still say "two persons" or "three persons," and so on. That's what I was taught in school and have not been able to unlearn. Most anchors are "people" persons, and they say "two *people*." But I haven't heard anyone say "one *people*." Yet.

It's easier to be a critic than a newswriter, but anyone who wants to be a better writer should be a keen critic.

"Above all else," the writer Allan W. Eckert quotes his father as saying, "you must be your own harshest critic, your own strictest editor, your own most demanding taskmaster."

And, he said, If you're honest with yourself in these respects, you will never please yourself entirely. But if you keep trying to do so, you can't help pleasing others.

YOUR TURN

Now it's your turn. I've said much of what I know about writing, maybe even more than I know, so I'm going to give you a chance to see for yourself what you know.

You can do this by rewriting the 11 stories printed in this section and comparing them with my rewrites. After you've written the first exercise, read my script, followed by my comments on why I wrote it the way I did. Then proceed to the second story, write it and compare what you've written with what I wrote. Do not write all 11 stories in a row and then compare them with my scripts. Do one exercise a time. That way, you may pick up a few pointers that you can put to use in your next rewrite.

This isn't a test, nor a drill. Call it an editorial checkup. Or a tuneup. But no matter what you call it, and you needn't call it anything, it gives you an opportunity to try out whatever know-how you've picked up in reading, or riffling through, this book. In this checkup, writing with speed is secondary. What's primary is getting the words right.

Here's the first piece of source copy. Your assignment: Write a 20-second story. Time limit: none. None, because what's paramount here is applying all the tips and rules, not in setting a world indoor speed record.

In these exercises—and in the newsroom—there is no single "right" version. There may be a few right ways to write a story, but there are an infinite number of wrong ways. My version is just that: my version. It may not be the best possible, even if one script could be designated "best." By now, I should be able to write an acceptable story. Chances are, over the years, I've written more stories than the average newswriter, made more mistakes, had more time to learn and had more opportunities to see how to get it right.

Treat all your source copy here as if it were fresh. Write your scripts for a late newscast. And write your scripts for a city other than the one where the stories occurred.

> CHICAGO (Reuter)—Binti, an eight-year-old gorilla with a baby of her own, cradled an injured boy in her arms after he fell into the gorilla's concrete enclosure on Friday, a zoo spokeswoman said.
>
> "Binti carried him to a shift door where zookeepers were able to take the child. She exhibited no aggressive behaviour," said Sondra Katzen, a spokeswoman for Brookfield Zoo in a Chicago suburb.
>
> Binti was reared by humans and has her own two-year-old baby, the zoo said.
>
> The spokesman said the three-year-old boy managed to climb over a fence guarding the walkway that takes visitors through the zoo's Tropic World, a popular facility that houses several species in addition to gorillas. The boy fell between 15 and 20 feet (4.6 to 6 meters).

My script is not intended for use as a template; you needn't hold your story up against mine to make sure it corresponds in every detail. But you would find that you've used most of the facts I did and approximated my pattern. Which gives you considerable latitude (but only 20 seconds' longitude). Here's how I wrote the zoo story:

> A boy fell into a wild-animal concrete pit in a suburban Chicago zoo today —and was saved. By a gorilla.
>
> The three-year-old boy had climbed over a fence at the Brookfield Zoo, then fell about 15 feet.
>
> The zoo says the female gorilla cradled the injured boy in her arms and carried him to a door, where zookeepers took him. No word on his condition.

A dramatic story. But I knew better than to call it dramatic. Rather, I tried to tell it so listeners could sense the drama. I started by trying to "see" the event myself. And I tried to tell exactly what I saw—with the action unfolding before your very ears.

The wire copy had been written for print clients, so I knew going in that I needed to make adjustments. And I soon realized that the copy was probably written hurriedly: it doesn't tell us who accompanied the boy to the zoo, how he was able to slip away, what other kinds of animals were in the enclosure, the extent of the boy's injuries, whether he was taken to a hospital, and it doesn't tell us his condition. But as happens too often in a newsroom with a deadline looming, we have to make do with slim pickings. And there comes a time when, as Prof. John Hohenberg used to say at Columbia Journalism, "You've gotta go with what you got."

I didn't use the name of the gorilla or her age because those details are secondary or tertiary. The script has room for only the primary. Not even for other primates. I didn't call the Tropic World a *gorilla* pen because the wire copy said the space was occupied by several species. For all we can tell, the gorilla shared quarters with some baaad beasts. (It's a jungle in there!)

I wasn't happy about writing *wild animal concrete pit,* but I had to jam several nouns into a small space. The source copy didn't say the boy landed on concrete, so I didn't guess; I wrote around it. And I was also uneasy about writing *the zoo says.* But I reassured myself with the knowledge that buildings do talk: "The Pentagon says," "The White House says," "The State Department says." Even countries: "China says." So where is it written that a zoo can't talk?

Enough about that. Too much. Onward.

Here's the next exercise—20 seconds in 25 minutes:

OKLAHOMA CITY (AP)—A prisoner being taken by federal marshals from Alabama to California bolted out of a moving plane's emergency exit after landing on Saturday and fled into the darkness, authorities said.

U.S. Marshal Stuart Earnest, said the escapee, 44-year-old Reginald D. Still, was en route from a federal hospital in Talledega, Ala., to Sacramento, Calif., where he was scheduled to go on trial on a charge of interstate transportation of a stolen motor vehicle.

Earnest said the plane contained 44 prisoners when it touched down at Will Rogers World Airport. No other prisoners tried to escape, he said.

Still wearing handcuffs and shackles, he leaped out of the plane's emergency exit, onto a wing and then the tarmac as the plane was braking, the marshal said.

> One of eight security people on the plane jumped out to chase the escapee, Earnest said.
>
> Federal marshals and local, county and state authorities fanned out across the airport property, southwest of Oklahoma City, in the search.
>
> Prisoners are normally transported by a Boeing 727, but a backup, a Convair 580 propeller, was being used Saturday because the jet was being repaired, authorities said.
>
> The U.S. marshal's service routinely transports prisoners every other day to courts and penitentiaries around the country. The transportation program is based in Oklahoma City, and prisoners on overnight trips often are housed overnight at a federal correctional facility in El Reno, 30 miles west of here.

Here's the way I wrote it:

> A plane with federal prisoners was taxiing at an airport near Oklahoma City this evening when a prisoner jumped off and escaped. While the plane was moving down a runway, he bolted through an emergency exit, landed on a wing, leaped to the ground and got away in the darkness, still in handcuffs and shackles.
>
> The plane had been taking him to California to stand trial for theft.

If you've found that one easy, you must have done something wrong; if you start your story by saying a prisoner jumped *out* a plane or even *off* a plane, many listeners might think the plane had been aloft. I wanted to make it clear the plane was on the ground, so my story takes a few extra seconds to get to the nub.

My second and third sentences are easy to follow (certainly easier than he was), they're energized by lively verbs, and the sentences flow in one direction. And you can see the action unfold. The last sentence in my script may seem anticlimactic after the exciting escape, but I wanted to let listeners know that the fugitive is not a killer, at least not yet.

■ I didn't use his name because he's a nonentity, and his name means nothing to listeners.

■ I didn't use his age because I thought it wouldn't tell anyone anything; everyone has an age. I would have mentioned the age of the lamster
only if he were a youngster or an oldster.

■ I didn't spell out the charge against him because it takes too much
time and would be unnecessary.

■ I didn't say *"car* theft" because a "motor vehicle" could be a car,
a van or a truck.

■ I didn't tell where the flight originated or its destination because
those places don't figure in the story.

■ I didn't identify the plane because it makes no difference whether
it's a Convair or an Electra, whether it's a jet or a prop plane, whether it's
taking off or landing. Instead, I focused on that minute of high drama and
moved in close.

■ I didn't report the number of inmates aboard the plane because
the story was about only one. If any other prisoners had tried to escape,
I would have said so, but why take time to report what didn't happen? I
was pleased to learn that someone has named a "World" airport for Will
Rogers, but I didn't mention it lest I run out of time before my story could
get off the ground. I'd have preferred to say "tonight," but I didn't know
the time of the escape, so I said "this evening." All I knew was that the
guy fled into the darkness. But the sun sets early in mid-December; "tonight" might have been wrong; "evening" seemed safer. The wire copy
moved at almost 11 p.m., but that doesn't mean the story just broke. It
could have been several hours old.

At a session of my broadcast newswriting workshop (advt.), I passed
out copies of that wire story to the news staff of a TV station and asked
everyone to rewrite this Saturday story into a 20-second script for use on
a late Saturday newscast. Here's the most inventive lead—and keep in
mind that the inmate who fled from the plane was charged with theft:
"When it comes to vehicles, Reginald Still apparently can take them
or leave them." Clever, eh? But what would you think if you were hearing
it for the first time, with no previous knowledge of the episode? The real
test is: What's a listener to make of it? It's easy for insiders to get a kick
out of that lead because we already know the story. For listeners, though,

this is the first exposure. So they can't savor the wordplay about "vehicles" and the inmate's being able to "take them or leave them." Sounds more like a final observation than an introduction, an epilogue rather than a prologue. Further, I wouldn't use the escapee's name so early. In fact, I didn't use it all. Why not? No listener has heard of him, no listener need hear of him. If I hear the name of an unknown in a lead, I assume he's a hometowner. In this case, the last name, Still, might worsen any confusion. "Still" is an adverb *(yet),* an adjective *(silent)* and common noun *(distillery).*

In case you're wondering how that inventive writer handled the rest of the story, here is his script in its entirety:

> When it comes to vehicles, Reginald Still apparently can take them or leave them. Still, an inmate being transferred from Alabama to California, tonight bolted out of a moving plane and fled into the darkness. Police said Still was wearing handcuffs and leg irons when he jumped out an emergency exit. The 44-year-old inmate was scheduled to stand trial on charges of stealing a motor vehicle.

Sounds as if he leaped from a plane in flight. The script doesn't say whether the plane was aloft or on the ground, just that it was moving. *Tonight* would fit better after *plane.* But one of the most important questions of all: *where* did this happen? No matter what you might think of that lead, the lack of the *where* leaves it nowhere.

How did that writer's deskmates do with the same story? Let's take a look at some of their opening sentences and my brief comments:

> It's the stuff movies are made of. . . .
> a prisoner escape from a moving airplane at an Oklahoma airport.

It's not the stuff good news scripts are made of. Why "movies"? Why not identify the city? Why four periods? Why not a comma or a dash? Why no strong verb, only linking verbs *(is* and *are)* and a verbal *(moving),* which does not behave like a verb? And why turn a good verb, *escape,* into a noun? So that lead gets two thumbs down.

> Right now, the manhunt is on for a
> prisoner who, handcuffed and
> shackled, lept from a moving plane.

"Right now"? That's no way to start this story—or any story I can think of. By the time this story is broadcast, the fugitive might be recaptured, so the manhunt would be over and "right now" would be wrong now. "*The* manhunt" should be "*a* manhunt." "Lept" (spelled *leapt*) should have been changed to the preferred past tense, "leaped." And there's no *where* there.

> Police in Oklahoma City are out
> chasing their very own Harry Houdini.

Why drag in Houdini? He was a great escape artist, but he died in 1926 and has not reappeared. So now he needs a label: "The master magician Harry Houdini" or something like that. In any case, Houdini has nothing to do with this case.

Use of *their very own* makes it sound as if the person they're chasing is a fellow policeman. No, I'm not going to call that story a Houdunit.

> A plane left Alabama today carrying
> 44 prisoners to California. When it got
> there, it had only 43.

The script is missing a lot more than one prisoner.

> Transporting prisoners from one place
> to another by jet seems to be an
> escape-proof method. That was until
> tonight.

Let's not speculate about what *seems* to be. Let's report what we know for sure. Let's tell the news. Right now.

> Police in Oklahoma City are still
> looking for a prisoner who jumped out
> of a moving plane.

"Still looking" makes it seem as if the escape was reported earlier and that this is a followup. The news is a prisoner's escape. When we talk about someone who jumped out a window, we dispense with *of*. On that basis (a leap of faith?), I'd delete *of* in the script. Better: "jumped *from* a moving plane."

> A federal prisoner, handcuffed and shackled, managed to escape from his captors by jumping from a plane tonight.

Where? Over Alaska? "Managed to escape" = "escaped." "Captors?" A captor is someone who has captured a person or animal. If anything, the marshals are losers.

> Federal marshals are wondering tonight how their man got away . . . shackled and in handcuffs.

The writer led with reaction, not action. The news is still the escape. Or Still, the escapee.

> Federal marshals in Oklahoma City are looking for an escaped convict.

Again, reaction, not action.

> An Alabama prisoner made a daring run for it as he was being flown to California.

A running jump?

> Federal marshals in Oklahoma City are hunting for a prisoner who escaped on a wing and a prayer.

He didn't get away on a wing, and he probably was too busy to pray. Which might make this a good place to bail out. Of the dozen or so other scripts on the escape, one or two came close, but I won't inflict any more on you.

The writers? All I'll say, to protect the guilty, is that they work in the Lower 48 (states, not markets).

Now, try your hand at this one, 20 seconds in 15 minutes for a Sunday night newscast.

> LONDON (AP)—Smiling to a cheering crowd, Princess Diana took home from the hospital Sunday her one-day-old second son, Henry Charles Albert David.

The baby, third in line to the British throne, will be known to his family simply as Harry.

Diana, 23, wore a red coat and cradled the infant swathed in a white shawl as she left the hospital 22 hours after a routine birth. Her husband, Prince Charles, 35, accompanied Diana and their new son home to their London residence, Kensington Palace.

The princess blushed as the crowd of about 1,000 people, some of whom had waited through the night outside London's St. Mary's Hospital, waved Union Jacks and called out, "Hurrah, Harry!"

The royal couple's first child, two-year-old Prince William, visited his mother and baby brother for 15 minutes earlier.

William, looking confused by the phalanx of photographers, arrived with Charles, but left holding the hand of his nanny, Barbara Barnes. He gave three small waves to a delighted crowd.

The baby, taken home in a three-car motorcade at the start of a life of wealth, privilege and constant publicity, bears the name of England's famed Henry VIII, who broke with Rome in 1534 because the Vatican would not give him a divorce.

"They chose the name Henry simply because they both like it and also because there is no other member of the royal family at present with that name," said a Buckingham Palace spokesman. "The other names all have family connections."

Prayers of thanksgiving were offered at Sunday church services around the country in the strongly monarchist nation for the birth of Prince Henry, who ranks behind Charles and William in the line of succession. He joins them as a Prince of Wales.

Bells pealed for three hours Sunday across the Gloucestershire village of Tetbury, where Charles and Diana have their country residence, Highgrove House.

The palace said the royal family will call the new prince Harry. The affectionate diminutive is in contrast to palace instructions that William must never be referred to as Bill, or Willy.

The new baby's second name, Charles, is both the name of his father and of Diana's only brother, Viscount

Althorp, 21. Albert was the first name of the baby's great-grandfather, who reigned as George VI, and of Queen Victoria's consort.

David, a palace announcement said, was for Elizabeth the Queen Mother's favorite brother, the late Sir David Bowes-Lyons.

David was also one of the names of Charles' great-uncle, Edward VIII, who abdicated in 1936 to marry a twice-divorced American, Wallis Simpson.

"The baby is fine! My wife is even better!" Charles shouted to the crowd outside the hospital after a three-hour morning visit Saturday.

The speed of the announcement of the names of the 6-pound, 14-ounce baby aroused speculation the princess knew from medical tests that it would be another boy.

William's names, William Arthur Philip Louis, were not announced until a week after his birth in the same private ward at St. Mary's on June 21, 1982.

Charles was with Diana, the daughter of Earl Spencer and a former kindergarten teacher whom he married July 29, 1981, throughout her nine-hour labor and the birth Saturday.

Queen Elizabeth II was due back in London next Friday from her Scottish residence, Balmoral, said a palace spokesman, who spoke on condition he not be identified.

The queen smiled and waved to villagers Sunday when she attended church in the nearby Scottish hamlet of Crathie. Prayers were offered for the baby, her fourth grandchild. Her only daughter, Princess Anne, 33, has two children, Peter and Zara Phillips.

The new prince pushes Charles' brothers, Andrew, 24, and Edward, 20, into fourth and fifth in the line of succession. Anne is now sixth.

Yes, this story is dated. In fact, even during marriage, Diana admits she was dated. But for our noble purposes, the story is as good now as the day the baby was born. It still puts us to the test, gives a workout to our mental muscles, and teaches us a few lessons about writing news.

Note that this AP story moved a day after Diana gave birth, but the birth itself had been widely reported on the day of delivery. Most of our listeners probably knew about it already, so our story shouldn't focus on

Diana's giving birth. It should carry a second-day lead, yet inform listeners who might not have known about it or who had forgotten.

Here's how I wrote it for air:

> Princess Diana of Britain went home from a London hospital today with her day-old son, Henry Charles Albert David. The new prince will be called Harry.
>
> Mother and son were escorted home by his father, Prince Charles. The family's first-born, Prince William, is second in line to be king, and now Harry's third.

As I look back, I wonder whether I squeezed in too many facts. In my defense, in case you take the offense: I needed the baby's name and his parents' names, and I wanted to point out that Harry was not Diana's first-born. I also wanted to let listeners know why this was more than a mere birth notice, that this baby might be king one day (but not a one-day king). Yet, look at all the facts I succeeded in keeping out.

If I could turn back the calendar, I'd re-do line 3 in the script to distance *day-old* from *today*. So in line 5, I'd substitute *day-old* for *new*. And in line 7, I'd delete *home;* it's implicit. Also, in the last line, I'd spell out the contraction so as not to hurry Harry. His new standing in the line of succession is too important to speed past.

Although listeners recognize the reference to "Princess Diana," her proper title was—and is—"Diana, Princess of Wales." But that sounds a bit starchy.

For the next story, write 20 seconds. Take 15 minutes.

> LONDON (AP)—Smuggled letters from Soviet dissident Andrei Sakharov reveal that he has been mentally and physically tortured by Soviet secret police while in internal exile in the closed city of Gorky, the weekly Observer reported Sunday.
>
> The newspaper said the documents "unmask the careful plan of KGB disinformation," including postcards and telegrams carrying his wife's name, that have for nearly two years suggested Sakharov was living without problems.
>
> Sakharov's stepdaughter, Tatyana Yankelevich, and her husband, Yefrem, received the smuggled letters and

photographs in two plain envelopes mailed from an unidentified Western country to the couple in Newton, Mass., the Observer said.

It quoted Yankelevich as saying, "How they got out of the Soviet Union I cannot say, but I know the source, and the source is reliable. They (the documents) have been carefully examined by the whole family and we are convinced of their authenticity."

Yankelevich, contacted in Newton by The Associated Press, confirmed that he had provided the Observer with the documents. "There were some financial arrangements, but I won't be able to discuss it," he said.

Sakharov, a physicist who led fellow scientists to produce the Soviet hydrogen bomb, has been in internal exile in Gorky, 260 miles east of Moscow, since January 1980.

He became a human rights activist in the 1960s and was ordered to Gorky after he publicly criticized the Soviets' military intervention in Afghanistan in December 1979.

The Observer said the letters, which it will publish in extract starting next week, detail the KGB's ill-treatment of Sakharov. They confirm reports that Sakharov was force-fed during two hunger strikes in 1984 and 1985 and was subjected to mental torture and physical violence while being treated at a Gorky hospital, it said.

The KGB is the Soviet security police and intelligence agency.

Sakharov spent several months on a hunger strike in an effort to get an exit visa for his wife, Yelena Bonner.

The paper said the main document is a 20-page letter written by Sakharov in October 1984 to Dr. Anatoli Alexandrov, president of the Soviet Academy of Sciences. In it, Sakharov appeals for his wife to be allowed to go to the West for medical treatment. Mrs. Bonner was granted an exit visa late last year, and she is now in Massachusetts, where she underwent a heart bypass operation.

Sakharov also describes how he was seized by KGB agents on May 7, 1984, and taken to Gorky's Semashko hospital, the paper said.

Sakharov wrote that hospital authorities "kept me by force and tormented me for four months. My attempts to flee the hospital were always blocked by KGB men, who were on duty round the clock to bar all means of escape," according to the Observer.

It said the letters "contain one of the most vivid testimonies of human suffering ever to have emerged in the Soviet Union."

Yes, this story also is dated. But as an exercise it's an evergreen— fresh at any time. We have to deal with a lot of facts here, and, as usual, we have to keep the best and ditch the rest.

Here's how I wrote it.

> A London newspaper says letters smuggled from Soviet dissident Andrei Sakharov confirm that the secret police have abused him mentally and physically.
>
> The paper says the letters knock down what it calls K-G-B disinformation—including postcards and telegrams—suggesting Sakharov has had no problems. He and his wife have been in internal exile, but she's now in this country for medical care.

Why did I write it that way? I led with attribution because I wouldn't assert on my own that Sakharov had been mistreated. Maybe he had been, maybe not. I needed to attribute it. And I know the rule: Attribution precedes assertion. I didn't identify the newspaper; most listeners have never heard of it. And those who have probably don't know whether it's reliable. I, for one, don't know. But I do know better than to take information printed by a newspaper and report it as fact. When I was a newspaperman, I once told a deskmate, in jest, "You can't believe what you read," and he riposted, "I don't even believe what I write."

I started my script by attributing the Sakharov story to a London newspaper. Another reason not to identify the paper; the *London Observer* sounds like a London observer.

The wire service used *tortured* in the lead, but I was leery of that. Not that I doubted that the KGB was capable of torture. But why did the body of the story refer to "physical violence" instead of "physical torture"? If the wire story had provided specifics, I might have accepted the word *tortured* without hesitation. I never want to deviate from the facts or go beyond the facts. But what were the facts? All I knew was what the wire service rewriter told me. And all he knew, probably, was what the newspaper said had occurred.

Had Sakharov used the word "torture"? Was that the translator's choice, was it the newspaper writer's characterization? Or was it the wire service's contribution? I didn't doubt that Sakharov had been deprived of his freedom, if it can be said anyone there in those days had freedom. And I'm sure he was treated outrageously. But "torture" is another matter.

If a member of my staff, someone in whom I had full confidence, told me she had learned conclusively that Sakharov had been tortured, I'd accept that. But I'm disinclined to place that much trust in a nameless wire service reporter who's rewriting a faceless newspaper reporter. So after my reasoning—and please don't call it tortured—I backed off from the source copy and moderated "torture" to "abuse." It wasn't just a matter of playing safe, although better half-safe than sorry; it was a matter of my trying to get as close as possible to what was true. Or what seemed true, or at least not untrue.

To simplify the story for the listener, I used only one name, that of the central figure, Sakharov. I didn't drag in a lot of other names that would only divert the listener's attention: his wife, Yelena Bonner; Afghanistan; Gorky; Semashko hospital; his stepdaughter, Tatyana Yankelevich, and her husband, Yefrem; the place where they were living, Newton, Massachusetts. But if you work at a station near Newton, that's another story.

Speaking of other stories—and labored transitions—let's turn to the next story. Please write 20 seconds. Take 15 minutes. Note: This story broke on a Friday but didn't move on the wires until Saturday. You are writing it for a Saturday night audience.

> MINNEAPOLIS (AP)—Drinking five or more cups of coffee a day appears to increase a person's chances of developing lung cancer, according to a researcher who says his study is the first to target coffee alone.
>
> "This is the first time that coffee has been implicated by itself" as a factor in lung cancer, Dr. Leonard Schuman, an epidemiologist at the University of Minnesota, said Friday.
>
> He said the study also found that the effects of coffee drinking and smoking may magnify each other.
>
> Smoking alone increases the risk of cancer tenfold, Schuman said. But men who smoked a pack or more a

day and drank five or more cups of coffee had a rate of lung cancer 40 times higher than men who neither smoked nor drank coffee.

Other studies will be needed to determine if the finding represents a cause-and-effect relationship, or is just a fluke finding from one statistical study, Schuman said.

The study didn't ask people to distinguish between regular and decaffeinated coffee, so that's another question that further research might tackle, he said.

Harvard University researchers in 1981 found a statistical link between coffee drinking and pancreatic cancer, but later studies have virtually killed that theory.

Schuman and his colleagues have been studying the dietary habits of 17,818 men, all age 45 and older, and tracking their death rates over the past 18 years.

Even after smoking habits and ages were taken into consideration, those who drank five or more cups of coffee a day were seven times more likely to have died from lung cancer than the men who drank no coffee at all, Schuman said.

"On the basis of this one study, I don't think it's warranted to say 'ban coffee from your diet,'" Schuman said after the findings were reported at a Society for Epidemiologic Research meeting in Chapel Hill, N.C.

However, moderation in the amount of coffee consumed, "like moderation in many other things, might be prudent for many reasons," he added.

"Smoking is still the most important factor in lung cancer," said Schuman. He served on the U.S. surgeon general's blue-ribbon committee of experts in 1964 that concluded that smoking is a major health risk.

Schuman's colleagues in the study are Dr. Robert Gibson of the University of Minnesota-Duluth and Dr. Erik Bjelke, who now lives in Norway.

Schuman said he didn't know what chemical in coffee might be responsible for any cancer risk, but it presumably would have to enter the bloodstream to reach the lungs.

Here's how I wrote it:

A new study says anyone who drinks five cups of coffee a day, or more,

may be increasing the chances of
developing lung cancer.

A University of Minnesota
scientist says his study is the first to
implicate coffee by itself. He also says
that if someone drinks too much
coffee and smokes, the combined
effects may be far worse. But he says
investigators must do more research.

That was the kind of medical story that needed attribution early and
often. So I started every sentence with attribution. And I avoided "yesterday." Instead, I started with the historical present tense, *says*. (And I'd
bet that you didn't notice the word *says* in four consecutive sentences.)
I didn't use the scientist's name because listeners wouldn't recognize his
name; it would only take time without shedding light. My last sentence
alerted listeners to *another* side of the story by starting with *but*. That's
important because it tells listeners that the findings are far from conclu-
sive. The last sentence in the script tends to chip away at the story, but
the sentence is important.

On to the next story. Make it 20 seconds, and try to write it in 25
minutes. Or less.

LOS ANGELES—More than 250 firefighters battled a
stubborn, smoky fire that swept through the Central Los
Angeles Library today, injuring 22 firefighters and
destroying thousands of books in the downtown landmark
building.

Neither Mayor Tom Bradley nor Fire Chief Donald
Manning could say what caused the fire, which broke out
shortly before 11 A.M. in the book stacks. It was
declared under control six hours later, after 49 fire
companies from across the city fought the blaze.

The 60-year-old library, which had 2.3 million
volumes, was listed on the National Register of Historic
Places and was declared a historic cultural monument by
the Los Angeles Cultural Heritage Board in 1967.

But the three-story building had also been designated
as unsafe by the Los Angeles Fire Department and had a
long history of fire violations. Mayor Bradley said some of
the violations had been corrected, and library officials said
fire doors were being installed when the fire broke out.

The interior of the library, which is situated amid a canyon of glass skyscrapers in downtown Los Angeles, was severely damaged. But its facade, although blackened and scorched, remained intact, in part because it was built of concrete, fire officials said.

"This is the most extremely difficult fire we have ever fought," Chief Manning said. "The men could not advance without the fire flaring up behind them."

The future of the library has been the topic of civic debate for the last 20 years. But, while various proposals were debated, the library began to fall into neglect, officials said.

About two years ago, a complicated plan involving the construction of three major buildings and the expansion of the library was worked out among private and public officials. The library staff was scheduled to move out next year for the expansion to begin.

Mayor Bradley, who arrived at the scene at 5 P.M., told reporters: "This magnificent building is something we have tried to save. We tried to get it up to safety standards."

Until the damage can be examined, the library's future is in doubt, the Mayor said, adding, "We will then decide whether to try to save it or to go forward with the remodeling."

Library officials said more than 300 employees and visitors were evacuated within minutes of the fire alarm sounding. Despite its landmark status, Chief Manning said, the building had no modern sprinkler system.

According to Robert Reagan, the library's public information director, steel fire doors were in the process of being installed between the book stacks and the public areas when the fire broke out. About half the work had been completed, he said.

Reagan said the library, the largest in the West, was "designated unsafe by the Fire Department as early as 1979." Violations were not corrected, he said, largely because of a lack of funds and uncertainty about its future.

The major fire violations, he said, were in the stacks that contained 85 percent of the library's books. The public has no direct access to the stacks.

The building, designed by the architect Bertram Grosvenor Goodhue and dedicated in 1926, was one of the few remaining buildings with open space in what is now the city's financial district.

From balconies and plazas of the glass skyscrapers that envelop the library, hundreds of office workers spent their lunch hour watching as smoke poured from the library's windows.

Firefighters were hampered by two factors: the desire to keep water at a minimum to decrease the water damage to the books and the fact that, for several hours, they were unable to bore a hole through the library's concrete roof to let the heat and smoke escape.

"It was like walking into a solid brick oven," said Capt. Anthony Didomenico of the Los Angeles Fire Department. Most of the injuries were caused by steam burns.

By day's end, neither fire officials nor library officials could estimate the amount of damage. The rare book collection, which is kept in a fireproof vault in the building's basement, was believed to be unharmed. But the general collection of books, many of which Reagan described as "irreplaceable," were probably ruined.

"We have a great collection of books here," he said. "How can I put a price on what is a priceless collection?"

Here's how I wrote it:

> A fire swept through one of the nation's biggest libraries today. The Central Los Angeles Library was damaged severely, and thousands of books were destroyed. 250 firemen fought the fire, and 22 of them were hurt.
>
> Firemen were hampered because they tried to hold down the use of water—to minimize damage to books.

By now, you probably see the way I attack a story: I go straight to the subject, go right to a verb and then to the object. Good old S-V-O: just the facts, no frills.

Punctuation is important. It tells anchors when to pause and when to stop. I mention that because of the dash I used in the last sentence. It gives the listener a chance to consider *water* and wonder for an instant why firemen tried to hold down its use. Then the listener is given the explanation.

The source copy said the library was the biggest in the West, so I broadened that and made it one of the biggest in the country. In reporting casualties, I ordinarily follow the rule "People before property." I would have written the story differently if any firemen had been killed or severely injured. Although the source copy tells of the injured in the lead, they're not mentioned again until almost the bottom. Most of the injuries, the copy says, were caused by steam burns. But in the absence of specifics, I assume none of the injuries were severe. Or severe enough to impress the reporter(s) covering the fire or the original writer and editor.

I also follow the rule "Keep like things together." I figured the reference to the books fitted better where I put it than if I had put it after the firemen. I didn't want to flit from saying the library was severely damaged to the sentence about the firemen and then go back to the destruction of books.

On to the next exercise. Or scrimmage. Write a 25-second story. This time, try to write it in less than 25 minutes. And try not to go into overtime.

WASHINGTON—Using free Washington Redskins tickets as bait, authorities arrested 100 fugitives who showed up Sunday at a pre-game brunch where police and federal marshals posed as waiters and served warrants.

U.S. marshals called it the largest mass arrest of fugitives in recent memory.

"It was like an assembly line," said Herbert M. Rutherford III, U.S. marshal for the District of Columbia. "It was party time, and they fell for it, hook, line and sinker."

"This ain't fair, this just ain't fair," said one prisoner who was led in handcuffs from one of two large buses that carried the prisoners to a local jail.

"They said they was takin' us to a football game, and that's wrong," said another man. "That's false advertising."

"I came to see Boomer, I came to see Boomer," said a third, referring to Cincinnati Bengals quarterback Boomer Esiason.

U.S. marshals, working with the Metropolitan Police Department, sent out invitations to 3,000 wanted persons. The invitations said that as a promotion for a new sports television station, Flagship International Sports Television, they were winners of two free tickets to the National Football League game Sunday between the Redskins and the Bengals.

The invitation said 10 of the "lucky winners" would receive season tickets to the Redskins' 1986 season and that a grand prize drawing would be held for an all-expenses paid trip to the upcoming Super Bowl XX in New Orleans.

The initials for the TV enterprise, F.I.S.T., also stand for the Fugitive Investigative Strike Team, a special U.S. marshals force.

About 100 fugitives responded to the invitation and appeared at the D.C. Convention Center for the special brunch. The building was decorated with signs saying, "Let's party" and "Let's all be there."

Some of the fugitives showed up wearing the bright burgundy and gold wool Redskins hats as well as Redskins buttons, while others were attired in suits and ties for the pre-game feast.

One marshal was dressed in a large yellow chicken suit with oversized red boots while another turned up as an Indian chief complete with large headdress.

Other marshals wearing tuxedos handed small name stickers to each of the fugitives.

Buses that were to take them to the game, however, took them to the police department's central cellblock several blocks away instead.

"When we verified their identity, we escorted them in small groups to a party room, where officers moved in from concealed positions and placed them under arrest," said Stanley Morris, head of the U.S. Marshals Service.

The sting netted 100 fugitives by 11 a.m., marshals said.

Arrested were two people wanted for murder, five for robbery, 15 for assault, six for burglary, 19 for bond or bail violations, 18 for narcotics violations, officials said. Others were arrested on charges of rape, arson and forgery. Two of those arrested were on the D.C. police department's ten most wanted list.

A similar scam in Hartford, Conn., in November 1984 invited people to attend a luncheon with pop singer Boy George. Fifteen were picked up by a limousine and arrested. Marshals said they used job offers as the bait to arrest about 90 people in Brooklyn last year.

"Redskin tickets are valuable. And when you're trying to get a person, you play on their greed," said Toby

Roche, chief deputy U.S. marshal for Washington, who coordinated the operation.

The cost of the project was estimated to be $22,100, or about $225 per arrest.

One man who got into the Convention Center before apparently being spooked by the circumstances was arrested on the street, still wearing his "Hello, my name is . . ." sticker.

That's a complex story to compress, and it offers a writer many chances to fumble—and to score. Here's how I tackled it:

> Three-thousand people in the Washington, D.C., area were notified they had won two free tickets to the Redskins' football game. About 100 of them showed up today at the Convention Center for the tickets and a pre-game brunch. But they were thrown for a loss: U-S marshals and police sprang their trap and arrested all of them as fugitives.
>
> Some were wanted for burglary, robbery or murder. Two of those caught in the sting were on the local list of Ten Most Wanted.

If my script is smoother than yours, it may be because I rewrote it for six months. And I'm still not sure I have it right.

New case. Again 20 seconds, but this time, 25 minutes.

SAN FRANCISCO (UPI)—A huge construction crane tumbled from the 12th story of a new financial district high-rise Tuesday, breaking into sections that bounced off neighboring buildings before smashing into rush-hour traffic, killing nine people, authorities said.

Fire Chief Fred Postel said five construction workers were believed buried under the debris and listed as missing.

The multi-story crane was being jacked up so construction crews could start work on another floor. Two sections from 75 to 100 feet long snapped off and crashed onto two buses and a taxi on California Street.

At least a dozen people were injured in the 8:15 a.m. mishap, police said.

Police Chief Frank Jordan said nine people were killed.

The falling crane slashed through the top floors of the corrugated metal and girders of a building under construction and being developed by the Federal Home Loan Bank Board. One part banged onto the 10th floor of a neighboring building. Another part glanced off another office building.

The remaining section dangled perilously from the 12th floor, and authorities ordered the evacuation of another 23-story building across the street. Hundreds of people worked there.

A motorized crane was brought to the disaster scene to stabilize the dangling section, police said.

The crashing crane sections struck a San Francisco Unified School District bus and a double-section San Mateo County Transportation District Bus.

The Fire Department said the dead included three ironworkers; a woman driving the school bus; a special education student on the school bus and a pedestrian. Jordan said three others also were killed.

The fire department said investigators were checking reports the crane operator was trying to pick up a load of metal and was unaware efforts were being made to jack up the crane for work on the next floor.

Bank employee Russ Yarrow said the accident "sounded like the Blue Angels (Navy Precision Flying Team) going over. There was a huge roar or like the sound of a power plant letting off steam—a huge roar just going and going.

"The crane came down and it sheared down through the top five or six floors of the building under construction," he said. "It cut through sheet metal. The girders were bent.

"It looked like a knife cut through butter."

Don Trabert, a stock firm employee in a nearby building, said he looked from his office window and saw two pieces of the crane dangling from the top of the building.

"I just heard a series of bangs," Trabert said.

One ironworker said operations had been under way to raise the crane to finish off the new high-rise office building.

"The crane operator was swinging the crane around and someone shouted, 'stop the swinging,'" one ironworker said.

Art Biada, a construction worker who had been on the job in the basement of the new building, said there was "a pretty wild noise." He added, "They were raising the crane and somebody made a mistake."

The back of the school bus was crushed. A cab also was smashed but the driver, Gerald Smith, managed to scramble out through a window and his passengers were freed by workers.

The dead ironworkers included the crane operator. Firefighters said the other two ironworkers had been in the vicinity of the crane cab.

Ray Cortez, 51, Daly City, Calif., was standing next to his cement truck when he heard a loud noise above him. He said he dived under his truck. "You only have maybe three seconds," he said. "You heard the noise and knew you had to do something." His truck was smashed by falling debris.

A gasoline can on the street burst into flames when struck by debris. The fire was quickly extinguished. A pedestrian walkway was flattened.

The workers on the 10th floor of one of the struck buildings were evacuated immediately. Some suffered minor injuries.

Crews had been attempting to boost the crane to add another floor to a planned 20-story building—a job a union official described as usually dangerous. The accident occurred at California and Kearney Streets. The area is served by cable cars but none was involved in the disaster.

"As they jump it (raise a crane), the possibility of accidents increases," said Dennis Madigan, business manager of Ironworkers Local 377.

Bob O'Reilly of New Canaan, Conn., said he was in a cab when the driver shouted. He said they jumped out and took refuge under an archway.

"We just bailed out and got out of there," he said.

Officials at San Francisco General Hospital said 11 people were taken to the emergency room for treatment. They said three were admitted in serious condition. One was the Samtrans bus driver, another was a construction worker. The third was a 12-year-old boy hurt while he awaited a bus.

A hospital official said the boy had "a lot of glass imbedded in his face and scalp."

It was the second major incident in two days in the bay area, which is still recovering from the disastrous Oct. 17 earthquake. Two people died and six others were injured Monday night when a bus chartered by ABC Television was struck by a commuter train at a south San Francisco rail crossing.

My script:

> A construction crane in San Francisco fell off a 12-story building into morning rush-hour traffic and killed nine people.
>
> At least a dozen people were hurt. And five construction workers are missing, perhaps buried in debris. Part of the crane hit a school bus and killed the driver and a student.
>
> Among the dead was the crane operator himself.

That wire copy presents a lot of choices because it's so full of facts, descriptions and quotations. Desirable, perhaps, for a newspaper, but too many details for us. So I cut the copy down to size.

I know listeners can't see the dateline on wire copy, so I worked it in near the top of my script. I dispensed with attribution. No need. At least not for what I wrote. And I know better than to slide into that dreary old formulaic approach: "Nine people were killed and at least twelve hurt today when. . . ." Don't go by the numbers. Start by telling what happened, where it happened, and then to whom it happened.

Listeners in other cities would be content with the amount of information in that script. But the closer you get to Frisco, the more information listeners would want. Almost every script could tell more, far more. Which is why you could write at the bottom of almost every script, "For further details, see tomorrow morning's newspaper."

Next exercise. Write this story for early evening, Tuesday, before the Pope makes his first stop. Length: 20 seconds. Time: 15 minutes.

VATICAN CITY (UPI)—Pope John Paul II left Rome
Tuesday for his 32nd foreign tour, traveling to
Bangladesh, Singapore, Fiji, New Zealand, Australia
and the Seychelles on his longest and one of his most
grueling trips.

The Pontiff, who left Rome's Leonardo da Vinci
Airport 20 minutes behind schedule, will spend the night
on his jet and land early Wednesday in the Bangladesh
capital of Dhaka, where he will make 12 hours of public
appearances.

John Paul will be traveling virtually non-stop to cover
the 30,000-mile itinerary in 14 days, and is to spend two
of the first three nights sleeping aboard the papal plane
to save time.

Among the highlights of the trip are scheduled
meetings with native Fiji islanders, New Zealand Maoris
and Australian aborigines, whose numbers and culture
were nearly eliminated after European settlers arrived in
the late 18th century.

Each of the three groups is scheduled to give John
Paul a traditional welcome. In Fiji he is to receive a whale
tooth, the local version of the key to a city, and sip a
watered-down version of kava, the powerful local brew.

In New Zealand he will touch noses with a group of
Maori tribesmen as a sign of trust, and in Australia,
aborigines will lead him along a traditional "meeting
path" as various tribes perform native dances and songs.

The trip—longest both in terms of distance and days
spent outside the Vatican—is the third to Asia and the
Pacific since he became pope in 1978. Half the trip will
be spent in Australia, with three days in New Zealand
and the remaining four days on brief stops in
Bangladesh, Singapore, Fiji and the Seychelles.

The Dhaka stop, during which John Paul is to ordain
local priests and celebrate Mass for the country's tiny
Catholic minority, could take on an unexpected
inter-religious significance, a senior Vatican official said
shortly before the trip.

A Moslem leader in Bangladesh recently contacted
the Vatican and asked to be present at the religious
services as a goodwill gesture in response to the Pope's
address to Moslem youth in Casablanca in August 1985,

and last month's inter-religious prayer meeting for peace in Assisi, Italy.

"This is the first time a Moslem leader has responded in such a way," the source said.

In Australia and New Zealand, church attendance has fallen off drastically in recent years and the supply of priests is fast dwindling.

Recent Australian polls show that less than 30 percent of the nation's 4 million Catholics attend Sunday Mass, while church members, as in other highly developed nations, widely ignore Rome's ban on artificial contraception.

My script:

> Pope John Paul left Rome today for Southeast Asia on his longest trip ever. He's flying first to Dhaka, the capital of Bangladesh, a Muslim country.
> Other highlights: He'll meet natives in Fiji, Maoris in New Zealand and aborigines in Australia, where he'll spend a week. His trip will take two weeks and cover 30-thousand miles.

You have plenty of facts to choose from. I probably chose all or almost all the essential facts; whether I put them in the right order and said what I should have said, I don't know.

The key to rewriting a story that's chock-full of facts lies in ruthlessly discarding the less important and perhaps even some of the important. We don't need to refer to him as John Paul *the Second*. (He can't be confused with any other living pope.) And we don't need to list every place he's visiting, the name of Rome's airport, the tardiness of his plane and a host of other petty details.

Although my version may not be creditable, it is acceptable. And I do deserve credit for not referring to the pope as *pontiff*. (An all-news station went so far as to call him *peripatetic*.) And in case you're uneasy about my second sentence, in which I have him flying, don't fret. If a nun can fly, so can a pope.

This script's cardinal virtue: it doesn't refer to the pope's 32d tour. That looks all right on paper, but when it's spoken, it sounds as though he's making the tour in 30 seconds.

Next exercise. You're writing this for a Sunday night newscast. Length: 20 seconds. Time: 15 minutes to air—no time to err. As they say in Wisconsin, "To err is human, to moo bovine."

KEYSTONE HEIGHTS, FL. (AP)—A 70-foot-wide sinkhole continued growing Sunday after swallowing one house and a carport and forcing evacuation of four homes in a retirement community, officials said.

The hole was about the size of a pickup truck when it was first discovered Saturday in this small town near Gainesville in northeastern Florida, said Mayor William Beam.

Three hours later, it had grown to 30 by 40 feet and had swallowed half of a small house owned by Keystone Heights administrator William A. Erickson.

Two hours later, the house was gone and the owners escaped only with their coats.

The carport of a second house also began slipping into the hole.

"It's still falling in, but gradual; not big hunks of stuff like (Saturday)," Clay County Public Safety director James Corbin Jr. said Sunday.

Corbin said he was not sure if other houses would follow the first house into the sinkhole. But he said the residents evacuated from four homes Saturday were moved as a safety precaution.

"We're preparing for the worst and hoping for the best," Corbin said. "What could you do?"

Clay County Administrator John Bowles estimated the hole was 45 feet deep.

A sinkhole is caused by the collapse of limestone caverns that lose water pressure that supports their roofs.

Much of Florida is susceptible to sinkholes, but central Florida and parts of northeast Florida, with limestone caverns 100 feet or more below the surface, are most vulnerable.

A celebrated sinkhole in Winter Park, near Orlando, grew to an estimated 400 feet across in 1981 and swallowed 250,000 cubic yards of property valued at $2 million, five sports cars, most of two businesses, a three-bedroom house and the deep end of an Olympic-size swimming pool.

Florida law requires that home insurers provide sinkhole coverage.

My version:

mb

OSGOOD — The swallows have come back to Florida. No, not the kind that flock to Capistrano but the swallows that gulp down homes.

V/O — The latest swallow—by a sinkhole—devoured a home at Keystone Heights, in northeast Florida. The residents escaped only with their coats. The hole is about 70 feet across and 45 feet deep. A sinkhole is caused when limestone caverns lose the water pressure that holds up their roofs. The most vulnerable places are in northeast and central Florida, where sinkholes most often pop up—or drop in.

I know: "Confidentially, it sinks." I said that just to beat you to the pun.

I could have written it as spot news or a feature. What emerged was a sort of newsfeature. Although you were asked to write 20 seconds, I wrote 30 seconds. The reason: My script had to accompany videotape that was scheduled in the lineup (or rundown) for :20. The anchor timed the lead-in at :08, so the V/O ran :22.

To give you an idea how someone else wrote this story, here's a script broadcast on network radio. It was based on wire copy that moved a couple of hours earlier than the copy reprinted above. Length: 30 seconds.

A sinkhole that's already gobbled up one home and a carport in a Keystone Heights-Florida retirement village is 70 feet wide ... AND GROWING. Keystone Heights is a small town near Gainesville in northeastern Florida. The sinkhole first appeared yesterday. It was just a few feet wide but began to spread rapidly. Four families have

evacuated the area. Sinkholes develop when the water pressure that supports limestone caverns drops. This happens a lot in Florida . . . especially in areas where rapid development is taking place.

What do you think of that script? If my approach has any virtue, it may be its odd twist. The radio script is written as straight news, which may be just as good a way, or better, to do it. But the first fact the radio script presents—*already gobbled up one home*—is not new. The next verbs, *is,* and [*is*] *growing,* are unobjectionable. But it's good to remember that *is* is weak and a verb that ends with *ing* is weaker than a finite verb, one with a tense. *Village* has too many attributive nouns, which serve as adjectives, piled in front of it. Why repeat the name of the town? No need for *small.* Did the four families evacuate *the area* or their homes? Also: how deep was the hole?

Last: 20 seconds, 10 minutes.

WASHINGTON (AP)—Amtrak will "starve to death" unless Congress identifies new funding to replace dwindling congressional allocations for the nation's passenger rail service, Amtrak's chairman told a Senate panel Tuesday.

During a Senate Commerce subcommittee hearing, Amtrak President Thomas Downs said funding cuts, combined with Congress' failure to identify a new funding source and allow for operational savings, are squeezing the rail service.

"Without the capital source and without legislative reform, we are dabbling with the edges of disaster for Amtrak," Downs said. "It will actually starve to death over the next five or six years."

Downs' comments came as lawmakers questioned Amtrak's plan to cancel four routes later this year.

"It can't be considered good policy to weaken the overall system in that way," said Sen. Kay Bailey Hutchison, R-Texas, chairwoman of the surface transportation and merchant marine subcommittee.

Downs agreed.

"I don't like losing any element of the system," he said. "I believe it weakens the national system."

But Amtrak faces a $243 million shortfall next year, Downs noted, even as Congress is contemplating a $50 million cut in federal subsidies. In a bid to save $200 million, the rail service has targeted four routes for elimination as of Nov. 10.

The lines are:

—Texas Eagle, three-times-weekly service between Chicago, St. Louis, Little Rock, Dallas, Fort Worth and San Antonio, will be discontinued between St. Louis and San Antonio.

—Pioneer, three-times-weekly service between Chicago, Denver, Portland, Ore., and Seattle, will be discontinued between Denver and Seattle.

—Desert Wind, three-times-weekly between Chicago, Denver, Salt Lake City, Las Vegas and Los Angeles, will be discontinued between Salt Lake City and Los Angeles.

—Lake Shore Limited, daily between Chicago, Boston and New York, will be eliminated between Boston and Albany, N.Y.

Asked by Hutchison and Sen. Ron Wyden, D-Ore., if the eliminations could be delayed for six months, Downs replied: "I haven't got the resources to do it . . . I cannot give what I haven't got."

Congress and the Clinton administration have directed Amtrak to achieve operating self-sufficiency by 2002. Even as Congress has cut Amtrak's federal operating support nearly 50 percent since fiscal 1995, lawmakers have yet to earmark a new funding source.

And, the rail service continues to await congressional approval of legislation that would allow it to greatly cut energy, labor and liability costs while gaining new freedom from red tape. The bill, which passed the House last year, remains mired in Senate squabbles.

Hutchison expressed support for one proposal: earmarking a half-cent from the 4.3-cent gasoline tax for Amtrak.

My version:

> Amtrak says its rail passenger service is approaching the end of the line.
> Amtrak's chairman, Thomas Downs, told a Senate subcommittee today that unless Congress finds new money, Amtrak will—in his words—"starve to death."

> He said it can keep running for
> only five or six more years. Congress
> is questioning Amtrak's plan to cancel
> four routes this year.

The wire copy tells us far more than we care to know, but we're grateful that it provides a plenteous supply of names, dates, places, numbers and quotations, if not excitement. But that's the nature of most news; it's not the fault of the news agency. A lot of news is humdrum. Our job is to write it the best way we can. And do the best we know how.

The wire copy doesn't have us panting because Downs's statement is self-serving: He's trying to scare up some dead Presidents (as slangsters call paper money). And he puts the date of Amtrak's demise at least five years into the future. In fact, into the next century. Between now and then, a lot can—and will—happen.

So the story has no drama, no air of urgency. In the first sentence, the wire copy describes Downs as Amtrak's chairman. But in the second sentence, Downs is Amtrak's *president.* Even if he's both (and he is), we shouldn't use both titles in a script because listeners might be confused—and wind up on a siding. As in every story, you want to keep 'em going full speed down the right track.

No matter how well you write, don't take someone else's script from an earlier newscast and rewrite it. If the story is newsworthy enough to be broadcast again, get the original writer's source material (perhaps wire copy) and rewrite that. Try to update or freshen it. And tell it in your own words.

The reason you shouldn't rewrite an earlier script: the writer might have omitted or downplayed something important, taken the wrong tack or made a factual error. You don't want to be confined to the four corners of that earlier script and risk perpetuating an error. So start anew. And make it new.

Exercise is good for us, so I hope you've learned as much from this chapter—and this book—as I have.

8

REAMS OF RULES

Here is a selection of the author's "WordWatching" columns—revised and expanded. They first appeared in Communicator, *the magazine of the Radio-Television News Directors Association.*

George Orwell himself might have been at a loss for words over 1984's orgy of Orwelliana, but as a resolute wordwatcher, he still has much to tell us. Not only did he coin words that have become catchwords—*Big Brother, doublethink, newspeak, unperson*—but he also wrote knowingly about using words.

Orwell worked in radio for the BBC as a writer, producer and broadcaster, so he knew broadcasting. His goal was to write plainly and clearly, to produce "prose like a window pane." In 1946, after writing *Animal Farm* and before writing *1984,* he set down some basic rules that are still sound and equally useful when writing for print or broadcast. These rules may not enable us to write as well as Orwell, but they can help:

- Never use a metaphor, simile, or other figure of speech which you are used to seeing in print. ["What a good thing Adam had," Mark Twain said. "When he said a good thing, he knew nobody had said it before."]

- Never use a long word where a short one will do.

- If it is possible to cut a word out, always cut it out.

- Never use the passive where you can use the active.

- Never use a foreign phrase, a scientific word, or a jargon word if you can think of an everyday English equivalent.

• Break any of these rules sooner than say anything outright barbarous.

Although Orwell presented these rules in an essay half a century ago, they're just as pertinent today. In the essay, "Politics and the English Language," he offered this advice:

• A scrupulous writer, in every sentence that he writes, will ask himself at least four questions, thus: What am I trying to say? What words will express it? What image or idiom will make it clearer? Is this image fresh enough to have an effect? And he will probably ask himself two more: Could I put it more shortly? Have I said anything that is avoidably ugly?

Orwell condemned slovenliness, vagueness and the use of ready-made phrases. He warned against "gumming together long strips of words . . . already set in order by someone else." Once a writer falls into that habit, Orwell said, it's easier and quicker for him to say, "In my opinion it is not an unjustifiable assumption that" than to say "I think."

As for the *not-un* formation, which is not uncommon, Orwell said you can cure yourself of the inclination to use it by memorizing this sentence: "A not unblack dog was chasing a not unsmall rabbit across a not ungreen field."

Orwell also pointed out the weakness of what he called "noun constructions," which rely on nouns instead of verbs. This is a noun construction: "There was a shooting in City Hall." Better: "A man shot a woman dead in City Hall."

"Noun constructions," known as "the nominal style," have been explored in *Journalism Quarterly*—and deplored. After elaborate research, Prof. Lloyd Bostian of the University of Wisconsin put into words and statistical tables what you probably know in your bones: "The nominal style is a poor choice for effective communication." But judging by what we hear on newscasts, too many broadcast writers don't know that the nominal style is ineffective or even that it exists.

Dr. Bostian wrote in *JQ* (Winter, 1983): "Nominal prose is potentially dull because it substitutes nouns for verbs, and we know that a high noun-to-verb ratio produces dull copy. In nominal style, Latin-root nouns contain verbs, and the only verbs are weak, primarily forms of 'to be.'

"For example, this sentence is nominal: 'The identification of writing faults is his goal.' The real action of this sentence is the verb 'identify' . . . hidden in the noun 'identification.' In active form, the sentence would read, 'His goal is to identify writing faults.'"

Bostian took two research articles and rewrote each in three styles, then tested them on students. Here are his lead sentences from an article on running, written in the various styles:

Nominal—"The finding of researchers is that more and more Americans are running for the achievement of physical fitness."

Passive—"It has been found by researchers that more and more Americans are running to achieve physical fitness."

Active—"Researchers have found that more and more Americans are running to achieve physical fitness."

In his analysis of the study, Bostian refers to "readers," but his conclusions can be applied with equal, perhaps greater, force to listeners:

"Readers prefer an active style; they judge it to be more interesting, and they can read it significantly faster.

"Active voice is especially advantageous when subject matter is dull or unfamiliar.

"Nominal style is clearly the poorest choice of the three styles. The combination of unfamiliar, low-interest material and the nominal style is disastrous."

If the nominal style impairs reading comprehension at the university level, you can imagine what that style does to *listeners* at any educational level. *Listeners* start at a disadvantage; unlike readers, *listeners* can't pause to go back in a story, can't refer to a previous word or line, and can't put the story aside to reread later. If *listeners* lose the thread of a story, they stay lost.

One way to help your newspeople write better is to tell them how they can get a paperback chock-full of useful tips on writing. The book, an easy-to-read 162 pages, is *The Word* by René J. Cappon, a general news editor. You can order it by mail from Associated Press Newsfeatures, 50 Rockefeller Plaza, N.Y., N.Y. 10020. Price: $7, including postage and handling. (*The Word* is also sold in bookstores as *The Associated Press Guide to News Writing*.)

Cappon wrote the book for print writers, but almost all of it can be extremely helpful for broadcast writers. Don't just take my word; get his.

Accuracy. Brevity. Clarity. They're our ABC's. But they're not so simple as ABC.

Accuracy depends on our dedication to facts: finding facts, focusing on facts and sticking to the facts.

But how can we achieve brevity and clarity? The paths are many, but the surest guidance comes from old pros. Our first advice comes from a master, Anton Chekhov, who spelled out the virtues of brevity and clarity in a letter to another Russian writer:

"Take out adjectives and adverbs wherever you can. . . . You understand what I mean when I say, 'The man sat on the grass.' You understand because the sentence is clear and there is nothing to distract your attention. Conversely . . . 'A tall, narrow-chested man of medium height with a red beard sat mutely, looking about timidly and fearfully' . . . doesn't get its meaning through to the brain immediately, which is what good writing must do, and fast."

But a word to the wise is often insufficient. So in this chapter I'm going to pass along more advice from more old pros, words that can guide us to brevity and clarity—with vitality. Not that advice or rules can make us better writers instantly—or even eventually—but they *can* point us in the right direction.

Some of the best rules for writing have been set down by Writer's Digest School. Like other rules quoted in this chapter, they're reprinted here word for word. Although all these rules were intended for people who write for the eye, in almost every case they also help us write for the ear. Writer's Digest says:

- Prefer the plain word to the fancy.

- Prefer the familiar word to the unfamiliar. [And use familiar words in familiar combinations.]

- Prefer the Saxon word to the Romance.

- Prefer nouns and verbs to adjectives and adverbs.

- Prefer picture nouns and action verbs.

- Never use a long word when a short one will do as well.

- Master the simple declarative sentence.

- Prefer the simple sentence to the complicated.

- Vary your sentence length.

- Put the words you want to emphasize at the beginning or end of your sentence. [The end is usually preferable.]

- Use the active voice.

- Put statements in a positive form.

- Use short paragraphs.
- Cut needless words, sentences and paragraphs.
- Use plain, conversational English. Write like you talk.
- Avoid imitation. Write in your natural style.
- Write clearly.
- Avoid gobbledygook and jargon.
- Write to be understood, not to impress.
- Revise and rewrite. Improvement is always possible.

A few of those rules echo *The King's English* by Henry W. Fowler and Francis G. Fowler. Their rules, published in 1906, include:

- Prefer the familiar word to the far-fetched.
- Prefer the concrete word to the abstract.
- Prefer the short word to the long.
- Prefer the Saxon word to the Romance.

The Fowlers define Romance languages as those whose grammatical structure, as well as at least part of their vocabulary, is directly descended from Latin.

The Fowlers also say, "Anyone who wishes to become a good writer should endeavour, before he allows himself to be tempted by the more showy qualities, to be direct, simple, brief, vigorous and lucid." (*The King's English?* Yes, and so's the Queen.)

Simple & Direct by Jacques Barzun also lists useful rules. Here are several:

- Weed out the jargon.
- Have a point and make it by means of the best word.
- Look for *all* fancy wordings and get rid of them.
- For a plain style, avoid everything that can be called roundabout—in idea, in linking, or in expression.
- To be plain and straightforward, resist equally the appeal of old finery and the temptation of smart novelties.

- The mark of a plain tone is combined lucidity and force.

- Read and revise, reread and revise. . . .

Later he wrote, the only general rule for good writing is "the search for complete adequacy," and he said, "Try to find out what you mean . . . and put it down without frills or apologies."

Some other practical rules are offered by John R. Trimble in his *Writing with Style:*

- Write with the assumption that your reader [think *listener*] is a companionable friend with a warm sense of humor and an appreciation of straightforwardness.

- Write as if you were actually talking to that friend, but talking with enough leisure to frame your thoughts concisely and interestingly.

- Use the fewest words possible and the simplest words possible.

- Read your prose aloud. *Always* read your prose aloud. If it sounds as if it came out of a machine . . . , spare your reader [again, think *listener*] and rewrite it.

- If you've written a paragraph that sounds heavy and tortured, put down your pencil and ask yourself: 'If I were actually speaking these thoughts to a friend, how would I probably say them?' Then go ahead and talk them *out loud,* and when you've finished, write down as nearly as you can recall what you said.

More good rules have been set down by Theodore A. Rees Cheney in his *Getting the Words Right: How to Revise, Edit & Rewrite:*

- Concentrate on the subject and eliminate digressions.

- Be sensitive to rhythm and sound. . . .

- Avoid ambiguity.

- Avoid things that kill emphasis: . . . passive verbs, abstract or indirect language, intensifiers, clichés. . . .

- Put important things anywhere but the middle.

- Bring emphasis by careful word choice and positioning.

And more good rules, from M. L. Stein's *Write Clearly—Speak Effectively,* tell us:

- Keep your sentences generally short, with one idea to a sentence.
- Get attention in your opening sentence by producing something interesting for the reader or listener.
- Be objective and impersonal so you can see facts and issues in proper perspective.
- Try [to] rid yourself of many of the bromides, truisms and platitudes that find their way into so much writing and speaking. Put your brain to work on new ways of saying things.
- Edit, edit, edit.

Have you noticed that most of these experts are singing the same song? In some places, they're singing in unison; in a few places, they differ on the lyrics. But, by and large, it's the same song.

Another member of the chorus, Robert Gunning, set down what he called Ten Principles of Clear Writing in *The Technique of Clear Writing:*

- Keep sentences short.
- Prefer the simple to the complex.
- Prefer the familiar word.
- Avoid unnecessary words.
- Put action in your verbs.
- Write like you talk. [He says the use of *as* instead of *like,* as many grammarians insist on using, would make the sentence ambiguous.]
- Use terms your reader can picture. [Think *listener.*]
- Tie in with your reader's experience.
- Make full use of variety. [He says, "You need a wide knowledge of the flexibility and variety of the language."]
- Write to express, not impress.

Another expert, Jefferson D. Bates, lays down his 10 rules in *Writing with Precision:*

- Prefer the active voice.

- Don't make nouns out of good, strong "working verbs."

- Be concise.

- Be specific.

- Keep related sentence elements together.

- Avoid unnecessary shifts [of number, tense, subject].

- Prefer the simple word.

- Don't repeat a word or words unnecessarily. [But Tim Wulfemeyer reminds us in his *Beginning Broadcast Newswriting*: "Don't be afraid to repeat words. If the word is the *right* word, don't hesitate to use it—more than once, twice, or even three times. If the word fits, write it."]

- Make sentence elements parallel.

- Arrange your material logically.

One of the country's leading authorities on writing, Roy Peter Clark, an associate director of the Poynter Institute for Media Studies in St. Petersburg, Florida, has listed some steps in writing that he says work well when used wisely. Although he's addressing print writers, what he says applies to us, and though he refers to "techniques," we would do well to consider them rules. He also provides explanations:

- Envision a general audience. *A journalist who writes for a general audience will find the language becoming purer and clearer. When I am struggling to make something clear, even to a general audience, I fantasize a conversation with my mother. If she asked me, "What did you learn at city council today?" I would not respond: "The city council agreed by a one-vote margin Friday to apply for federal matching funds to permit them to support a project to aid small businesses in the black community by giving them lower interest loans." I might be more inclined to say, "Well, Ma, black business people are struggling, and the city council thinks it has found a way to help them out." Sometimes, when you imagine telling a story to a single human being, your voice changes and your language becomes more simple and direct.*

- Slow down the pace of information. *Too much writing on difficult subjects is of the "dense-pack" variety: information stuffed into tight, dense paragraphs and conveyed at a rate that takes the breath away.*

- Don't clutter leads with confusing statistics, technical information or bureaucratic names.

- Remember that numbers can be numbing.

- Translate jargon.

- Consider the impact.

- Eliminate unnecessary information.

The record for the number of writer's rules between two covers probably should go to Gary Provost for his *100 Ways to Improve Your Writing*. We'll trim them to 15:

- Write a strong lead.

- Don't explain when you don't have to.

- Write complete sentences.

- Keep related words together.

- Respect the rules of grammar.

- Prefer good writing to good grammar.

- Use dense words. [A "dense" word, he says, is one that crams a lot of meaning into a small space. For example, "once a month" can be reduced to "monthly." And "people they didn't know" = "strangers."]

- Use short words.

- Use active verbs.

- Use strong verbs.

- Use specific nouns.

- Use the active voice—most of the time.

- Say things in a positive way—most of the time.

- Put emphatic words at the end.

- Stop writing when you get to the end.

Writers tend to be unruly, so most of us can benefit from practical rules. Not that good writing can be achieved by rules alone. But writers who heed sound rules are most likely to produce sound copy.

Some of the soundest rules were set down by Douglas Southall Freeman, and he put them to good use. He won the Pulitzer Prize twice. His 20 rules:

- Above all, be clear.

- Therefore, use simple English.

- To that end, write short sentences.

- Do not change subject in the middle of the sentence unless there is (a) definite antithesis or (b) no possible way of changing the subject. If you must change subject, always insert a comma at the end of the clause that precedes the one in which you make the change.

- Do not end sentences with participial phrases. Beware such construction as "The mayor refused to discuss the subject, *saying* it was one for the consideration of the council."

- Do not change the voice of a verb in the middle of a sentence. If you start with an active verb, keep it active. It is sloppy to say: He went to Hopewell and was met by. . . ."

- Seek to leave the meaning of the sentence incomplete until the last word. Add nothing after the meaning is complete. Start a new sentence then.

- Avoid loose construction. Try never to begin sentences with *And* or *But.* [But as first words in broadcast sentences, *and* and *but* are permissible, even desirable.]

- Never use vague or unusual words that divert the reader's attention from what you are reporting.

- Make every antecedent plain: Never permit 'it' or 'that' or any similar word to refer to different things in the same sentence.

- Where you write a clause beginning with *which,* do not follow it with one that begins *and which.* Never write a sentence such as "The ordinance which was considered by the finance committee *and* which was recommended to the council. . . ."

- Avoid successive sentences that begin with the same word, unless emphasis is desired. Especially, in quoting a man, never have one sentence begin "*He* said" and then have the next sentence start "*He* stated."

- In sentences where several nouns, phrases or clauses depend on the same verb, put the longer phrase or clause last. For instance, do not say, "He addressed the general assembly, the members of the corporation commission, and the governor." [As Freeman suggested, the example should be rewritten to go from short to long: "the governor, the general assembly and the members of the corporation commission." That rule has given us "life, liberty and the pursuit of happiness."]

- If you are compelled, for condensation, to use many long sentences, relieve them by employing very short sentences at intervals.

- In conditional sentences, seek to put the conditional clause before the principal clause. An *if* clause at the beginning of a sentence is better placed than at the end, unless the whole point of the sentence lies in the *if.*

- Be accurate in the use of synonyms and avoid overloading a sentence with a long phrase employed as a synonym. You will do well to buy and keep on your desk a copy of [*Roget's Thesaurus*]. . . .

- Avoid successive sentences with the same form and conjunction. One of the surest ways to kill interest and to make a story dull is to use a succession of compound sentences, the clauses of which are connected by *and.* Change the conjunction and the form of the sentences as often as possible.

- Shun the employment of nouns as adjectives; it is the lowest form of careless English. There always are better ways to condense than to pile up nouns before a noun and to pretend they are adjectives.

- Avoid successive words that begin or end with the same syllables, for instance *re* or *ex* at the beginning of words and *ly* or *ing* as the final syllable.

- Try to end every story with a strong, and, if possible, a short sentence.

Freeman wrote the rules in the 1920s, when he was a newspaper editor in Richmond, Virginia. He called them "The *News Leader's* Twenty Fundamental Rules of News Writing"; and he applied them in writing his Pulitzer-winning biographies of Washington and Robert E. Lee. The rules are just as good now as they were then.

If Freeman had expanded on his rule about the sequence of words in a sentence, he could have added that elements in a series should be listed, where suitable, in ascending order of impact. That gives the last-named element the most emphasis: "I came, I saw, I conquered." Exceptions: A series shouldn't deviate from any logical—or chronological—need. And you can't set up a series in the order of climax if the elements are unrelated or unimportant: "He bought milk, tea and soup."

A newscaster said terrorists had singled out Americans for "threats, taunting and terror." The sequence should have started with the mildest misdeed, "taunts," which is a noun, not "taunting," a gerund. Then the series should have stepped up to the next more serious offense, "threats," and peaked (as it did) with the strongest word, "terror." (I disagree with the writer who says, "No one needs to know what a gerund is, except people taking a test that asks: 'What's a gerund?'")

When you don't build up to the strongest word in a series like that, your sentence stumbles. That happened to Chicago's late Mayor Richard J. Daley in his lament about critics: "They have vilified me, they have crucified me, yes, they have even criticized me."

A later editor of the *News Leader,* the columnist James J. Kilpatrick, also laid down some "ought tos":

- We ought to master our tools. [He's alluding to *words.*]

- We ought to pay more attention to cadence. [He quotes Barbara Tuchman: "An essential element for good writing is a good ear: One must listen to the sound of one's prose."]

- We ought to pay closer attention to the arrangement of our words and clauses.

- We ought to keep in mind that words have nuances; words carry connotations, and words that may be appropriate in one context may not be appropriate for another. We ought constantly to search for the right word.

- We must copy-edit, copy-edit, copy-edit!

Kilpatrick also laid down some "ought nots":

- We ought not to use clichés.
- We ought never to fall into gobbledegook.
- We ought not to mangle our sentences.
- As a general rule, we ought not to use euphemisms.
- We ought not to pile up nouns as adjectives.
- We ought not to coin words wantonly.
- We must not break the rules of grammar.
- We ought not to be redundant.

- We ought not to use words that have double meanings. [He's talking about ambiguity, not suggestive remarks.]

- We ought not to write portmanteau sentences. [That's a sentence, he says, in which a writer "tried to pack everything he owned into a single traveling bag, and he left ties, socks and shirttails sticking out."]

In *The Writer's Art,* Kilpatrick elaborates on these and other rules, provides examples of usage (and abusage), and offers insights that can help good writers become better.

Man cannot write by rules alone, but rules can help.

9

WHO SAYS?

An 11 p.m. newscast on TV in New York City began:

> **Good evening. The United States and Iran . . . locked in aerial combat over the Persian Gulf . . . with oil prices skyrocketing and Western economies sagging.**

Jolted by this ominous opening, I strained to catch every word as the co-anchor picked it up:

> **That's the fear tonight . . . in the wake of a series of air attacks on oil tankers in the Persian Gulf. . . .**

What? The newscast starts with a slam-bang lead, boldly describing U.S.-Iranian combat, but retreats from *aerial combat* by saying it's just a *fear.* Nowhere in the long package does anyone—other than an anchor— express such a *fear.*

The script—and I quote from it exactly (including ellipsis points)— goes on to say that at the State Department, *concern over the Persian Gulf was evident.* But the script doesn't mention how that *concern* was apparent. Nor how *concern* became *fear.*

The effect of that scary lead is that it alarmed *me.* Many people, after hearing only the first few seconds of the newscast, might have started talking or shouting to other people about the news of U.S. combat. In the hubbub of the household, they might not have heard the next anchor's saying it was only a *fear.* They might not have listened carefully to the rest of the story and realized that *fear* was expressed only by the anchor. Many listeners—and half-listeners—who caught the mention of *fear* were probably left worried and confused. Some might have even become fear- ful themselves. All were misinformed.

What bothers me is the apparent willingness of the anchors, producer(s) and writer(s) of the newscast to ignore one of the basic questions a reporter should ask: "Who says so?" If they had paused to ask, "Who says he fears U.S.-Iranian combat?" they would have realized that their imaginative lead was just that—merely their imagination. If they did ask—and answer—that question and decided to go ahead anyway with the fabrication, they ignored their obligations to their news director and to their public.

They could have tested the validity of their approach by applying a basic rule of broadcast newswriting: Start the lead by identifying the source of the assertion that someone fears the entry of this country into the fighting. Apparently, the information the newsroom had available, probably wire service stories, didn't identify or point to anyone who had articulated such a fear. So by that time they should have concluded that their hard-hitting lead was hollow. And they should have shot it down.

Few leads are as misleading as that one, but I do hear many that are unsatisfactory because they make startling, controversial or questionable assertions without first saying who's doing the asserting.

And some leads start with quotations (without first saying who's being quoted). The offense is compounded when the quotation contains a "you" or an "I," or both, as in this broadcast script:

'If you don't come here this year when I want you to, I won't go there next year.' So says President Reagan to President Mikhail Gorbachev. Reagan doesn't want Gorbachev here in September. He says it's too close to the Congressional election in November.

Besides starting with a quotation, this script, reprinted in its entirety, has several problems. It didn't identify the country headed by Gorbachev, who was *not* president. Usually, we don't have time for propriety, but I think it's desirable, on second reference, to grant the President of the United States the courtesy title of Mr.

On first hearing this item—and there is no second chance—a listener would wonder who *you* is—or are. And he'd wonder who *I* is. And where *here* is. After the listener hears "So says President Reagan," the listener has to try to go back in his mind and fill in the pieces in the puzzle and, at the same time, keep up with the flow of the story. The writer probably intended the *he* in the script to refer to Mr. Reagan, but *he* refers to the last person named, Gorbachev.

When we converse, we naturally put the source first: "He told me. . . ."; "She told him. . . ."; "I told them. . . ." People are attuned to this pattern of conversation, which is why it makes sense for broadcast newswriters to follow the same pattern and write the way people talk. But writers for print routinely hang attribution at the end of a sentence (frequently with "according to"). Or they tag the tail of a 25-word sentence with "he said."

Broadcaster writers must keep in mind that they're not writing for the eye but for a much different sensor, the ear. But they shouldn't overdo attribution. Not every story, let alone every sentence, needs attribution. When you have a story where the facts are public knowledge and indisputable— say, two cars collided on Main Street—you needn't attribute the story to the police. But if the police say one driver had been drinking, or the police affix blame, you'd better attribute that assertion to the police.

When attribution is essential, it should precede the assertion. Experts are seldom unanimous, but they agree on this rule: Attribution precedes assertion. Here's what they've said over the years:

"Attributions must precede quoted material." Edward Bliss Jr. and James L. Hoyt, *Writing News for Broadcast.*

"When attribution is needed, name the source at the beginning of the sentence if possible, and never any later than the middle." E. Joseph Broussard and Jack F. Holgate, *Writing & Reporting Broadcast News.*

"Attribution precedes statements 90-plus times out of 100, and always before statements of opinion—a criticism, attack, prediction, etc. . . ." Charles Coates, *Professional's TV News Handbook.*

"In broadcast news the attribution is placed at the *start* of the sentence." David Keith Cohler, *Broadcast Newswriting.*

"Put attribution first." Carl Hausman, *Crafting News for the Electronic Media.*

"The attribution should always come at the beginning of the sentence." Irving E. Fang, *Television News, Radio News.*

"Never lead with a quotation. Always give the source of the information before you give the information." Daniel E. Garvey and William L. Rivers, *Newswriting for the Electronic Media.*

"When you name the source of your information at the beginning of a sentence, you give your listeners and viewers a foundation for believing or rejecting it." Roy Gibson, *Radio and Television Reporting.*

"Because of the characteristics of the broadcast medium, it is confusing for the listener to hear the source for a statement at the end of that statement." Mark W. Hall, *Broadcast Journalism.*

"Put the attribution high in the story so your audience will not have to wait to figure out where the report came from. And put the attribution at the head of the sentence rather than at the end as is done in newspapers." Phillip O. Keirstead, *Journalist's Notebook of Live Radio-TV News.*

"You say who said it before you relate what he said." Carolyn Diana Lewis, *Reporting for Television.*

"In all cases, attribution precedes the comment." Peter E. Mayeux, *Broadcast News Writing & Reporting.*

"Begin sentences with a source, with the attribution." Melvin Mencher, *News Reporting and Writing.*

"Attribution always should precede the quotation . . . attribution must always precede the indirect quote." The Missouri Group: Brian S. Brooks, George Kennedy, Daryl R. Moen and Don Ranly, *News Reporting and Writing.*

"Put attribution at the top. Although there are occasional exceptions to this, most of the exceptions you hear on the air are examples of a writer opting for effect over responsibility." Robert A. Papper, *Broadcast News Writing Stylebook.*

"Place the name of the source you are quoting at the front of the sentence, not at the end." Frederick Shook, *Television Newswriting: Captivating an Audience.*

"Broadcast stories usually *sound* more natural if you name the source at the beginning of the sentence." Frederick Shook and Dan Lattimore, *The Broadcast News Process.*

"The best way to avoid . . . confusion is to lead with the source attribution." G. Paul Smeyak, *Broadcast News Writing.*

"Sentences are clearest when the attribution is placed at the start of the sentence." Mitchell Stephens, *Broadcast News.*

"In placing the source first, the radio writer again aligns himself with the conversationalist and departs from newspaper style, which in itself was a departure from the earlier oral style." Carl Warren, *Radio News Writing and Editing.* (It came out in 1947—apparently the first year in which a book was published on broadcast newswriting.)

"It is best to let the listener-viewers know who is talking before you tell them what is being said. This means the writer begins with an attribution." J. Clark Weaver, *Broadcast Newswriting as Process.*

"Attribution in broadcast copy, if used in the lead sentence, is always at the top of the sentence." Ted White, *Broadcast News Writing, Reporting and Producing,* 2d ed.

"Name the source at the beginning of a sentence if this can be done without awkwardness. And it generally can be." Arthur Wimer and Dale Brix, *Workbook for Radio and TV News Editing and Writing.*

"We ALWAYS report attribution at the beginning of a sentence, because that's the way we report it in our everyday conversations." K. Tim Wulfemeyer, *Broadcast Newswriting.*

"The general rule for broadcast writing is that the attribution comes first." Steven Zousmer, *TV News Off-Camera.*

"Getting attribution into your copy early on in the story is a cardinal rule that almost never should be violated." *The Associated Press Broadcast News Style Book* (1976).

"The source belongs at the beginning of the sentence." *The United Press International Broadcast Stylebook.* (1979. And yes, the AP and UPI even had different styles for "stylebook.")

This rule was stated even more forcefully in a book, *Television News Reporting* by the staff of CBS News, published in 1958. True, no committee ever won a prize for writing, and no one ever erected a statue to a committee, but this book deserves our attention:

"When writing for television, always say *who* before you say *what* someone said or did. . . . The viewer is entitled to know the authority for a statement or action first so that he can gauge what importance to attach to it as the newscaster relates it. . . .

"Do not make the mistake of leading a story with an interesting quote and then identifying the speaker in the second sentence. Almost inevitably, some viewers will miss the connection and will accept the quote as the newscaster's own opinion."

In other words: Attribution precedes assertion.

Quote, Unquote

Quoth a network newscaster:

> **Gorbachev delivered his sharpest attack yet against President Reagan's 'Star Wars' plan, warning of, quote, 'rough times ahead' if President Reagan and his aides, quote, 'continue along the perilous path they have laid.' Unquote.**

To *quote* or not to *quote?* That is the question: whether 'tis nobler in the mind to *quote* or take another tack to avoid a sea of troubles.

That and other quotidian questions about quotations vex many a writer, so let's see what experts say. And let's start with one of the earliest efforts to quash *quote:* "Thoughtless use of such hackneyed terms as 'quote' and 'end quote' tend to interrupt the listener's thought. They have a barking, staccato sound no matter how softly they are spoken. They call attention to themselves and detract from the story." The criticism comes from *A Manual of Radio News Writing* by Burton L. Hotaling. It was published in 1947.

Another expert on the same wavelength was the first news director of CBS, Paul W. White. He wrote in *News on the Air,* also published in 1947: "Remember that since the word 'quote' is foreign to the ear as far as ordinary conversation is concerned, it probably always is disturbing to the listener. . . . Please, please don't use 'unquote.' "

"Such phrases as 'and I quote' and 'end quote' are . . . shunned by skillful writers," Mitchell V. Charnley said in *News by Radio,* published in 1948. "The need for them can be avoided in most cases by careful use of the more conversational devices." (Until 1947, Charnley said, publications on handling radio news were scant: apparently only two mimeographed handbooks printed before World War II and two pamphlets issued by news agencies during the war.)

"Avoid the words 'quote,' 'unquote' and 'end quote. . . .' This style has become trite and stilted." 1947. Baskett Mosse, *Radio News Handbook.* He said that a half century ago.

"*Never,* under any circumstances, start a sentence with a direct quote and tack the source on the end. . . . This method . . . violates a fundamental rule of good broadcast writing." 1962. *The Associated Press Radio-Television News Style Book.*

"It is old-fashioned to say 'quote' and 'unquote.' " 1967. *Broadcast Writing Style Guide,* U.S. Defense Information School.

More often than not, says the 1972 *AP Broadcast News Style Book,* using direct quotations in stories is "lazy writing."

"The oldtime use of quote-unquote has long gone by the boards. . . ." 1976. *The Associated Press Broadcast News Style Book.*

"Don't use the hackneyed QUOTE-UNQUOTE." 1982. E. Joseph Broussard and Jack F. Holgate, *Writing and Reporting Broadcast News.*

"Never use the words *quote, unquote* and *quotation.*" 1982. Frederick Shook and Dan Lattimore, *The Broadcast News Process.*

"The use of the terms 'quote' and 'unquote' is cumbersome and lacks finesse." 1984. J. Clark Weaver, *Broadcast Newswriting as Process.*

"You should avoid using the expression 'quote . . . unquote.' 1984. Ted White, Adrian J. Meppen and Steve Young, *Broadcast News Writing, Reporting, and Production.*

"Avoid the use of 'quote-unquote.' " 1986. Mark W. Hall, *Broadcast Journalism.*

"Do not EVER say 'quote' and 'unquote.' That is a holdover from the ancient days of sending news by telegraph when the sending operator wanted to be certain the receiving end knew the limits of the quoted material." 1987. R.H. MacDonald, *A Broadcast News Manual of Style.*

"These words [*quote* and *unquote*] are jarring to the ear; they are abrupt and interrupt the flow of the story. Rather than clarifying, they may well confuse the listener. Even more stiff and formal are the phrases: 'and I quote' and 'end of quote.'" 1988. Roger L. Walters, *Broadcast Writing.*

The same disdain for *quote* and *unquote* is also expressed in the most recent books. *Broadcast News,* 3d ed., published in 1993, says, "This heavy-handed device [*quote*] has become antiquated." The author, Mitchell Stephens, suggests the use of "more subtle and less formal alternatives."

These attributing phrases inform listeners in a conversational way that they're about to hear a direct quotation:

He put it this way. . . .
In her words. . . .
The governor's exact words were. . . .
As he put it. . . .
. . . what she called. . . .
These are the mayor's words. . . .

In other words, there are many other words. Yet some writers use *quote* and *unquote* so often you'd think they're trying to fill a quota. Maybe they need to consider a few more quotations:

"NEVER use the old 'quote, unquote' method." 1993. K. Tim Wulfemeyer, *Beginning Broadcast Newswriting,* 3d ed.

"It is awkward and unnecessary to start and end a quotation with the verbal quotation marks *quote* and *unquote.*" 1994. Edward Bliss Jr. and James L. Hoyt, *Writing News for Broadcast,* 3d ed.

"Do not use phrases like *quote* and *end quote* or *unquote.*" 1996. Peter E. Mayeux, *Broadcast News Writing & Reporting,* 2d ed.

When should a writer use a direct quotation? "Only when it's neat, compact and the wording is exceptional," says Mitch Stephens. "Otherwise, paraphrase."

In *Crafting the News for Electronic Media,* Carl Hausman says, "You do not read 'quote' and 'close quote' or similar indicators over the air, except when the quote is of such a controversial or bizarre nature that you want to ensure that listeners or viewers completely understand that these are the newsmaker's words and not yours." One such extraordinary remark could be handled this way: "President Nixon said—*quote*—'I am not a crook'—*unquote.*" If you wrote, "President Nixon says he's not a crook," you'd drain the remark of its tang.

So let's rewrite what the newscaster said in the excerpt at the outset: "Gorbachev made his sharpest attack yet on President Reagan's 'Star Wars' plan. He warned of [here the newscaster can pause or punctuate with his voice] 'rough times ahead' if President Reagan and his aides continue on what he called their 'perilous path.'"

And now if you need help in your newsroom to give *quote-unquote* its quietus, you can quote our quorum.

The Wrong Stuff

By the time we reached Easter, I'd had it up to my keister. Not with bunnies and bonnets but with political clichés. And the worst was yet to be. With the national conventions approaching, clichés were already flying through the air like an acrobatic team, Thick and Fast.

As an old city editor of mine is reputed—or disreputed—to have said, "We need some new clichés." Or we need to try harder to resist the first cliché that comes to mind. Clichés spring to mind because we've heard them so often they've saturated our consciousness, ready for instant retrieval. But we should be on guard against them precisely because of their instantaneity and ubiquity.

Here are some of the political clichés that ricochet and re-echo through our minds, clichés that we should not use at the drop of a hat in the ring:

Front-runner. Put it on the back-burner. Who knows for sure which candidate—or non-candidate—is ahead until all the delegates or voters have cast ballots? As an article in the *Washington Journalism Review* said, "Hart's New Hampshire surprise did not show that reporters need better ways to pinpoint the leader; it showed the error of trying to do so at all." When Sen. Gary Hart dropped out of the race for the Presidency in 1988, it was called a *Hart-breaker.* We also heard *Hart attack, Hart-stopper, Hart failure.* Bypass 'em. Puns on people's names age rapidly. And most people whose names lend themselves to puns have heard them all—many times. Just don't "Kick that Block!"

The last hurrah. When Edwin O'Connor wrote *The Last Hurrah* in 1956, the phrase was fresh. But it has long since gone stale. Like *It's all over but the shouting,* it deserves its own bye-bye.

An idea whose time has come. When Victor Hugo (or his translator) wrote, "Greater than the tread of mighty armies is an idea whose time has come," he expressed an idea with originality. But his line has been trampled by his followers' footsteps. Even the variations since it was written in 1852 have become tiresome: "an idea whose time has come again," "an idea whose time has come and gone," "an idea whose time will never come." For all of them, original and variations, time has run out.

The right stuff. Clichés don't have it.

On the campaign trail. Too tired for *the comeback trail.* Why not merely say the candidate is campaigning?

On the hustings. It's an outdated and wordy way of saying someone is on the road campaigning. What *are* hustings? And where are hustings? (Not to be confused with the Battle of Hustings or Hustings-on-Hudson.)

On the stump. Worn to the stump.

A real horse race. Fits the definition of a cliché by Eric Partridge: "So hackneyed as to be knock-kneed and spavined." When tempted to use it, just say neigh.

Political warhorse. Ready for pasture.

Neck and neck. Ditto.

Won his spurs. Pack it away with the buggy whip.

Homestretch. Save it for Hialeah.

Beauty contest. Save it for Atlantic City.

Dark horse. Has been ridden into the ground, but because it packs a lot of meaning in two short words, still good for more outings. (Didja hear the one about the dark horse that won a beauty contest? A chestnut came in second. That, of course, is a color of another horse.)

Political animal. A bone-weary critter ready for the glue factory.

Stormy petrel. Out of petrol.

Crossed the Rubicon. Next time it crosses your mind, ask the first five passersby what the phrase means.

Stemwinder. That word may still be a favorite of politicians and political reporters. But I've never heard anyone else say it—or understand it. Its time has passed.

_____ *is expected to win.* Expected by whom? As Confucius should have said, "Man who lives by crystal ball ends up eating glass."

Warts and all. See a dermatologist. Better yet, a dictionary or a thesaurus. What's wrong with calling an appraisal "frank" or "blunt"?

Has worn two hats, kept a high profile and *kept the political pot boiling.* They're all burned out.

Political litmus test. How many listeners know what a litmus test is? It flunks *the acid test.*

Current incumbent. A redundancy. An incumbent *is* the current occupant of an office.

Margin. It's not a cliché, but it is a word that reporters covering elections and polls misuse often. If Clyde gets 500,000 votes and Merrill gets 400,000, some reporters would say, "Clyde won by a five-to-four *margin.*" Wrong. He won by a five-to-four *ratio.* A margin is the difference between two sums (100,000); a ratio is a proportion.

Open secret. If it's open, it's no longer secret.

Topic A. Passé.

Flushed with success. Use it only if you're writing about a prosperous plumber.

Bandwagon, for example, is a cliché I wouldn't retire (even if it needs new tires). It works: it's not wordy; it saves many words. It presents a clear, colorful picture. And it's a lot shorter and faster than this definition of *bandwagon* (from William Safire's *Political Dictionary*): "a movement appealing to the herd instinct of politicians and voters to be on the winning side in any contest."

I don't want to inveigh against all clichés, but I do want to veigh in against almost all of them. When they were coined, they might well have sparkled. Their popularity, though, has been their undoing; now they're tarnished. They may be tried and true (like that cliché) but they're so trite they lack bite.

Non-Starters

There is a quick, easy way to start a story or a column: "There is. . . ." Which is why so many writers start their scripts that way:

"There's a big fire near City Hall."

"There's a shooting at the courthouse."

"There has been a train collision near Dullsville."

Now let's toss out the wordy, murky *there is* and go straight to the news with a vigorous verb:

"A fire has broken out near City Hall."

"A lawyer has been shot in the courthouse."

"Two trains have collided near Dullsville."

These revised sentences are much stronger than the originals because they do away with "there is," which is indefinite, indirect and indolent. The new leads start with what should be the subject of the sentence. Instead of relying on the static "is," they move the action along with energetic verbs. As David Lambuth says, if you have a nail to hit, hit it on the head.

A simple explanation for the weakness of "there is" is offered by Lambuth in *The Golden Book on Writing:* "The habit of beginning statements with the impersonal and usually vague *there is* or *there are* shoves the really significant verb into subordinate place instead of letting it stand vigorously on its own feet. In place of saying *A brick house stands on the corner,* you find yourself lazily falling into *There is a brick house which stands on the corner.*" Lambuth goes on to say that in that last sentence, your attention is first drawn to *there is,* and from that to *stands,* which should have the whole emphasis, because it's the one definite statement in the sentence. (Lambuth's book, now in paperback, was first published in 1923. That may explain why *house* is followed by *which* instead of the now-preferred *that.*)

"Both [*there is* and *there are*] are dead phrases and should be used as a last resort," says John R. Trimble in *Writing with Style.* "Eliminating them through recasting," he suggests, "usually results in sentences that are more vivid, concrete and terse. There are many exceptions, though, and this sentence is one of them."

"*There* itself is not bad," says Theodore A. Rees Cheney, "it's the company it keeps that gets it in trouble. *There* usually hangs out innocently on the corner with other idlers, verbs like *is, was, are, have been, had been,* and other weak verbs of being." In *Getting the Words Right: How to Revise, Edit & Rewrite,* he says, "These colorless verbs merely indicate that something exists, nothing about how it exists, how it behaves . . . nothing to pique our interest."

Equally wasteful in starting a story—or sentence—is *It is.* So experts advise against it. (To be precise, against *it is;* usually, it's also a good idea not to start with an indefinite pronoun like *it.*)

When *there* is used with *is* or any form of *to be* to introduce a sentence, *there* is called an expletive. So is *it* when coupled with a form of *to be,* as in *it is.* The wordiness—and unworthiness—of this kind of beginning can be seen in the Latin origin of *expletive:* "added merely to fill up." So the best rule for newswriters is: Make sure your scripts have their expletives deleted.

Newswriters should also be alert to other weaknesses in their scripts. "Be especially ready to revise a sentence," Frederick Crews writes in *The Random House Handbook,* "if you notice that its main assertion:

- has as its verb a form of the colorless, inert *to be* (*is, are, was, were, had been,* etc.);

- conveys action through a noun rather than a verb (*there was a meeting* instead of *they met*);

- has its verb in the passive voice;

- begins with one of the delaying formulas—*it is, it was,* etc.

- contains one or more *that* or *what* clauses, suggesting a displacement of your main idea to a grammatically minor part of the assertion; or

- seems to go on and on without interruption, requiring an effort of memory to keep it together." (His example: *It is what she recalled from childhood about the begonia gardens that were cultivated in Capitola that drew her to return to that part of the coastline one summer after another.*)

Of those six danger signals, Crews says, the last one *always* calls for revision. The other five are just warning flags: "When you have made an indistinct assertion, it will probably show more than one of the features we have named; and you can make your assertion more distinct simply by replacing those features."

"Bring" and "Take"

What do you think of this lead by a networker?

> **An American airlift advance team has arrived to help bring food to millions of Ethiopians dying from famine.**

Please don't say it's strictly from hunger. But surely it needs help. First, people die *of* an ailment, not *from.* Second, *famine* is not something that anyone dies of. People die *in* a famine. Further, the sentence confuses *bring* and *take. Bring* (like *come*) implies movement toward the speaker; *take* (like *go*) implies movement away from the speaker. You ask someone to *take* your letter to the post office; you ask him to *bring* back stamps. A reporter at the airfield where the advance team landed would have been justified in using *bring,* but the newscaster in New York City should have used *take* or *deliver.*

In the impromptu give-and-take between co-anchors or between an anchor and a reporter, there are far more chances for lapses than in a written script. That's why written words are, with exceptions, preferred. An anchor ad-libbed about some new electronic devices:

> **Actually, I have heard that some of our correspondents actually will carry these on stories.**

One sentence, 15 words, two of them *actually*! When you delete *actually,* you'll see that the sentence means the same thing without *actually.* In 95 cases in 100, *actually* adds nothing. Usually, it detracts. Used twice in one sentence, it distracts.

A good rule to bear in mind is one that writers can apply to every word in a sentence: If it's not necessary to put it in, it *is* necessary to keep it out.

Misuse of words in newscasts is hardly news, but this jarred me. In a story about the stock market, a reporter said,

> **Add to this the possibility of a disappointing Christmas for retailers, the lingering problem of the Federal deficit and the uncertain tax outlook, and you see why some analysts say the rally could *run amuck* by next week.**

The reporter was rambling *and* scrambling. He probably wanted to say the rally could run out of steam, or stumble; *run amuck* means to be in a frenzy to kill. But even Wall Street's high muckamucks mustn't run amuck, especially if they want to make a killing.

Today

Today, wordwatchers, let's look at *today.*

It's a daily irritant for writers who wonder where in a story to insert *today* and whether to use it at all. It also annoys listeners who dislike having *today, today, today* tapping a tattoo on their eardrums.

"In the broadcasting business," Allan Jackson of CBS News once wrote, "the customers (your listeners) assume you're talking about what happened today; in fact, by the very nature of the medium, they assume you're talking about what is happening not only today but, to a large extent, right now. Allan died about 20 years ago, but his advice is timeless.

The first editor of the "CBS Evening News with Walter Cronkite," Ed Bliss, told me that his chief chore in scrutinizing the scripts of the three writers was deleting *today.* Although Ed was jesting, he made it clear that the overuse of *today* is nothing to wink at. Using *today* in the first story of a newscast seems reasonable, maybe in the first two stories. But in his *Writing News for Broadcast,* Ed advises, "Avoid a succession of leads containing the word *today,* especially in news summaries when repetition of the word becomes painful."

"It is a mark of the amateur to use *today* in every story you write," according to another textbook, *Broadcast News Writing, Reporting and Production* by Ted White, Adrian J. Meppen and Steve Young. "Your listeners," they write, "assume that your stories deal with events that are taking place today without your reminding them every 20 seconds."

On evening newscasts, *this evening* or *tonight* in a story may make a script seem newsier. But some stations, in an effort to make their late newscasts seem different from their evening news and more up-to-the-minute, put *tonight* in every story. So even if a story is fresh or has a new angle, this approach palls.

For example, an anchor on a late newscast reported, "A British researcher said tonight. . . ." That was the first time I ever heard of a researcher who made public his findings just before dawn, as it was in Britain—unless he held a news conference at 3 a.m.

When we talk about the time and *today* and *tonight,* we should use our local time. Occasionally, a writer will see a story from Moscow that says the Kremlin said something *tonight.* The time in Moscow when the Kremlin spoke might have been 7 p.m. But in Washington, D.C., that's mid-morning. Yet, a few U.S. newscasters will go on the air at 6 p.m. or later and say, "Moscow said *tonight.* . . ." I'd say the person who writes it that way is either thoughtless or careless with the truth.

A careful writer would make his script read, "Moscow said *today.* . . ." But in most cases, the writer could skip the time element and use the present tense: "Moscow *says.* . . ." The illogic of using any but local time is apparent in this imaginary lead: "A top Russian official said *tomorrow.* . . ." Only infrequently is it necessary to say that it's *tomorrow* in Moscow and that something occurred at dawn there.

If a story—or a producer—does cry out for a *today* or a *tonight,* where in a sentence do we put that adverb? If you use *today* or *tonight* in the first sentence, use it *after* the verb. It makes no sense to use *today* before the verb, before we even tell listeners what the action is.

We hear stories that start, "The White House today said. . . ." The use of *today* near the top delays listeners from learning why they should keep listening. If you must use *today* in a story like that, you can make it, "The White House said today. . . ." *Today* is one of those words so commonplace in newscasts that they induce yawns, according to Mitchell Stephens in *Broadcast News.* "They are best kept out of the lead," he writes, "or at least out of the first few words of the lead—what might be called the 'lead's lead.' News is what is special about a story, not what is common to every story."

Avoid putting *today* at the end of the first sentence unless it's especially short. Putting *today* at the end can be awkward and make the story wrong. Yet I heard this on a network newscast:

Another Lebanese died of injuries received in that terrorist bombing of the U.S. embassy today.

Sounds like the bomb went off today; but no, the Lebanese *died* today.

As for starting a story with *today* or *tonight,* don't, unless it's intended as a transition from a closely related story with a different time element. Another possible exception: to draw a sharp contrast, perhaps something like this: "Today, Mayor Meyer passed a tough physical. Tonight, he dropped dead." But I'd probably write it this way: "Mayor Meyer is dead. He died tonight of. . . ."

Another angle on *today* comes from the newsman Jerry Bohnen, who says he tries to avoid *today.* He says *today* is too broad and covers too great a time span. Instead, he prefers to "narrow the time frame" for the listener. Rather than say, "A judge will decide *today,*" Jerry favors saying, "A judge will decide *this afternoon.*" Although that's longer than a simple *today,* it is more specific and more immediate. If you have time, his approach may occasionally be appropriate. On an evening newscast, though, I wouldn't say that something happened *this morning.* That's too long ago, too long to say and immaterial. Nor, on an evening newscast, would I say that something happened *this afternoon.* It's wordy and immaterial. *Today* would suffice.

In most cases, it's unimportant whether the mayor said something at 10:30 a.m. or 4:30 p.m. But if the story just broke and the news is significant, I might consider featuring the time element: "Mayor Trumbull says he's resigning. *A few minutes ago,* he said his doctor advised him to move promptly to a warmer climate." Or: "Mayor Trumbull is planning to resign *within the hour.*" Or "Mayor Trumbull and Governor Graham are meeting *now.*" I think those words, where appropriate, heighten the now-ness of news.

Unless you're writing for an early morning newscast, using *yesterday* or *last night* in a lead is undesirable: listeners want to know what went on today and, if possible (and pertinent), what's going on right now. If you're dealing with a *yesterday* story, write a second-day lead, starting with the *today* angle. If it's a *yesterday* story that has just come to light, focus on today's disclosure or use the present perfect tense: "A man *has been* shot dead. . . ." If you must use *yesterday* or *last night* to avoid misleading listeners, use it in the second or third sentence.

Whatever you do, don't put two time elements in the same sentence. This network example offers the worst of times:

The Chinese Air Force pilot who crash-landed his twin-engine bomber in South Korea *last night today* asked for political asylum in Taiwan.

Better: "The Chinese Air Force pilot who landed his bomber in South Korea has asked for political asylum in Taiwan." Or: ". . . is now asking for. . . ."

Another lead that causes a listener's mind to swivel:

And in the news *this morning,* in New York City, four men armed with handguns *last night* made off with a Wells Fargo truck containing 50-million dollars.

There's no need to say *in the news* in a newscast. And there was no need to say *this morning;* listeners who have windows, alarm clocks or calendars can be expected to know that. And the writer can get to the heart of the story sooner by not using the company's name in the first sentence. The story is about the robbery; whether it was Brinks or Purolator or Wells Fargo is secondary. Better: "Gunmen in New York City have stolen an armored truck with 50-million dollars."

Speaking of Brinks, here's a network lead:

Correspondent _____ _____ begins our coverage of President Reagan on the brink of the summit.

Brink of the summit? Surely they weren't practicing brinkmanship. A brink is the edge at the top of a steep or vertical slope. A canyon or a chasm has a brink or two. And *brink* also can be used figuratively to mean "verge": "on the brink of bankruptcy," " brink of tears," "brink of war," "brink of day." But "*brink* of the summit" is faulty—logically and geologically.

The launching of a space shuttle reminds me of another problem: a reliance on clichés by some newscasters. They describe launchings as "picture-perfect," "letter-perfect," or "textbook-perfect." For most of us, a simple "perfect" is sufficiently perfect. And when a shuttle is aloft, some newscasters say the crew has "a mixed bag" of assignments, or "a laundry list" of tasks, or "a shopping list."

Even when writers string clichés together like beads, I can usually figure out what they're trying to say. But this lead left me dazed:

> **Like the sailing ship she is named after, the new shuttle
> Discovery will begin its first mission of exploration
> tomorrow.**

Did the writer mean that Henry Hudson's ship, *for* which the shuttle was named, would also be sailing into space? Don't look for an answer in this space.

When a U.S. balloonist reached Europe, a network newscaster reported he had crossed the Atlantic *successfully.* That's like the news item we've heard—more than once—that someone has swum the English Channel *successfully.* But have you ever heard of someone who has swum the Channel *un*successfully?

Tonight

A new blight is blanketing the land: *Tonight* Shows, featuring *tonight: tonight* this, *tonight* that, *tonight* the world. Night after night, newscasters start stories with *tonight* and pepper story after story with *tonight.* So many *tonight*s are sprinkled in newscasts you'd think some stations were plugging a new product named Tonite. Intended as a stimulant, it's now a depressant.

The writers' intentions are good: They want to make their late newscasts differ from their early 'casts. To do that, some take the trouble to try to find out what's new—if anything. Some merely reword the early scripts. But many who update early stories think the best way to go is to insert *tonight.* Some go through such contortions to stress *tonight* they twist their sentences out of shape. And when writers inject *tonight* into certain stories, they also twist the truth.

Let's look at several broadcast examples:

> **Two top school officials in Du Page County tonight are
> pleading not guilty to charges they used school funds to pay
> for activities at sex clubs.**

Where are they pleading, in night court? They almost certainly entered their plea that day, not at night. So the use of the present progressive tense, *are pleading,* which stresses the continuity of the action, is suspect. Further, the adverb *tonight* (or *today*) is best placed after the verb. The script would have been strengthened by making it "*their* activities." I assume they're charged with spending the school's money on their own activities.

> **In Chicago politics tonight, the mayor and his City Council
> opponents are locking horns once again. Aldermen from
> the council's majority bloc forced adjournment of today's
> council meeting, just 23 minutes after it began.**

In the first place, the "in" lead is weak, the word *politics* a waste. (Who'd
ever start a story about the President by saying, "In national government
tonight"?) In the second place, if the meeting broke up hours ago, during
the day, how could they still be locking horns *tonight?* If you keep seasoning your scripts with contrived *tonight*s, how do you point up the
freshness of a genuinely new story that *did* break tonight?

And *locking horns* should be consigned to the cliché closet, unless
you're writing about trombonists at a jam session. Or about moose or elk.
As for that unnatural *tonight,* let's respect our listeners' intelligence and
not try to hornswoggle them.

> **In DeKalb County tonight, just outside the town of
> Somonauk, the search goes on tonight for a seven-year-old
> girl.**

This was the lead story, so one *tonight* might be all right, but two in one
sentence? After all, listeners know that *are still searching* has to be *now,
right now, at this very moment,* and they also know that when it's 10 p.m.
and dark outside, they're engulfed by night. So they don't need to be
reminded repeatedly.

The first four words of the script hold no attraction for listeners.
Starting with *in* is pointless. And there's no reason to turn a good verb
like *search* into a noun. And no need for *the town of.* Also, *outside* can be
reduced to *near.* Better: "Police and volunteers in DeKalb County are still
searching near Somonauk for a seven-year-old girl."

> **Actor Stacy Keach is a free man tonight. Keach was
> released from a prison in England this morning after
> serving six months of a nine-month sentence for smuggling
> cocaine.**

On a 10 p.m. or 11 p.m. newscast, why mention *this morning* unless the
time element is significant?

If you're trying to avoid *today* in the first sentence of a script in the
belief that *today* sounds too long ago, use the present perfect tense. It
shows an action has been perfected, or completed, at the time of writing

or speaking but is still pertinent; it can also show that an action is continuing into the present. Use of the present perfect tense also enables you to avoid that dirty word *yesterday* in the lead.

It's true that Keach *"is* free tonight," but *is* is weak. Let's make use of the present perfect to improve that script: "The actor Stacy Keach has been freed from prison. He was released in England today after serving six months for smuggling cocaine." The length of his sentence is immaterial unless you can say why he didn't serve the full term. Maybe the facts warrant your writing, "Because of good behavior, Keach was freed three months early." That way, you're doing the math for the listener and simplifying the sentence—yours.

> **Tonight, all is right in the world. The swallows have returned to San Juan Capistrano.**

After the first sentence, listeners may wonder whether all's right with their hearing. They've been hearing a steady stream of what's wrong in the world, so that sentence may throw them. The anchor's delivery *might* make it acceptable. But if the writer's going to use that line, he probably should use it the way it's most widely known: "All's right *with* the world." There's nothing wrong with saying "All is right *in* the world," but listeners familiar with Browning's line might think the anchor is misquoting it. The broadcast script works if the writer reverses the order of the two sentences and says: "The swallows have returned to San Juan Capistrano, and all's right with the world." The swallows have been returning there for more than 200 years, so you might wonder what makes this story news, what makes it different tonight? The probable answer: videotape—today's.

10

LEADING QUESTIONS
(AND OTHER PROBLEMS)

What do you think of question leads? And of these broadcast examples?

> **The Achille Lauro is docked safely in Port Said this morning. But where are the hijackers? Have they already gone free?**

You're asking *us?* We tuned in to find out.

> **First, amazement. Then, outrage. Tonight, above all, confusion. Who, if anyone, has custody of the four Achille Lauro hijack murderers who took partly paralyzed 69-year-old Leon Klinghoffer from his wheelchair, shot him, killed him and tossed him overboard? Who, if anyone, will bring the murderers to justice?**

Why the time-consuming hard sell? *Amazement, outrage, confusion?* Who's going to stop asking us and start telling us?

> **What do Coca-Cola, Caterpillar and General Electric have in common? They're just a few of the American companies represented in Moscow at a round of talks on increasing U-S—Soviet trade.**

How do writers hatch so many inane question leads? Trick questions no listener could answer, guess at or even care about? If the story's worth telling, go ahead and tell it.

> **Did Ponce De Leon ever find the fountain of youth he was seeking in Florida? A Philadelphia man says he ran into the 500-year-old Spanish conquistador back in 1973, and he looked <u>marvelous</u>—not a day over 23.**

You don't think I could make that up, do you? Or would want to.

> **What went wrong? That question tonight confronted doctors after a sharp reversal in the condition of a man being kept alive by the only mechanical heart of its kind.**

When a listener hears that question before he knows what has happened, he can't have the slightest idea what the anchor's talking about. Better: "The first man with the so-called Penn State heart has taken a bad turn, and his doctors are trying to find out what went wrong."

Something else wrong with that script: *tonight* should be placed after *doctors.* But is this an honest *tonight,* used because of a development tonight? Or is it a fishy *tonight,* inserted to try to make a day-time development seem fresh? In any case, the sentence would be improved if the verb were used in its present tense: *confronts.*

> **Now, what did the United States know during the hijack in progress and when? How did this affect what Egypt ended up doing and what the United States may have been planning to do?**

You're asking *me?*

> **When did NASA know about problems with the shuttle's rocket boosters, and what did the agency do about it?**

Why not skip the questions and go straight to the news? Better: "The commission on the Challenger explosion will try to find out today when NASA learned about problems with the shuttle's rocket boosters. And what the agency did about them."

> **Question: What did the French president and the prime minister know and when did they know it?**

Question? Dear anchor, don't you think listeners can recognize a question by the word order and the rising inflection? And without being told they're about to be asked a question? Isn't there a better way to start this story than with a question, a question that echoes one first asked during Watergate, one that through overuse has become waterlogged? Another overusage that has become soggy: "Smith's throwing arm is the big *question mark.*"

> **Should a nurse be paid as much as a prison guard? That's
> the contention of the American Nurses Association. . . .**

Should a writer be paid for generating that *non sequitur?* No one can
contend a question.

> **Here's a riddle: What totally American art form has been
> overhauled by some people in Argentina who want to bring
> it back home to America right after they market-test it in
> France?**

Market-test or *test-market?* Do you "drive-test" a car or "test-drive" it?
A riddle? That question is no riddle; it's a muddle.

> **Of course, they play the same courses, they use basically
> the same equipment, but how different is women's golf, that
> is, big-time women's golf, from men's golf? We're going to
> be putting that question to two of the very best women on
> the golf tour in just a few minutes.**

The opening *of course* is way off course. That's no way to start a story or
an intro. Didn't the anchor consider the peril of a premature pronoun
(they), one that precedes the subject? In this case, the peril is more pronounced because the anchor never does say who *they* are. As for the
opening question in the script, that isn't the way I'd put it—or putt it.

> **What looks like a large potato and travels at high speeds?**

A promo for "M*A*S*H"? The newscaster's answer to his own half-
baked question: Halley's Comet.

> **Is it good news or bad news: the falling dollar and the
> rising yen?**

True or false: the newscaster was writing under the influence of Sam
Goldwyn? Reportedly, he said, "For your information, I would like to ask
a question."

What's wrong with question leads? When was the last time you
started a conversation with a question? (Except for "How are you?")
When was the last time you bought a newspaper to read its questions? Or
turned on a newscast to catch the latest questions? Who needs rhetorical
questions? We turn to newscasts for answers. Any other reasons question

LEADING QUESTIONS ■ 163

leads are objectionable? Yes; question leads sound like quiz shows or commercials. Question leads don't inform, they trivialize the news, can be hard to deliver and don't go straight to the point.

So why do writers persist in whipping up question leads? Is it because they themselves don't know the answers? Or mistakenly think a question is a good hook? Or do they persist because it's easier for them to ask a question than burrow through a jumble of facts and think through a good lead?

Is a question lead ever acceptable? Perhaps, if the anchor isn't playing games with the listener and if the question is either one that a listener can answer, almost instantly, or one that provokes thought. But not too much thought, lest the listener lose the thread. In almost every case, though, answers beat questions. No question about it.

Questions for Yourself

The art of writing—as an editor somewhere says every seven seconds— lies in rewriting what you've already rewritten. True, broadcast writers barely have time to write, let alone rewrite. But when they do have time, or can make time, rewriting usually improves their scripts. Which is why the text for today's sermon is itself a rewrite: "Writers of the World: Repent and Rewrite."

How can writers find time to rewrite? One way is to start writing earlier. Or curtail or rearrange other activities. Another way is to avoid dawdling.

Before we rewrite, we should examine our scripts for signs of sloppy—and sleepy—writing. In the pressure-cooker atmosphere of a newsroom, we often put down the first words that come to mind and lapse into constructions and locutions that are weak and wordy. But if we read—and reread, and rethink—our scripts carefully, we can see the soft spots. Some need to be cut out, others need to be fixed. Before we turn in copy, we should ask ourselves at least three questions, according to René J. Cappon, author of *The Word:*

Have I said what I meant to say?
Have I put it as concisely as possible?
Have I put things as simply as possible?

One of the most common problems in scripts is wordiness. In a medium where time is precious and scripts should be brief and brisk, a good writer makes every word count. Generally, the fewer words a writer uses to tell a story, the stronger the impact. Suppose you discover a fire and shout, "A conflagration is consuming the premises." If no one responds, make it short and simple: Try "fire!" That'll get action.

The first words to look for when you review a script are words that don't count—except in adding to the word-count. "Stretchers" is what Sheridan Baker calls them. "*To be,* itself," he says, "frequently ought not to be." In *The Complete Stylist and Handbook,* Prof. Baker offers examples of sentences where *to be* should be deleted: "He seems [to be] upset about something," "She considers him [to be] perfect," "This appears [to be] difficult."

"Above all," he writes, "keep your sentences awake by not putting them into these favorite stretchers of the passivists, *There is . . . which, It is . . . that,* and the like." And he advises that if you can, cut every *it* not referring to something. Some *it*'s and *there*'s are immutably idiomatic: *It is raining, There is nothing to do.*

And Baker says, "Next to activating your passive verbs, and cutting the passive *there is*'s and *it is*'s perhaps nothing so improves your prose as to go through it systematically also deleting every *to be,* every *which, that, who,* and *whom* not needed for utter clarity or for spacing out a thought. All your sentences will feel better." And sound better.

Also watch out for signs of what Baker calls "the of-and-which disease": "The passive sentence also breaks out in a rash of *of*'s and *which*'s, and even the active sentence can suffer. Diagnosis: something like sleeping sickness. *With*'s, *in*'s, *to*'s and *by*'s also inflamed. Surgery imperative."

The skills of a surgeon—or a rewriter—were needed on a network newscast that was slowed and sapped by a slew of stretchers, several in one segment:

> **Elsewhere in the country, in Clinton County, Missouri, today, there was a violent protest against the forced sale of a family farm. About 300 people from an agriculture protest group . . . tried to keep officials from carrying out the sale. They failed. The sale went on. There were a few arrests, and there were no injuries.**

Let's take a look: no need to start a story with "Elsewhere" or "Elsewhere in the country." Almost every story comes from somewhere else. Although I wouldn't start with "Elsewhere," I wouldn't start with "In [place-name]." Why not? Because one of my first broadcast editors (at CBS News), Bob Siller, told me not to do it. He said it's a lazy man's way of starting a story. After his instruction sank in, I realized that anyone could start any story that way: "In Katmandu, Nepal. . . ."; "In Timbuktu, Mali. . . ."; "In Tippecanoe, Indiana. . . ." (But no man can do what Katmandu.)

A place-name itself isn't news. What happened there *is* news. So for me, the *in*-lead doesn't make the cut. It's best to go ahead and tell the story as directly as possible. The writer should try to put the place-name at or near the top. But not at the end of a long first sentence. And if the writer delays the place-name too long, listeners may assume the news occurred in their area. So you can take care of that quickly. At the top: "Denver police say." Or near the top: "Police in Denver say." But "In Denver, the police say" is a non-starter.

Yet, starting a story with *in* can be acceptable, even desirable in specific circumstances. With a series of fast reactions or related developments, it makes sense to use an *in* after an umbrella lead: "The United Nations called on all members today to send food to the hungry people in Starvania. In Washington, President Parker said. . . . In London, Prime Minister Munster said. . . . In Paris, French President du Jour said. . . ."

In the broadcast about the forced sale of a farm, not many people are going to turn up the sound when they hear an item that starts out talking about a distant county. Better: "Protesters [at least this word holds promise of action] in Clinton County, Missouri, tried to block officials from selling a family farm." (*Why* was the family forced to sell its farm?)

I'm not sure how to rewrite the next sentence because I don't know what an "agriculture protest group" is. Does it protest agriculture? Does it protest the use of the word "agriculture" instead of "farming"? Or are farmers protesting the use of "agricultural implement" instead of "farm tool"?

As for the two *there were*'s in the story's last sentence, let's recast that sentence: "Police [or sheriff's deputies] arrested a few people [protesters? farmers? members of the family?]." I wouldn't take time to write that no one was hurt. It's news that no one was hurt only when the story is about an event in which someone might have been expected to be hurt, yet, remarkably, no one was.

Starting a sentence with *there were* or *there is* is weak. Experts have noted that *there is* lacks substance, that it delays the action in a sentence and shoves the significant verb into a subordinate place; and that it's a dead phrase. There are exceptions, though, like this sentence.

After two *there were*'s in the last sentence of that script, the anchor was dragging. And he began the next item the same way:

There is a report of poisoned water today, water that may
[should be the past tense *might*] **have been poisoned by toxic**
waste. The Interior Department has ordered the closing of. . . .

Better: "The government has ordered the closing of a California
wildlife refuge because its water may be poisoned. The cause is said to be
toxic waste. . . ." If the refuge had already been closed, I'd write, "The
government has closed. . . ." Whatever strength that news had was
leached out of it by the anchor's first words, *There is.* Also: When the
anchor said there's a *report,* did he mean a reporter has turned in a story
about the purported poisoning? Or did the anchor say *report* because it's
only a rumor? The story was probably reported by a wire service, so,
chances are, the script was based on wire copy. But news agencies aren't
in the business of circulating rumors, so his use of *report* was probably
thought-free.

As they say euphemistically about a new show in rehearsal that's
found wanting, that script "needs work." That means reworking. Which
means rethinking and rewriting. But the outlook for that network anchor's
improvement seems favorable. As Samuel Johnson said, "It is only by
writing ill that you can attain to write well."

Hit List

Some sportswriters work so hard trying to reach listeners they must think
a metaphor is something you shout through. Occasionally, a figure of
speech, like a metaphor or simile, can bring copy to life but only if it's
fresh or at least not stale. Too often, though, writers fall back on a device
so worn-out its fizz has fizzled.

No central registry keeps track of every use of a metaphor (an im-
plied comparison) or simile (explicit comparison). Yet even half-listeners
can sense that "war of words" is overworked by newscasters. A word
doctor would pronounce it dead. If it is dead, it needs burial. If it's only
overworked, it needs a rest. Yet a network anchor said someone had *trig-
gered a war of words.*

The first use of "war of words" is attributed to Alexander Pope (not
to be confused with Pope Alexander). According to the *Oxford English
Dictionary,* the English poet used "war of words" in 1725. So that metaphor is more than 270 years old. Not even the comedian Milton Berle—
known as the Thief of Bad Gags—would take material that old—not even
from a Youngman. (As for "trigger," that word is so misused and overused, I avoid it unless I'm writing about Roy Rogers' horse.)

"Metaphor" comes from the Greek word for transference. And Pope has been praised for his ability to transfer the fury of fighting to speech. And for the first recorded use of "war of words," he certainly deserves credit. So does the first wordwatcher who recognized Pope's imaginative phrase and used it himself (with or without credit). But by now, it has become a lame warhorse, trotted out so often by so many writers that it's ready for the glueworks.

Instead of striving for originality and shunning clichés, unthinking writers turn every clothesline quarrel, as we used to call a backyard shouting match, into a "war of words." These overkillers should be reminded of Strunk and White's advice in *The Elements of Style:* "Use figures of speech sparingly." Orwell, as we know, put it more sternly: "Never use a metaphor, simile or other figure of speech which you are used to seeing in print."

Some that fit Orwell's injunction are listed by Harold Evans in *Newsman's English.* Here is a partial list of what he calls "stale expressions":

bewildering variety	lashed out
bitter end	leaps and bounds
brutal reminder	left up in the air
built-in safeguard	lending a helping hand
burning issue	matter of life and death
checkered career	move into high gear
cherished belief	not to be outdone
city fathers	over and above
conspicuous by its absence	pros and cons
cool as a cucumber	proud heritage
coveted trophy	red faces
crack troops	red-letter day
daring daylight robbery	reduced to matchwood
deafening crash	64,000-dollar question
doctors fought	spearheading the campaign
dramatic new move	speculation was rife
finishing touches	spirited debate
fly in the ointment	spotlight the need
foregone conclusion	storm of protest
give the green light	upset the apple cart
hook or by crook	voiced approval
in full swing	wealth of information
in the nick of time	

If we use those phrases in casual conversation, no one is going to get his *nose out of joint.* But if we use those phrases in news scripts, we risk being written off as hacks. "They [clichés] are so smooth from wear," says *The Written Word,* "that they slip off the tongue or pen with great ease, and that can be the undoing of an unwary writer or speaker. . . . The temptation [to use them] is great merely because many of the expressions in question are catchy (or once were), and to an untrained user of language their surface appeal and never-ending appearance may seem a recommendation in itself. . . . *Do one's thing, bite the bullet* and *keep a low profile* suggest that such expressions seem to age very fast through relentless use." That guide's list of clichés includes:

agonizing reappraisal
agree to disagree
as a matter of fact
brave the elements
bright and early
by the same token
calm before the storm
can't see the forest for the trees
easier said than done
fall on deaf ears
few and far between
go over the top
handwriting on the wall
hit the nail on the head
hit the spot
hue and cry
if the truth be told
in no uncertain terms
it stands to reason
land-office business
on cloud nine
part and parcel
point with pride
rain cats and dogs

separate the men from the boys
separate the sheep from the
  goats
sick and tired
silver lining in the cloud
stagger the imagination
sweet smell of success
take a dim view of
that's for sure
truth is stranger than fiction
uncharted seas
understatement of the _____
view with alarm
what with one thing or another
when all is said and done
  [more is said than done]
when you come down to it
wide-open spaces
you can say that again
you win some, you lose some
you're damned if you do,
  you're damned if you don't
your guess is as good
  as _____

The journalism educator Curtis D. MacDougall offered some figures of speech (in *Interpretative Reporting*) that he said "are whiskered with age and mark their innocent user as callow":

ax to grind
blessing in disguise
clutches of the law
crying need
hail of bullets
in the limelight

police combing the city
slow as molasses in January
threw a monkey wrench into
watery grave
worked like Trojans

His book also lists what it calls "shopworn personifications":

Dan Cupid	Lady Luck
Father Time	Man in the Street
G.I. Joe	Mother Nature
Jack Frost	Mr. Average Citizen
John Q. Public	

Some metaphors and clichés can be classed as "journalese," the superficial style of writing characteristic of many newspapers and magazines. Prof. MacDougall's list of words that have lost their effectiveness through repetition includes:

brutally murdered	mystery surrounds
death car	police dragnets
feeling ran high	sleuths
gruesome find	swoop down
infuriated mob	

Other words and phrases in that category are presented by E. L. Callihan in *Grammar for Journalists:*

a shot rang out	pitched battle
caught red-handed	pool of blood
fusillade of bullets	reign of terror
hail of bullets	shrouded in mystery
miraculous escape	

Still more trite expressions are listed by Richard D. Mallery in *Grammar, Rhetoric and Composition:*

as luck would have it	it stands to reason
beat a hasty retreat	looking for all the world like
clear as crystal	method in his madness
deadly earnest	powers that be
doomed to disappointment	psychological moment
dull thud	riot of color
Grim Reaper	venture a suggestion
irony of fate	

The editorial consultant Albert Toner has listed hundreds of once-bright words and phrases that have lost their luster and become clichés. "How many of these tranquilizers," he asks, "do you mistake for stimulants?"

back-to-back
back to basics or square one or
    the drawing board
beautiful people
can of worms
close encounters of any kind
collision course
comparing apples and oranges
conventional wisdom
couldn't agree more/care less
cutting edge
cutting-room floor
different drummer
doing something right
down the tubes
extra mile
eyeball to eyeball
fast lane
fat city
father figure
forget it
game of inches
game plan
garbage in, garbage out
goes with the territory
hard ball
hearts and minds
hit the ground running
interestingly enough

like gangbusters
mind-boggling
moment of truth
name of the game
nation that can go to the
    moon
only game in town
one-on-one
Operation Whatever
pecking order
Project Anything
psychic income
reinventing the wheel
rubber chicken circuit
says it all
since sliced bread
single most
slippery slope
smart money
smoking gun
state of the art
tell it like it is
tip of the iceberg
up for grabs
very private person
wall-to-wall
where it's at
won't fly/wash

The *Associated Press Guide to News Writing* lists more:

beauty and the beast
beyond the shadow of a doubt
bite the dust
blazing inferno
blessed event
blissful ignorance
bull in a china shop
club-wielding police
colorful scene
dread disease
drop in the bucket
glaring omission
glutton for punishment
last but not least
leave no stone unturned
limp into port

long arm of coincidence (law)
paint a grim picture
pay the supreme penalty
picture of health
pre-dawn darkness
proud parents
radiant bride
rushed to the scene
scintilla of evidence
spotlessly clean
sprawling base
supreme sacrifice
tender mercies
trail of death and destruction
walking encyclopedia

How many of these trite expressions have you heard in newscasts? They're among many listed in *Words into Type,* a reference book for editors:

aired their grievances	long-felt need
beginning of the end	masterpiece of understatement
built-in safeguards	proud possessor
charged with emotion	ripe old age
failed to dampen spirits	shot in the arm
grind to a halt	superhuman effort
herculean efforts	unprecedented situation
hurriedly retraced his steps	untiring efforts
ill-fated	vanish into thin air
iron out the difficulty	voice the sentiments
keep options open	wrapped in mystery
leaves much to be desired	young hopeful
lend a helping hand	

As far as exhausted expressions go, that's not *the whole kit and caboodle, not by a long shot.* But those samples provide enough *food for thought* to help writers think more about what they write—which is, after all, *the bottom line.* One of the most fertile fields for clichés is the athletic field. Sportswriters, says Callihan, must learn to avoid words and expressions like these:

apple	pellet
battled furiously	pigskin
chalked up a victory	pill
charity toss	rifled the ball
horsehide	tangle with
in the shadow of their own goal posts	

Some sportswriters seem to think that writing in simple English might cause them to be benched, so they do their double-barreled damnedest. They say a batter has *belted a four-bagger, clouted one for the circuit, poked one out of the park,* or hit a *roundtripper, a tater, a goner, a dinger, a grand slam,* even a *grand salami.* (I never sausage a thing.) They'll go to any lengths—even *the length of two football fields*—to sidestep simplicity.

The sports producer William Weinbaum tells of a few old standbys that sportscasters rely on to avoid that dreaded word *homer:* "You can hang a star on that baby," "It's see ya later time," and "That dog will hunt." Intent on grandstanding, they ignore the easiest—and best—way to say it: "He hit a home run." After some of the offenders condescend to write "hit," I recommend they learn to use "win"—as a verb. I keep hearing about teams that *triumphed, grabbed a win, rolled up a victory,* or *handed a defeat to.* I'd like to hear more about teams that just *won.* And teams that simply scored runs, goals, baskets and touchdowns. "When sportscasters try to be too cute," Weinbaum says, "they come across as clowns." And imitators come across as clones.

Even more tiresome is the use of sports jargon in non-sports news. So resist the lingo of the jargonauts, where all the world's a game and all the men and women merely players.

Now that we've disposed of that "mixed bag of leftovers," a term minted by a newscaster (a mixed metaphor like that is what Theodore Bernstein calls a "mixaphor"), let's look at another case of wrongdoing, one that was broadcast:

> **New York City detectives today will pick up self-admitted**
> **subway vigilante Bernhard Goetz, who waived extradition**
> **at a court appearance in Concord, New Hampshire.**

Obviously—except to the writer who wrote the copy, the editor who edited it, the producer who produced it and the anchor who delivered it—no one can admit to wrongdoing but oneself. So "self-admitted" is tautological. A logical thought would have prompted someone to delete "self"; it should have been self-evident.

After a second look at the broadcast sentence, I'd rewrite it and try to place *today* (as I always do if I use it) after the verb: "New York City police are going to bring back the so-called subway vigilante, Bernhard Goetz, today from New Hampshire. He waived extradition at a hearing in Concord." I substituted "police" for "detectives"; it's shorter. Besides, they didn't have to do any detecting.

A network newscaster reported that indictments against a mess of mobsters had been "handed down." Rub out "down" and make it "up." A grand jury hands *up* indictments to a judge; a judge hands *down* rulings. That's today's final decision.

Once Is Enough

Ever hear a newscaster speak of an *acute* crisis? Or a *new* record, a *controversial* issue or a *final* outcome? If so, you've heard a redundancy, something said superfluously. Using too many words to express an idea or repeating needlessly is objectionable—unless you're talking about Pago Pago, Sirhan Sirhan, or Walla Walla.

In newscasts, economy in language is not merely desirable, it's essential. Redundancies waste time, blur meaning and lessen impact. The fewer words used to tell a broadcast news story, the clearer and more forceful the communication. Flab weakens communication and crowds out other news. With leaner stories, you can fit more stories into a newscast and make your newscast newsier.

I was nudged into writing about redundancies by a suggestion from a wordwatcher, Mike Berriochoa of central Washington. He passed along a few redundancies he had come across: a forest fire that's *fully* surrounded, a burning home that's *completely* engulfed, then *totally* destroyed.

Other redundancies we have to guard against:

all-time record	disappeared *from view*
new bride	invisible *to the eye*
new baby	*major* breakthrough
new recruit	*major* milestone
build a *new* jail	*mental* attitude
circle *around*	*value* judgment
square-*shaped*	judgment *call*
green-*colored*	*temporary* reprieve
large-*size*	*temporary* suspension
friendly *in nature*	while *at the same time*
short *in stature*	widow of *the late*
few *in number*	*advance* planning
wide variety	*positively* identify
head honcho	grocery *store*
state of Ohio	*invited* guests
capital *city*	fall *down*
sworn affidavit	lose *out*
funeral *service*	pay *out*
self-confessed	continue *on*
asphyxiated *to death*	cancel *out*
smothered *to death*	lift *up*
strangled *to death*	*up* above
suffocated *to death*	*down* below
originally established	*exact* same
first began	*necessary* requirements
first discovered	*serious* danger
first *and foremost*	*old* adage/proverb
bouquet *of flowers*	*grateful* thanks
foreign imports	*basic* fundamentals
root cause	*usual* custom

customary practice
still remains
component parts
appointed *to the position of*
commute to *and from*
shuttle *back and forth*
join *together*
eliminate *entirely*
so *consequently*
cirrhosis *of the liver*
death by *lethal* injection
strictly prohibited
surrounding circumstances
depreciate *in value*
opening gambit
undergraduate *student*
fellow classmate
doctor *by profession*
true facts
over-exaggerate
exact address
violent explosion
vitally necessary
nodded *her head*
shrugged *her shoulders*
winked *an eye*
a smile *on her face*
Easter *Sunday*
Christmas *Day*
legal contract
personal opinion
as a *general* rule
general public
general consensus
consensus *of opinion*
repeat *again*
total extinction
total monopoly
totally annihilate
totally destroy
flaming inferno
passing fad
ten acres *of land*
a distance of five miles

seems *to be*
appeared *on the scene*
they're *both* alike
definite decision
ever since
awkward predicament
hired mercenary
pair of twins
grand jury indictment
county coroner
at *the corner of* Oak and
  Polk
for *the purpose of*
future outlook
future prospects
minor quibble
may *possibly*
short *space of* time
in *a period of* 90 days
in three months' *time*
it's raining *outside*
joint cooperation
mutual agreement
previous police record
previous experience
past history
past record
puppy *dog*
glance *briefly*
reason *why*
each *and every*
completely full
patently obvious
close proximity
close scrutiny
intents and purposes
ways and means
compromise *solution*
*eye*witness
ultimate outcome
end result
final climax
final completion
complete stop

Some redundancies show up in ads, repeatedly: *advance* reservations, *pre*-reserved seating, *free* gift, *full* quart, *hot*-water heater, *new* innovation, *extra* bonus, and kills bugs *dead*.

When we're chatting, we use casual speech, which is harmless *enough*. "A man who never said an unnecessary word," Bergen Evans observed, "would say very little during a long life and would not be pleasant company."

I used to order a tunafish sandwich. No more. Since a friend pointed out my offense, I've cut back to just tuna—and hold the *fish*. But an anchor who says tuna*fish* shouldn't be canned. Yes, we should guard against wasting words. Air time is precious. The battle cry of Strunk and White in *The Elements of Style:* "Omit needless words."

Strunk and White also say: "Avoid foreign languages. . . . Write in English." When the crew of the space shuttle Discovery went aboard for the second time after its first liftoff was postponed, a newscaster said the astronauts must have "a feeling of déjà vu. . . ." What he meant, I suppose, was that they felt a sense of having endured a pre-launch wait before. But that common use of "déjà vu" is wrong. "Déjà vu" is the *illusion* of having already experienced something that is, in fact, being experienced for the first time.

Often, when newscasters use a foreign word, they misuse it or mispronounce it. Even when listeners hear it right, many misunderstand it or don't get it. After all, how many listeners are familiar with French idioms? Even if a newscaster knows how to use "déjà vu" correctly, he shouldn't use it on the air. Next time you hear the phrase, and you will, remember what Yogi Berra said (or is said to have said): "It's déjà vu all over again."

More important than knowing a few foreign words, writers should know the meaning of English words and how to use them correctly. Yet we often hear mistakes that writers could catch merely by checking a dictionary. I heard a newsman report on the murder of a Denver talk-show host:

Someone fired a salvo of bullets from a high-caliber gun. . . .

According to the *Naval Terms Dictionary,* a salvo is one or more shots fired simultaneously by the same battery (set of big guns) at the same target. So one gunman using one gun could not have fired a salvo, no matter what his caliber.

In another misfire, a network correspondent said,

So what's Hollywood been up to in the year since Bob Dole fired his barrage of criticism?

A barrage is a heavy curtain of artillery fire, or a rapid, concentrated discharge of missiles. So one man, even a machinegunner, can't fire a barrage.

While discussing gunfire, let's target newscasters who overdo the word "war." Let's save "war" for armed conflict between nations, even gangs. When listeners keep hearing of "the war against scofflaws," "the war against jaywalkers," "the war against crabgrass," they get war-weary. What prompts me to start a campaign (no, I don't declare war) against the spread of "war" is the misuse I keep hearing. A newscaster said the President's chief economic adviser had often "warred" with the Administration. Not "disagreed with," "argued with," or "stood up to," but "warred." Now that's overkill.

Just as bad, sometimes, is underkill. For example, the first sentence in a story on a network newscast:

There were no surprises at Wimbledon today.

Sounds like an imaginary newspaper banner: "No One Hurt in No Plane Crash." The tennis lead has several faults: It starts with "There were," and says nothing. Although the tennis results may come as no surprise to the newscaster, the average listener would regard it as news. Better: "The tennis star Martina Navratilova was favored to win at Wimbledon today—and she did. She won her fifth singles title there, her third straight."

A network evening newscast:

To no one's surprise, Ross Perot says he's in.

A common fault with those last two broadcast leads: they're negative. Strunk and White urge: "Put statements in positive form. Make definite assertions. Avoid tame, colorless, hesitating, noncommittal language. . . . Consciously or unconsciously, the reader is dissatisfied with being told what is not; he wishes to be told what is."

A post-convention boomlet is not unexpected and certainly not unwelcome for the vacationing Mondale. . . .

That construction, expressing an affirmative by negating its opposite, is hard for a listener to sort out. And two double negatives in a row, as in that sentence, leave me out of sorts. And might well leave Orwell unwell, as well.

Writers in broadcast newsrooms often work in a din and under stress. So they sometimes turn in copy that's not so strong as it could be. For example, here's a lead sentence I heard on a network newscast:

A prominent international bridge player told today how she was threatened with death by kidnappers in Washington, D.C.

That could be strengthened by building up to the strongest words, *threatened with death,* instead of burying them in the middle of the sentence. Also, it's undesirable to put the place-name last. Better: "A prominent international bridge player told today how kidnappers in Washington, D.C., threatened her with death."

If the writer of the first version had reread his script just once more, perhaps he would have spotted those weaknesses before he heard them on the air. I ought to know. I was the writer—and still am. Or am I being redundant?

11

BAD NEWS

We start with some bad news,

the anchor said somberly on his network newscast.

I was only half-listening, but that grim opening hit me like a bucket of ice cubes. The news sounded grave. Was it an assassination? A terrorist bombing? A disaster? The anchor went on to report that the actor James Mason was dead.

I wondered, for whom was that news bad? Presumably, family, friends and fans. But the death of one person, even a personage, is generally accepted by listeners as just another news item; we've become accustomed to a cascade of calamities, catastrophes and cataclysms. As good an actor as Mason had been, by the time he died, he was no longer a big name on moviegoers' mental marquees. Opening the newscast with a story on Mason's death would have been all right if the newscaster had reported it straight—without telegraphing us that he was going to deliver "bad news."

Whenever I have to write an obituary or any story, I'm still guided by a rule I learned in school: Don't label the news as good or bad. What's bad for some listeners is good for others. Heavy rain can be bad for pedestrians, motorists and sunbathers; but it can be good for farmers, taxi drivers and umbrella vendors.

"Good news" abounds on broadcasts when the prime interest rate drops. But for listeners, a drop in the prime has both positive and negative sides. Anyone who takes out a home improvement loan will benefit right away. And if other borrowing costs start to fall again, consumers could save interest on adjustable rate home mortgages and similar borrowings. But for many listeners, lower rates are "bad news." Many consumers like high interest rates because it enables them to earn strong returns on their investments, such as money market funds and U.S. government securities.

I was also taught not to tell an audience that a story is distressing, or amazing, or amusing; stick to the facts and just tell the news. If the "good news" or "bad news" is tied to a specific person or group, characterizing the news may be valid. For example: "Mayor Murphy received good news today from his doctor." Or "The I-R-S has bad news for taxpayers." Otherwise, a newscaster should let listeners decide whether it's good or bad. But how many listeners do you think are sitting out there with clipboards checking off each story as "good" for them, "bad" or "indeterminate"?

Anchors should also avoid "good news–bad news" leads, such as "Governor Graham has good news and bad news for farmers. The good news is. . . ." The "good news–bad news" approach is suitable for a comedian. But some newscasters have used it so much and for so long that it has lost whatever appeal it had—and has simply become bad news.

The "good news–bad news" approach has been traced back to Biblical times. When Moses came down from Mount Sinai with the Commandments, he reportedly told his people, "I have good news and bad news. The good news is that I got them down from 40 to 10. The bad news is that adultery is still included." (You know that commandment: Thou shalt not *admit* adultery.) I said "reportedly" because a news director who reads that may wonder, "If a minicam wasn't there to shoot it, did it really happen?"

But I did hear this one myself: A network newscaster said diplomats had worked out an agreement and had "initialized" it. *Initialized?* The suffix *ize* has long been fused onto nouns and adjectives to turn them into verbs: *apologize, burglarize, computerize, hospitalize, jeopardize, legalize, pasteurize, polarize, synthesize,* even *decriminalize.* I won't itemize them, but writers should realize they can't slap on an *ize* indiscriminately, especially if an existing verb does the job. "Initialize" is not needed because an established verb, *to initial,* already means "to sign one's initials."

A community newspaper in St. Louis told of someone who had been "funeralized." And a local newscaster spoke of "unionized" teachers. This usage seems strange; it made me think of teachers who had been processed in some way.

Another misbegotten verb is *finalize.* It has the ring, or thud, of bureaucratic jargon, and we already have ways to convey the action intended by *finalize:* "end," "make final," "put in final form," "finish," "complete," "wrap up." Under *finalize,* the *American Heritage Dictionary* (1992) says the verb "is frequently associated with the language of bureaucracy and so is objected to by many writers." And the *AHD* says *finalize* was unacceptable to 71 percent of its Usage Panel. But the 1969 *AHD* reported *finalize* was found unacceptable by 90 percent of the Panel; so opposition to *finalize* has slipped about one percentage point a year. The final word isn't in yet, so let's wait till the fat lady croaks.

Another problem I don't sympathize with or temporize about: what some grammarians call "stacking." That's the practice of piling adjectives and nouns-as-adjectives in front of nouns. One of the most horrendous examples was uncorked by a network newscaster who spoke of

a new and improved revised downward federal budget deficit forecast.

Rather than punctuate that, I'll puncture it. When the anchor reaches the first noun, *budget,* the average listener probably thinks that's the subject of the sentence. But it's quickly followed by another noun, *deficit,* so he realigns his train of thought, if he can, and surmises that the story is about a budget deficit. Wrong. All those adjectives and nouns modify what it's really all about: a *forecast.*

A listener can catch a couple of adjectives before a noun, but seven adjectives are far too many, especially those seven. What makes it even tougher to untangle is that two of them *(budget, deficit)* are nouns pressed into service as adjectives. The sentence should be rewritten—and the writer sentenced.

A newspaper *reader* might be able to thread his way through that terrible thicket of words because he'd first see the headline, read the sentence at his own pace, reread whatever isn't clear and then perhaps rip it out of the paper for another read-through. Any story written that heavy-handedly ought to be ripped out—and up. But a *listener* who wanted to figure out that sentence as it was spoken would have had to be a Champollion (the French Egyptologist who deciphered the Rosetta stone). Or have total recall—with instant replay.

The problem with that kind of over-writing is that a listener can't grasp it instantly. The problem with that writer was not that he wasn't trying. He was trying too hard. Maybe he wanted to make himself heard by hammering out a punchy sentence, one that would put a dent in the listener's mind. But no one will ever remember it, and children will never recite it. And that's *my* forecast.

Wasting Time

Many newscasters fritter away time by talking too much about time. Example: "The space shuttle Mercury will be landing later today."

Later is unneeded. As soon as we hear *will be,* we know that the shuttle has not landed yet, is not landing now, but that it *will be* landing. Because it *will be,* the landing will have to take place in the future—and, we hope, not in the pasture. Everything that happens after the anchor or reporter speaks must be *later.* It's inevitable. So if an event will take place today after the newscast, there's no need to say *later.*

We hear morning newscasts say the President will meet with his advisers "*later* today." If he's going to be meeting today, it must be *later* (not *later on*). Later, we hear stories telling us he met with advisers "*earlier* today." If he has *met* with them, the meeting is already past-tensed. Whatever happened before the newscaster spoke *had* to have been earlier. So why say *earlier?* Sometimes we hear a story like this:

> **The Union Carbide Company says it will resume**
> **production of the deadly chemical . . . at its plant in**
> **Institute, West Virginia, *some time* today.**

If the writer had spent some time thinking, she might have realized that everything occurs at *some time.* Perhaps she wanted to suggest that the time of the resumption is unknown or indefinite. So what? Even if she knew that production would resume at 2 p.m. or 3:30 p.m., she needn't take time—hers and ours—to tell us the precise moment. What's important is that the factory will resume production today. Mention of the time may be essential when a newscaster is reporting an impending community event, like a town meeting. But in 99 stories in 100, it's a waste of time.

Are there any exceptions to the advice against writing *earlier today* and *later today?* Yes. Almost every bit of advice or rule is subject to exception. Example: "The President will meet with his cabinet this afternoon and will confer *later today* with his National Security Council." But sooner or later, we have to deal with other words that add nothing to a sentence. And if they don't add, they detract. Here's a Washington correspondent's opening line:

> **Well, needless to say, they were not encouraged here by**
> **Nabih Berri's comments.**

If something is needless to say, there's no need to say it—nor to say it's *needless to say.* And we have no need to hear it. But if the story's worth reporting even though the reporter doesn't think much of it, he shouldn't dismiss it on the air by introducing it with a put-down. And when that correspondent said *here,* did he mean *here in the studio?*

Obviously is another wasted word. If something is obvious, why say so? A fact may be obvious to the reporter. And to some listeners. But not to all. If it's obvious to everyone, there's no need to say so. Of course not. Aha! Another superfluity: *of course.*

Here's another example from a network newscast:

> **Today is Good Friday, *of course,* the day when Christians around the world. . . . And, *of course,* at sundown tonight** [*tonight* is not needed] **Jews begin the celebration of Passover.**

The curse of *of course* is that it sounds apologetic and condescending. It sounds as if the newscaster is sorry he has to say something that everyone knows. But on another level, it sounds as if his message is: "You undoubtedly know this already, *of course;* you know you do, but I'm going ahead because not everyone knows as much as you and I do." Or it may sound as if he means, "*I* know this, *of course,* but I'd better inform you." Listeners who didn't know about today's religious holidays might well resent the *of course* because they'd think it implies they should have known.

Often, the information that a writer couples with *of course* is not obvious or widely known. Even when dealing with a widely known fact, a writer should skip the *of course* and tell the story straightaway. Better: "Today is Good Friday, the day when Christians. . . ." Or: "Christians are observing Good Friday." The use of the present tense says it's going on at this very moment, so there's no need for *today.*

One way for a writer to deal with a widely known fact that many people may not be mindful of is to mention it only in passing, not as the news itself: "The celebration of Good Friday by Christians today coincides with the start of the Jewish Passover. The two holidays fall on the same day only once every. . . ." That way, the coincidence becomes the news. Yet the listener learns—or is reminded—that today is Good Friday and the start of Passover. In my book, but not in the Good Book, the *news* value of both holidays has—through the ages—depreciated.

Of course is a short form for another phrase that popped up in a network story about the airlines' frequent flyer programs:

> **But, *as we all know,* you can't get something for nothing forever. The I-R-S is now pondering whether frequent flyers should pay income tax on all those trips.**

Sounds as if the reporter knows she's going to dispense an obvious truth, so she wants to assure the listener that she's no fool, that she knows that what she's about to say is clear to everyone. The truism that you can't get something for nothing is about as profound, informative and newsy as saying, "Nothing lasts forever." Or, as many a Wall Street sage says when a growth stock falters, "No tree grows to the sky." Even the frequent flyer programs don't give away anything; airlines have built the cost of the programs into the price of tickets. "You can't get something for nothing" is old hat; *you can't get something for nothing forever* is battered hat.

Also a waste of words, not to mention an assault on reason, is the lead that goes like this—and, in fact, went like this:

> **Everyone this morning's talking about the big fight last night. . . .**

Not everyone was talking about it. I didn't even know there'd been a fight. And not everyone who did know that was still talking about it. Any assertion that brooks no exception or qualification is an assertion that bears scrutiny. Although it's safe to say that *everyone* is mortal, any sentence that uses *everyone* is risking an implosion.

A network example, this one about the stock market's steady advances early this year:

> ***Everyone* is looking for an even bigger winning streak.**

If everyone on Wall Street—and elsewhere—were of one mind, the market might stand stock-still. Everyone doesn't think alike anywhere; unanimity exists only in the graveyard.

Another broadcast generalization:

> **All of Britain is talking about a royal scandal. . . .**

Whatever the scandal, I can't imagine that everyone in Britain was talking about it. Or knew about it. The *royal scandal* dealt with a member of the royal family—through marriage—who had confirmed that her father had been a member of the Nazi S.S. She herself was not a Nazi, and her father was long dead. So who was scandalized? Was *everyone* in Britain talking about it? In a nation with so many subjects?

The flip side of *everyone* is *no one*. One of my favorites—but not everyone's—often appears in stories about escapees: *"No one* knows where he is." *He* knows where he is. And his whereabouts may be known by a friend, a relative, someone harboring him without knowing he's wanted. If the police knew where to find him, he wouldn't be a fugitive. By definition, a fugitive is someone who has fled and whose whereabouts is usually unknown. A fugitive doesn't broadcast his escape or departure. And *needless to say,* he goes without saying.

Empty Words

Quick. Name anyone in public life who isn't "controversial"—or any subject, from abortion to zip codes, that's not "controversial." If Mother Teresa went on a newscast and said, "God bless America," someone would complain. Listeners complain about every blessed thing.

Almost everything in the news is controversial, which means that almost every item is subject to or marked by controversy. Controversy is "a dispute, especially a lengthy and public one, between sides holding opposing views." And in some minds, "controversial" has come to mean "disapproved of" or "causing criticism." Whatever writers may mean when they insert "controversial," many seem to think it's a flavor enhancer that's bound to spice up a script:

> **Senator Edward Kennedy's controversial tour of South Africa has ended on a controversial note.**

What made Kennedy's tour "controversial"? Most Americans probably didn't even know about it. And of those who did, probably few cared. At least, not enough to create a controversy. And how did the senator's tour end on a "controversial" note? According to the network newscast, about 100 demonstrators prevented him from making a speech in the black township of Soweto. Is the stifling of a speech "controversial"? True, there was a ruckus. But the relatively small group heckling Kennedy hardly caused a controversy; and listeners in the States hadn't even known about the dustup.

In any case, nothing justified that script's use of *controversial* twice in one short sentence. The writer probably used the word because it popped into her head, and she figured it would add punch to the story. Instead, she should have taken the time to construct a strong sentence, relying on nouns and verbs, not mindless hype.

The *New York Times*'s in-house monitor, *Winners & Sinners* (now defunct), said, *"W & S* would be hard pressed to cite a word that tells less, yet appears more often, than *controversial."* *W & S* also said that during a lull on night rewrite, two reporters tapped the *Times*'s Information Bank computer to see what the staff had been calling "controversial." They found that in two recent weeks, "controversial" had been applied more than 30 times—to Robert S. McNamara, McGeorge Bundy, the suffragist Lucy Stone, a fumble by a football player, pet projects of legislators, a U.S. stamp honoring the memory of St. Francis of Asissi, banks' alliances with brokerages, an endorsement by N.O.W., a new building in Portland, Oregon, an umpire's home-run call, Linda Ronstadt's "new wave" album, remedies for the rising cost of health care and the N.C.A.A. No wonder *W & S* called "controversial" an empty word. Not only has overuse drained it of meaning, but "controversial" has also become a sort of cliché, constantly on call to try to prop up a story. But its emptiness leaves it impotent.

Listeners are showered by hollow words, the latest outpouring inspired by the Presidential inauguration. Take "pomp and circumstance." In his *Dictionary of Clichés,* Eric Partridge defines "p. and c." as "splendour of the whole and magnificence of the details." But the average listener doesn't know what "circumstance" means, even circumstantially.

Here's an example of its use on a newscast:

Soviet Defense Minister Dmitri Ustinov is being buried in Moscow's Red Square today with the full pomp and circumstance that his motherland can offer.

What does "circumstance" add to that sentence? Color? Detail? For me, it adds only pomposity. And prolixity. When I hear "pomp and circumstance," I think of Sir Edward Elgar's march, composed in 1901. Shakespeareans might think of the line from *Othello:* "pride, pomp and circumstance of glorious war." In the 17th century, "circumstance" meant any formal show or ceremony. But now the *Dictionary of Word and Phrase Origins* by William and Mary Morris says that meaning is archaic.

The sentence about Ustinov's burial has another problem: Instead of saying *the full p. and c. that his motherland can offer,"* it should say *"all* the p. and c. his motherland can offer." In fact, Ustinov received all the p. and c. Moscow *did* offer, not all that Moscow *could* have offered.

Editors should also rule out old sayings served up as fresh dressing for what's supposed to be news. Here's how a network anchor began a story:

Haste makes waste, as the saying goes. . . .

Haste does make waste; it also makes for reliance on clichés. Centuries ago, that line was good, so good it became a proverb. And its popularity has turned it into a cliché. Air time is too valuable to waste; as the saying goes, *"Time is money."*

But the writer who relied on "Haste makes waste" might not regard it as a cliché. Opinions vary. What constitutes a cliché is the subject of a verse printed by Roy Copperud in his *American Usage and Style:*

> If you scorn what is trite
>   I warn you, go slow
> For one man's cliché
>   Is another's *bon mot.*

With the approach of April 15, dedicated wordwatchers should keep a sharp watch for clichés that tax us all. One that's recycled annually is T.S. Eliot's line from *The Waste Land:* "April is the cruelest month." Even as you read this advisory from WordWatching Central, a newscaster somewhere is probably delivering that line as if it were newly born. Instead, after a life of over-employment since its birth in 1922, the line deserves retirement, *not with a bang but a whimper,* another Eliot inspiration that deserves a long rest. So do most variations: "For the Chicago Cubs, September has become the cruelest month."

Another certainty with the advent of April is that many newscasters will work into a story or a lead-in Benjamin Franklin's wrinkled adage: "Nothing is certain but death and taxes." And clichés.

But the cartoonist John Caldwell has managed to turn clichés inside out and upside down: "The early dog gets the worms," "There is no free brunch" and "What goes up must calm down."

As Prof. Ted Peterson says: "If you must perpetrate a cliché, rework it for freshness. For instance: When a veterinarian removed the bladder from a cat, he remarked, 'Just a case of letting the bag out of the cat.' Get the idea?"

Got it.

Ms. Guidance

At the risk of being ex*Communicator*ed, at least from this issue on women and minorities, I want to say I'm a *Ms.*ogynyst: I don't like "Ms." No, I don't mean I personally dislike Mss. or whatever they call themselves. I just dislike the courtesy title "Ms." I don't hear it, I don't say it, I don't write it. Network newscasters rarely use it, perhaps because of misgivings over the buzz-saw sound: "Miz." But in workshops and classrooms I'm often asked about "Ms." In reply, I can't do any better than quote Trevor Fishlock, who wrote about "Ms." in the *Times* of London:

"It is artificial, ugly, silly, means nothing and is rotten English. It is a faddish, middle-class plaything, and far from disguising the marital status of women, as is claimed, it draws attention to it. It is a vanity." Fishlock ended his 1980 essay by saying, "There is an important battle to be fought for all women, not just a tiny elite." But, he said, "Ms. is one of the excesses of the revolution and should be junked." The *Times* did junk it. And many U.S. publications also junked it. Which prompted the author Willard R. Espy to observe that "Ms." will probably last longer in junk mail than anywhere else.

According to a 1985 survey of copy chiefs of the top U.S. newspapers and magazines, "Ms." was on its way out, at least in print. Three years earlier, the annual survey found that "Ms." was acceptable to 57.3 percent of those surveyed. But the new survey said only 28.4 percent of the 200 respondents would let it stand in copy; 76.1 percent would change or omit it. The survey, conducted by Richard L. Tobin, who taught journalism at Indiana University, was published in the April 1985 issue of *Quill.*

The 1996 AP stylebook advises using "Ms." for an unmarried woman only if she prefers it. The *New York Times Manual of Style and Usage,* published in 1976, was more restrictive: "As an honorific, use it only in quoted matter, in letters to the editor and, in news articles, in passages discussing the term itself." But 10 years later, the *Times* reversed itself. An Editors' Note in mid-1986 said: "Beginning today, The New York Times will use 'Ms.' as an honorific in its news and editorial columns. Until now, 'Ms.' had not been used because of the belief that it had not passed sufficiently into the language to be accepted as common usage. The Times now believes that 'Ms.' has become a part of the language and is changing its policy. The Times will continue to use 'Miss' or 'Mrs.' when it knows the marital status of a woman in the news, unless she prefers 'Ms.' 'Ms.' will also be used when a woman's marital status is not known, or when a married woman wishes to use it with her prior name in professional or private life." That prompted Gloria Steinem to express gratitude that she would no longer be referred to as "Miss Steinem of Ms. magazine."

And the *Times* of London also changed its stance. Its *Guide to English Style and Usage,* revised in 1992, tells the paper's staff to use "Ms." on subsequent mentions for unmarried women only when they express a wish for that appellation (as the *Times* terms it). "In stories originating in America, however," says the stylebook, "use Ms. in preference to Miss unless requested otherwise."

Whatever the policy of publications, few people use "Ms." as a spoken form of address. Or say it at all. Some of the copy chiefs who replied to the survey quoted in *Quill* said their newsrooms had dropped all courtesy titles, including "Mr.," "Mrs." and "Miss," except for certain types of stories, like obits and engagements.

In writing for broadcast, I use "Mr." in a second or subsequent reference to the U.S. President. In a second mention of a woman in a story, I use her title, if any, or I refer to her as "Miss" or "Mrs." When a newscaster refers to a woman only by her last name, I sometimes wonder whether he's referring to her or to her husband. For example, in the Patty Hearst case, hearing "Hearst" made me think of her father or grandfather. Newscasters would have dispelled confusion about the cast of characters in that case by using a simple "Miss" before her name. In any case, if you abandon "Ms.," you won't be amiss. (As for how to deal with other disputed words in the debate over sexist and alleged sexist language— including *snowman, statesman, fisherman, manhole, maiden voyage* and *motherland*—that's a whole other book. A mankiller.)

Arguably also confuses me. It's a word I've been seeing and hearing more and more. When the trial of Claus von Bülow on the charge of attempted murder was moved to Providence, R.I., a network correspondent said,

Newport has lost what is arguably the socialite trial of the century.

Arguably is so mushy that even dictionaries disagree on a definition. *Webster's New World* gives only one definition for *arguably:* "as can be supported by argument." My favorite desk dictionary, *American Heritage,* defines *arguable* as "open to argument."

In *Power Language,* Jeffrey McQuain classifies *arguably* as a Janus word, named for the Roman god of doors, who was represented by two faces looking in opposite directions. McQuain—research associate for William Safire's weekly *New York Times Magazine* column, "On Language"—says *arguably* can mean "easily argued for" *or* "easily argued against." In a *New Yorker* humor piece about clichés, Roger Angell wrote that *arguably* "allows me to say something and then partly take it back." And the *Wall Street Journal's* in-house bulletin said (Sept. 5, 1996), "One could argue that *arguably* is the most overworked adverb extant."

The network correspondent who used *arguably* might have thought, "I want this story to sound important. This may be 'the' trial of the century; I can't say so with certainty, though I can try." But that's an assertion not susceptible of proof. No one can pin it down. For casual listeners, the newsman *was* calling it the trial of the century. Few people notice *arguably;* fewer still realize it's being used as an escape hatch. Which is why the journalism educator Mel Mencher says *arguably* means "Don't hold me responsible if I'm wrong."

Another argument with that script: Was the von Bülow trial "bigger" than the sensational trial of Harry K. Thaw, the socialite who murdered architect Stanford White because of his affair with Thaw's wife, Evelyn Nesbitt Thaw (made into a movie, *Girl In the Red Velvet Swing*)? "Bigger" than Gloria Vanderbilt's scandalous custody trial? "Bigger" than the stock fraud trial of socialite Richard Whitney, the president of the New York Stock Exchange sent to Sing Sing? "Bigger" than the trial of Miss Hearst? Even if the von Bülow trial isn't the "biggest," it's big enough. Anyway, what does "biggest" trial mean? Whatever *socialite trial of the century* might mean, if it means anything at all, the correspondent needn't have embroidered his script.

As Einstein put it, "If you are out to describe the truth, leave elegance to the tailor."

World's Biggest Snow Cone?

Some newspapers run children's pages with a picture-puzzle asking, "How many mistakes can you find?" So I'm going to challenge grownups with a word picture: How many mistakes can *you* find?

> **Five years ago today, with unprecedented fury, Mount St. Helens erupted, decimating 150 square miles of lush green forest.**

That's the lead of a story broadcast by a TV network reporter. Although she didn't sign a consent card for this autopsy, she should be gratified that she's contributing to the advancement of newswriting. We can't tell from her lead whether she meant that the fury was unprecedented for Mount St. Helens or for all volcanoes everywhere. In either case, she was wrong.

The most destructive eruption in modern times was that of Krakatau in 1883. The volcano, in Indonesia, generated tidal waves that killed 36,000 people. The *Encyclopedia Britannica* says, "The enormous discharge threw into the air nearly five cubic miles of rock fragments, and the fine dust [caused] spectacular red sunsets all over the world through the following year."

But the *biggest* blowup in modern times was that of Tambora, also in Indonesia. According to the U.S. Geological Survey, Tambora's eruption in 1815 disgorged more than seven cubic miles of material. Mount St. Helens spewed less than one cubic mile. And, more important, the USGS says the 1980 eruption wasn't even Mount St. Helens' biggest blowup.

That reporter would have been on safe ground if she had just told her story without straining, if she hadn't tried to punch it up with *unprecedented.* When an editor sees *unprecedented,* his mental alarm should go off. Other absolutes and superlatives should also set off his alarm: *only, unique, first, fastest, fattest, foulest* and other *est* words. An editor should ask: How do we know this is the world's *biggest* snow cone? Even if we're satisfied it is, does that make it worth reporting? If we can't confirm it on our own, are we attributing it properly? How do we know this is the world's *thickest* waffle? Or that it's the *first* time anyone has hijacked a bandwagon? Is there a central registry that keeps track of everything everywhere forever—accurately? (An exception: sports, where statistics are part of the game, and statisticians seem to record even the cap size of batboys.)

A reporter on the scene of the Mount St. Helens eruption couldn't know or easily obtain the history of volcanoes (unless she's a closet volcanologist). Even the people I spoke with at the Geological Survey had to dig out the information and call me back. But a prudent reporter doesn't trot out *unique, unparalleled, unprecedented, unsurpassed,* or any other such word without knowing that it's correct—*and* worth mentioning.

Another problem with the reporter's lead: she misused *decimate.* Originally, it meant to kill every tenth person. But now it is sometimes used to mean the destruction of a large part of a group. Yet even a volcano can't *decimate* trees, only people. The reporter might have meant "devastate," meaning "destroy" or "lay waste." (I've also heard a newscaster tell of a building in Beirut that had been "decimated" and a network correspondent speak of an effort in Washington to "decimate" a plan.)

By starting the volcano story with "Five years ago today," the reporter deprived the anchor of the anniversary angle for the lead-in. Ordinarily, a correspondent in the field (or forest) should start with what will become the second sentence of the story. She does that by picking up from—or playing off—the anchor's lead-in. That's quite a trick, because the anchor's lead-in is usually written after the correspondent's piece has been put into the lineup.

Another point: The first sentence in the script can be improved by changing the participle to a finite verb, one with a tense. And by using only one adjective: "The volcano blew up with great fury—and destroyed [not *decimated*] 150 square miles of forest." That's shorter, sharper, stronger.

My suggested anchor lead-in—based on hearing the whole story: "Mount Saint Helens erupted five years ago today, but nearby residents are, in a sense, still feeling after-shocks. Jane Jones has the story in Washington state."

One way to make sure that the lead-in and the script dovetail, says a former CBS News producer, Norman Glubok, is for the correspondent to submit, with her script, a proposed anchor lead-in. Once the correspondent thinks through what her story is all about, she'll know how to write the lead-in, and that'll give her a head start on writing her script. If the story is about a volcano, a correspondent can expect the anchor to identify the volcano in the lead-in. So the correspondent can start her script with "the volcano," skipping the name. But she should make sure that she leaves the anchor a strong fact or two for the lead-in. In most cases, she should omit those facts from her script. Otherwise, when the piece is broadcast, she'll be the one who'll sound repetitious.

Speaking of blowups (and if you like that transition, you'd better raise your standards), a news director, Dick Nelson, asked me about my reference to a story on the blowup by the so-called subway vigilante Bernhard Goetz. Dick wants to know whether it's permissible to call Goetz a vigilante.

"Vigilante" was first used more than 100 years ago to refer to a member of a "vigilance committee." The committees were formed, mostly in the South and West, to see that criminals were punished. Often, punishment was inflicted by members themselves, occasionally on suspects who were blameless. One case of frontier justice administered by vigilantes was reported in Denver's *Rocky Mountain News* on May 31, 1862: "The vigys pointed to an empty saddle and gave him just 10 minutes to skedaddle." *A Dictionary of Americanisms* by Mitford M. Mathews also offers examples showing "vigilante" has been used in this century. And in recent years it has been widely used to describe people who take the law into their hands.

I'm not keen about writing *subway vigilante* (when I used it in a column, I was quoting someone else), but I think it's acceptable—at least in this case. The term has been so widely applied to Goetz, people know in an instant who he is and what he did. It's not as if we were declaring him guilty; he acknowledges being a vigilante. But I'd precede that label with *so-called* to remind listeners we hadn't declared Goetz guilty, that we're merely using a standard label.

By using the shorthand device *subway vigilante,* we capture an event that would otherwise take many words to describe. Let's try it without the shortcut: "The man who shot four teenagers in a New York City subway train, Bernhard Goetz, was arraigned today and pleaded not guilty." Now, using our shorthand, let's set the scene swiftly: "The so-called subway vigilante, Bernhard Goetz, has pleaded not guilty."

I, too, can be insufficiently vigilant. The newsman Alan Cohn pointed out my incorrect reference to Claus von Bülow's "murder trial." Von Bülow was tried for *attempted* murder. I plead guilty.

Ups and Downs

A network correspondent reported that a nationally known candidate was "mired down." But the newsman mucked it up. Someone who's mired *is* already down—stuck or sunk in mud. Although the use of a superfluous adverb, such as *down,* isn't on the up and up, it seems to be popping up more and more.

So a watchword for wordwatchers is: Tighten copy. (If you tighten it *up,* you may not wind up a titan.) Some verbs—occasionally called merged verbs—do take an adverb or preposition: cave *in,* look *over,* sound *off,* and perhaps what that correspondent had in mind, *bog down.*

We often hear newscasters talk about factories that have been closed *down* or opened *up,* and in those cases, *down* and *up* should be offed. In *The Careful Writer,* Theodore M. Bernstein calls these adverbs and prepositions "verb tails." He puts them in three categories: necessary (bottle *up,* break *in,* burn *down*); usually unnecessary (check *over,* head *up,* hide *out*), and unnecessary but idiomatic (slow *down,* hurry *up,* visit *with*). When a reporter is unsure whether a certain verb needs a tail, he can look it up in a good dictionary.

No newsroom should be without a good dictionary. Better: Every newsroom should have a good dictionary. The second sentence is easier to understand and more emphatic. (Not for nothing do Strunk and White stress that writers should put their sentences in a positive form.)

Sometimes, I hear a story open in slo-mo, then slip into no-mo:

> **A package of military aid for El Salvador has been the subject of much debate in Congress lately. Today is no exception. House Speaker Thomas O'Neill predicts. . . .**

The first sentence isn't news. Someone might try to justify it by calling it background, but it shouldn't be thrust into the foreground. At least, not with that flimsy construction. The first verb, *has been,* is a form of *to be;* like other linking verbs, it's anemic. It links but doesn't move. And the script's second sentence says feebly, "Today is no exception."

Unfortunately, we often have to write stories about the unexceptional, but we don't ballyhoo their banality. Instead, without exaggerating, distorting or misrepresenting, we try to pump life into stories that are dead, dying or dormant. If we put aside its dubious news value (a prediction doesn't carry much weight), we could improve that lead and yet follow the writer's pattern: "Congress has been debating military aid for El Salvador, and today House Speaker Thomas O'Neill predicted. . . ." But whenever possible it's important to start a story by telling listeners something they don't already know. Using only the facts available in that script, we can strengthen the lead by starting with a today angle: "Congress resumed debate today on military aid for El Salvador."

Another broadcast item began wimpishly:

> **The diplomatic chill continues between the superpowers.**

That's not news; it's olds. If something *continues,* it has been going on, and it still goes on. So it is not new or news.

News generally reflects change. Except for a siege, a strike, a fast, a drought or other long-running story, no change means no news. So *continues* is static. It doesn't advance the story—if there's any story at all. And it doesn't arrest or engage the listener. Even if a newscaster is dealing with a story that changes only by millimeters, like that of hijackers holding a plane on a runway, he should search for a new angle or a new approach, and he should use vigorous verbs. *Continues,* as I say continually, is as colorless and spineless as a jellyfish.

Having a good dictionary in a newsroom isn't enough. Writers should be encouraged to consult it. One way to arouse their interest may be to post a sign at the dictionary stand that warns: Don't Open This Book! My experience in newsrooms—broadcast and print, network and local—is that the best writers go to dictionaries most. And writers most in need of dictionaries go least. This philosophizing is inspired by another broadcast lead I heard:

Power and influence win their magic in many different ways.

I wasn't sure whether the newscaster had said *"win* their magic" or *"wend* their magic," but both would have been wrong. If only someone in the newsroom assembly line had wondered about *"win* [or *wend*] their magic" and wended his way to a dictionary, the newscaster might have been able to *work* his magic.

Another writer who should have checked his dictionary (but not at the door) said that at the national convention in Dallas (I won't identify the political party or the offending party), *the crescendo rose.* A crescendo is a gradual increase in the volume of sound. So it's the nature of crescendos to rise. And of diminuendos to fall.

A more common error was committed at the convention by a correspondent who said,

But they come to Dallas . . . to bake in the 106-degree heat. . . .

Whatever they might have been cooking up, they didn't go to Dallas to bake. They did bake, but their goal was to stay cool.

One last note: Some newswriters have too many ironies in their fire. In fact, they often have no ironies at all, but they're quick to describe various occurrences as ironic. Perhaps William S. Gilbert was poking fun at a predecessor of theirs when he wrote of "an unlettered man of letters, attracted, like a magnet, to irony." *Irony* is the use of words to convey the opposite of their literal meaning; an irony is also an incongruity between what might be expected and what does occur. The *BBC Style Guide* says of *ironically:* "Overused. Irony is a subtle concept: it is not the same as paradox and it does not mean coincidence. It's probably a word to avoid."

Here's what a reporter broadcast after an Amtrak train jumped the tracks:

More than half those on Train Number 60 were from a group ironically called Adventures Unlimited.

Apparently, the members of that group were looking for a new adventure, and they found one. Their name is not ironic, and their being thrown by an iron horse is not ironic. After all, they were seeking adventure, and they found it.

I thought I was rolling on the right track until I received a card from Ridge Shannon of Shawnee Mission, Kansas. He said my use of "refer back" in a column was redundant. He's right, and I'm contrite.

"Out of" Abounds

If there's anything some writers never run out of, it's *out of:*

"A story *out of* the White House tonight that. . . ."

"A report *out of* London today. . . ."

"News *out of* Hollywood. . . ."

Out of? News comes *from* somewhere. I've never heard anyone else use *out of* that way, except sheriffs in Westerns: "The word outta Fort Dodge is that them varmints is up to no good."

Although some newswriters have made *out of* common, that doesn't make it acceptable. As the columnist William Safire says: "Common usage excuses; good usage demands."

But even with the substitution of *from,* those leads need to be rewritten. Instead of telling the news, they start by saying they're *going* to be telling the news. People tune in newscasts expecting to hear newscasters deliver the news, so an anchor shouldn't start by talking *about* the news but start *with* the news.

Newscasts consist of stories, so there's no need to start with the word *story.* And the lead that tells of a "report out of. . . ." has another flaw. The noun *report* can mean a rumor or a factual account. So when we hear of a "*report* from" somewhere, we have no idea whether it's well grounded or unfounded. We also hear sportscasters describe an athlete as "*out of* Peoria." Peoria is not something you run out of. And certainly nothing you can run out and get more of, like beer. No matter where you're *from.*

More writing that needs righting:

> **Qaddafi also denied that Palestinian terrorist Abu Nidal lives and operates out of Libya.**

The sentence has a past-tense denial of present-tense action. So it makes more sense to start with the present tense: "Qaddafi also *denies.* . . ." Also: The writer meant ". . . lives *in* Libya and operates out of Libya." This use of *out of*—after a verb like *operates*—is standard, but *from* is faster.

> **The Census Bureau *is out* tonight *with* word of a baby boomlet gone bust. . . .**

Is out with seems to be getting into more newscasts. But it's blander than bean curd. Like other forms of *to be, is* conveys no motion, no action. It's inert. Better: "The Census Bureau *says* the baby boomlet has gone bust." Not good, but better. Let's take up a new battle cry: "Out, out, damned *out with!*"

> **Police said the exact number and extent of their injuries**
> **was not immediately available.**

That sentence has what an ad for zippers used to call "gaposis." The gap can be filled by rewriting: "Police said the number *of injured* was not. . . ." But even after closing the gap, we still have a sentence that lacks zip. Better: "Police say they don't know how many people were hurt—or how badly."

> **People came from as far as Chicago and Oregon to catch**
> **one furtive, faraway glimpse of the future queen.**

Furtive = stealthy. The correspondent should have sneaked a look in a dictionary. The people he spoke of didn't travel that far to catch a *glimpse;* they traveled that far to get a good look, but they wound up far away. The people who traveled to Springfield, Virginia, from Oregon came from a lot farther than Chicago, so the correspondent had no need to mention an intermediate place—like Chicago. Also, cities and states shouldn't be mixed. If it had been desirable to mention a half-way place, he should have changed "Chicago" to "Illinois."

The faulty construction in that excerpt is heard often: "She returned home *to* find her husband dead." Should be: "She returned home *and* found her husband dead."

The script was also wrong to refer to the Princess of Wales as "the future queen." Wrong in 1986, even wronger today. In my column of June 1986, I wrote: "She may or may not become queen—and definitely not '*the* queen.' If Diana were to die while Elizabeth is still queen, or if Prince Charles dies, Diana won't become queen. And if they're divorced, or if he renounces the throne, she won't become queen."

Later, John McFadyen of Toronto told me then that if Charles did become king, Diana would not necessarily become queen. So I wrote: "She would become queen only if Charles exercised his royal prerogative to have her named queen. His mother, Queen Elizabeth, whose royal birth makes her *the* queen, has not chosen to have her husband, Prince Philip, elevated to king. So calling Diana 'the future queen' is presumptuous."

Although Diana and Charles have been O.B.E.—Overtaken by Events (not the Order of the British Empire)—it's useful to retain that paragraph because it still carries a lesson: Make sure you know what you're talking about. And focus on what has happened and what is happening, not on what might happen over the horizon.

> **A murder today is sending shock waves through a quiet Abington neighborhood. The body of a woman was discovered at about three-thirty this afternoon in the basement of her home in the 21-hundred block of Rush Road. Police say 44-year-old Marge McAndrews was stabbed to death. Her body was found by her 18-year-old daughter. Police aren't sure what happened, but it appears that the woman surprised a burglar. The search is on for her killer.**

Like too many first-day leads, this one focuses on reaction instead of action. The writer should zero in on the murder, not on "shock waves"— whatever they are, other than vintage journalese. The time when the body was found is irrelevant. If the writer had wanted listeners to know of the recency, he could have said "this afternoon" or "in mid-afternoon." Or "within the past hour" or "a short time ago." The hour and minute add nothing; everything happens at one time or another.

Who was the victim? Occupation? Family? Was it one of her kitchen knives? Rather than write "Police aren't sure," I'd write, "Police say they think Mrs. [?] McAndrews surprised a burglar." The script's last sentence, about the search for the killer, isn't worth using. Searching for a killer isn't unusual. It's customary. When a Boy Scout helps an old woman cross the street, that's not news. But if he trips her, we have news. So if police *refuse* to search, that's news.

> **The Soviet Union shot two astronauts into space. . . .**

Moscow calls them cosmonauts. So do we. *Shot two astronauts into space?* Was it a shoot-'em-up?

12

A "GUILTY CONVICTION"
(AND OTHER OFFENSES)

Some newspeople have demonstrated that they deserve network recognition—for boners, boo-boos, bloopers and blunders:

> **In the Bronx this morning, a guilty conviction.**

WordWatcher's verdict: guilty of aggravated redundancy.

> **This fellow . . . did the exact same work in the exact same shop. . . .**

Verdict: guilty on two counts of aggravated redundancy.

> **Police say the fireman was knocked from an aerial ladder by a hose when he fell to the ground.**

Huh?

> **Pan Am will continue to service its other routes.**

Correct: "Pan Am will still *serve* its other routes." A mechanic *services* a plane; a boar *services* a sow.

Reporting from Geneva on the arms control talks several hours after the death of Soviet President Konstantin Chernenko, a correspondent said:

> **The new negotiations are expected to last for years. In any event, Chernenko would have been unlikely to live to see the end.**

Do negotiations *last?* Or do they *drag on?* An ice cream bar *lasts.* Chernenko *unlikely* to live? He didn't live until that newscast. At least, the newsman didn't say Chernenko's death was a turning point in his life.

> **Communist forces entered the city from six different directions.**

All directions are different, so *different* is superfluous. In another newscast:

> **They make speeches in seven different languages.**

Same problem. And this:

> **Four explosions in three different parts of Belgium. . . .**

No different.

> **For the second time in the past four days, federal authorities are landing a knockout blow on a local outlaw motorcycle gang.**

If the first blow had been a knockout, there would have been no need for a second knockout. Also, the opening phrase—"For the second time in the past four days"—delayed the action and diminished its newsiness. If the writer had had room, he could have gone on to say, "It was the second raid in four days." He did go on to mention

> **four separate indictments.**

At least, he didn't say the feds arrested "13 separate people."

> **The rock group Wham! [has started] their history-making tour of China.**

The collective noun *group* takes the singular, so *their* should be *its*. News-writers don't determine who "makes history"; historians do. No one, not even Wham!, enters history books by whim. I don't want to slam Wham!, but I doubt that it will make even a footnote. Except in a history of hype or a history of histrionics.

> **[Edgar Degas] will be 150 years old this year.**

No matter what the anchor meant to say (in 1985), that sentence would have made the French painter the oldest living master. The anchor was wrong on two counts. Degas was born in 1834, so this was the 151st anniversary of his birth. And he died in 1917, so he stopped at age 83. That means he wasn't able to reach 84, let alone 150—or 151.

There was even a new American record established in Potsdam today.

A record set today *is* new, so *new record* is redundant.

Firemen tonight called to the scene of. . . .

By omitting *were* before *called,* this incomplete sentence sounds as if firemen responded to the fire by phone. And when they go to a fire by firetruck, firemen go straight to the fire; they don't bother with *the scene of* the fire.

It's May 29th, if you're just getting up.

And if I've been up for an hour, it's still May 29.

A 44-year-old mother and nurse was found stabbed to death by her daughter.

Did the daughter commit the crime? Or did she discover it? Sharp-eyed Emerson Stone has found another ambiguity (*triguity?*) in *by,* which means "next to"; he asks whether the writer meant the mother and daughter were found side by side. In fact, the daughter found the body.

The lead should not have compounded the confusion by identifying the victim as both mother and nurse. And the victim's age should not have preceded what happened to her. Age isn't more important than everything else in the story. In fact, age isn't exciting; everyone has an age. I'd use the victim's age—but later in the script. Better: "A nurse has been found stabbed to death in her home. Her daughter found the body. . . ."

Emotions run so high in these games, where hopes soar one minute and are dashed the next. _____ _____ has been on this emotional roller coaster with the Villanova fans. What's the mood in Lexington, _____ , or need I ask?

The only place so awash in emotion is Clichéville. Never let emotions run high. And never let them on a roller coaster.

A story about the arrest of a suspect in a fire that killed seven persons:

His name is 18-year-old Walter Craig.

Imagine squeezing *18-year-old Walter Craig* onto a nameplate.

It happened last night at 13th and Locust in City Center, Philadelphia. A fight between a pair of transvestites ended in death for one and arrest for the other.

Transvestites may pair up, but they don't come in pairs. (Socks, gloves and bookends do come in pairs.) Also, the lead is weak. Avoid starting a story with the indefinite pronoun *it*. I'm not saying never. (Almost never do I say never.) And I wouldn't use "last night" or "yesterday" in a first sentence. Another problem: The only verb in the second sentence is *ended,* a poor choice in reporting a killing.

A transvestite is someone who dresses in the garb of the opposite sex; in a story like that, the sex should be specified. Better: "Two male transvestites started quarreling in City Center, Philadelphia, and one was stabbed to death. The other one has been charged with murder. The fight occurred last night at 13th and Locust. . . ."

In a story about the President's impending visit to Bitburg, West Germany, a newscaster said a certain development had

reawakened the furor.

For all we listeners could tell, he might have spelled it "Führer" (although I wouldn't have been able to detect that umlaut). If the writer had read his copy aloud carefully before he broadcast it, he could have caught that unfortunate ambiguity. Another newsman referred to a high-powered broadcaster as a "broadcasting magnate." Which made me think of a magnet used in a speaker.

These cases of hearing something other than what the newscaster meant should remind us of the risk in using homophones: words that sound the same but whose meanings differ. Other words to watch out for—and listen for—when we read our scripts softly to ourselves before turning them in:

accord/a chord	faint/feint
aides/aids/AIDS	farewell/fare well
attacks on/a tax on	formally/formerly
breadth/breath	half/halve/have
censer/censor/censure/sensor	hear/here
cite/sight/site	heroin/heroine
complement/compliment	malicious/militias
council/consul/counsel	passed/past
cymbal/symbol	pedal/peddle/petal
deceased/diseased	rain/reign/rein
defuse/diffuse	raise/raze

sects/sex	to/too/two/tutu
soar/sore	where/ware/wear
their/there/they're	wholly/holey/holy
threw/through	

Yes, we do need to use most of those words. But we need to make sure that they're not combined with other words that lead to ambiguity or hilarity. The homophones in that list are just a few of the many lurking in our keyboards, but enough are there to remind us of all the double meanings we must guard against. We must keep in mind that what makes sense to the eye can cause double trouble for the ear. An amusing example of the confusion caused by homophones occurs in a skit by the comic Benny Hill. Two workmen drag sacks of telephones into a room and put them on a table. Hill snaps peevishly, "I told you, two *sax*ophones!"

Not by the Numbers

Bits and bites from broadcasts:

> **Indeed, Europe is said to have larger banks but fewer of them. We have more banks but they are smaller than those in Europe.**

That second sentence is a funhouse mirror of the first, which indicates a lack of reflection. The item is reminiscent of a parody of T. S. Eliot: "As we get older, we do not get any younger."

And when I hear a newscaster use *we,* I wonder whether he's referring to himself, his station or his nation. According to Mark Twain, the only people entitled to use *we* are presidents, editors and people with tapeworms. (How about pregnant women?)

> **Twenty-seven people are dead, 43 injured, the result of a bus accident in Mexico. Police say the crowded bus blew a tire and went spinning off a highway 150 miles west of Mexico City. The bus crashed at the bottom of a gorge.**

Stories that start with numbers leave me numb. My mind needs a warmup before I hear the final score. Any form of *to be* is weak, so saying people *are* dead is lifeless. The accident was dramatic. But *are,* the only verb in the first sentence of that script, lacks ardor. Also, by putting the place-name last in that first sentence, the writer keeps the listener wondering whether the accident occurred in her town or even in her country; she doesn't find out until the sentence ends. And that's too late.

Another drawback: After the newscaster gave us the outcome in his first breath, the sentence rolled downhill. A writer can create a strong sentence by building up to the high point, not down from it. Better: "A bus in Mexico blew a tire, spun off a highway and plunged into a gorge. Twenty-seven people were killed. Forty-three were hurt." Or the jiffy version: "A bus accident in Mexico has killed 27 people."

> **More than 40 people were injured today when a couple of bombs exploded aboard a truck transporting military explosives through Oklahoma. _____ _____ reports it could have been much worse.**

Like the previous story, this anchor lead-in starts with a number and proceeds in reverse chronological order. *Then* it tells us what caused the casualties and where. Also regrettable: The script talks about *explosives* that *exploded.* And the story would have more impact by starting with the most vivid aspect and using a vigorous verb: "A truck carrying military explosives in Oklahoma blew up today, and more than 40 people were hurt."

The newscaster's intro to the correspondent says *it could have been much worse,* which is inane. After just about any accident, someone can say it might have been much worse. Or can say, "It didn't have to happen."

Here's how another newscaster reported the story:

> **There's now a crater 30 feet wide and 18 feet deep on a highway near the town of Checotah in eastern Oklahoma. It was created today when a car going the wrong way on an entrance ramp hit a military truck carrying ten bombs. Some of them detonated. . . .**

Detonated? Why use a Latin-root word when *blew up* does the job? Almost any lead that starts with *there is* or *it is* should be changed. The writer backed into that story. His script could have been worse, but not much worse.

> **According to court documents, Whitworth relayed his information to Walker in Hong Kong when the carrier pulled in for a port visit.**

The most important element in the sentence is the circumstances of the alleged transfer. But buried in the middle of the sentence, *Hong Kong* is passed over quickly, so it lacks importance. The key facts in the news item could have been highlighted by progressing chronologically and building up to the main idea: "Court documents say Whitworth gave Walker the information when the carrier visited Hong Kong." (With Walker convicted of running a spy ring for Moscow, can he be labeled *Johnnie Walker Red?*)

There's new concern this week about an old air-safety problem, near-misses in the sky.

If two planes nearly miss but don't miss, they collide. If they nearly collide, they have a near-collision, not a "near-miss." Isn't a "near-miss" a bride who was almost jilted?

If you write that two planes collided over Yellowstone National Park, the *over* conveys the idea that the collision occurred in the air instead of on the ground. So steer clear of "near-miss" and "mid-air collision." Also avoid "near-panic" and "near-riot." The law says a riot is a violent disturbance by three or more persons. So is a "near-riot" a ruckus caused by *two* persons?

Are you ever bothered by airline people's use of English? When I make a flight reservation and the agent recaps my itinerary, she sometimes tells me I'll be "arriving *into*" a certain city. Sounds scary. When I board, a flight attendant often says the plane will be taking off "momentarily." "Momentarily" means "*for* a moment," not "*in* a moment," as I hope the attendant intends. And when the attendant explains the safety features, demonstrates the oxygen mask and points out the elastic tabs "on either side," that, too, is disquieting: "either" means "one *or* the other," not "both." Even more disquieting: Mary P. Clunis says she was sitting in a plane when the pilot announced over the P.A. that this would be his last flight. Gulp!

Aren't you troubled when you hear a flight attendant say, "We'll be on the ground shortly"? (Sounds like the sailor who offers mock reassurance to his shipmates during a storm: "We're only one mile from land—straight down.") I've also heard an attendant say, "If you're terminating in Chicago. . . ." Many terminators have populated Chicago (or depopulated it), but should airlines encourage that sort of thing? They could ease my anxiety by brushing up on their English. The columnist William Safire paraphrases Admiral Nelson at Trafalgar: "English expects all of us to do our duty."

Why do airline personnel use such highfalutin language? Occasionally, I hear: "The fasten-seatbelt sign is still *illuminated.*" Five syllables when one would do the job: *on*.

Another example of airlinespeak appeared on signs at Nashville airport: "The airlines have implemented enhanced security procedures designed for the protection of customers and employees. We regret any inconvenience you may experience as a result of increased security surveillance."

That high-flown jargon should be brought down to earth: "We're taking stronger steps to protect you. If you're inconvenienced, we're sorry." My revision may not be worthy of chiseling in marble, but at least it's only 12 words (the original is 29 words). Halving the word-count and simplifying the language help make the message clearer, crisper and comprehensible.

Another airline abomination: "de-plane," as in "Passengers will de-plane through the front exit." Can't they just *leave?*

> **United Airlines had better luck getting planes into the air today than it did yesterday. . . .**

That script about the pilots' strike is chilling. It suggests that the airline relies on luck.

> **Today begins a special time for Polish-Americans, a time to celebrate their culture as part of Polish-American Heritage Month.**

Today begins? The *event* begins. Today we can begin the beguine, and the beguine can begin the day. But *today* can't begin anything. Not in English.

Word Champs

Let's mark the end of the year by awarding No-bell Prizes. These prize-winning scripts were broadcast by networks as *news*—not parody.

The first non-bellringer takes the prize for misleading lead-in:

> **Japan's drive to be number one, the excellent Japanese education system, teenage suicides, schoolyard bullying and extortion at school. Some or all of these elements are in tonight's report from Tokyo by _____ _____ .**

After the anchor broadcast that item, I wondered whether the writer would be emboldened to write a lead-in like this for a shootout: "Sex. Drugs. Greed. Violence. Sudden death. Some or all those elements figure in the story from. . . ." *Some or all* sounds like the legalistic language of a contract. In fact, the correspondent said nothing about "Japan's drive to be number one."

Even if the writer had written the lead-in accurately, he would have done it incorrectly. Starting with a list and *then* telling listeners why is like giving a recipe and finally telling what it's for.

Prize for startling comeback:

> **At least three people were dead tonight and three more missing as. . . .**

Were dead—but no longer dead? Those who were killed *are* dead; the dead *were* oil workers. Even if the writer had lined up his tenses correctly, he got off to a weak start because he began with numbers and backed into the action.

Prize for resistible lead:

> **In the 'what-else-is-new?' department, the U-S dollar rose again today.**

Prize for negating the positive:

> **The chairman of the P-L-O, Yasir Arafat, had no kind words for President Reagan today.**

No kind words is negative. Be positive. The lead would be far stronger this way: "The chairman of the P-L-O, Yasir Arafat, denounced President Reagan today as 'a robot and a parrot.'"

Prize for superfluous use of prepositions:

> **European space scientists phoned NASA today for emergency help in fixing their . . . space probe that's meeting up with Halley's comet. . . .**

Anyone who says *meet up with* is going to collide with me.

Prize for ambiguity:

> **For the first time since 1962, it appears that a woman will be executed next month.**

Sounds as if the newscaster is a forecaster.

Prize for poise in the heat of battle:

> **The lobby of the Commodore Hotel became a battleground as Terry Waite held a news conference with the foreign press about the fate of four American hostages. . . . It was a**

classic Beirut scene—Waite trying to be calm as Druse and Amal militiamen fought an intense street battle outside.

Was the battle in the street or the lobby?
Prize for quick-change artistry:

What was a tragic accident on Sunday has now become a possible murder investigation.

It's a strange world, but how does an accident become an investigation? And is that a possible murder or a possible investigation?
Prize for absurd word:

That's an embarrassment, a *pozzible*—a puzzle and a possible future trouble spot for. . . .

That ran on a network? *Impozzible.*
Prize for sensitive opening line:

We had hoped not to have to report it, but an Ohio doctor said today, 'There were just too many strikes against him.' He was speaking about that little boy. . . .

Prize for redundancy:

Hundreds of worried parents stood face to face with armed soldiers outside a Soweto police station.

Armed soldiers? Are they comrades-in-arms of *armed* gunmen?
Prize for impossible questions put to listeners in a lead-in:

What's cutting into the steelhead trout population in the ship canal? Some deadly disease? Or is it only Herschel and his friends? Only Herschel?

Why ask *us?*
Prize for gratuitous explanation:

Now, we didn't lead with this next story because, frankly, we feel strongly about not raising any false expectations.

When I hear someone say "frankly," I wonder whether he's saying that because he's usually not frank.
Prize for mangling syntax—consumer reporters' division:

**Well, first I want to tell you these are not new products.
These are when you borrow it from somebody else.**

Prize for mangling syntax—anchors:

**Foreigners found themselves jeered at, spat at and had their
cars overturned.**

Did the foreigners arrange to have their cars overturned to collect
insurance?

Prize for most informative first sentence:

**Winter kills and snow is dangerous. Yet another reminder
has happened in a small town along the coast of the Japan
Sea. . . .**

Reminders don't *happen.* And a sea does not have a coast; a country does.
Japan Sea? Is that anywhere near the Sea of Japan?

Prize for hype and tripe:

**By the rules, what goes up must come down, but that was
before the rule-breaking, record delay-breaking bloops [*sic*],
foul-ups and bleepers mission of space shuttle Columbia.**

By staying in space longer than planned, Columbia didn't break any
rules. No rule says an object in space must return to earth—and when.

Prize for iffiness:

**And if you love the ancient canal city of Venice, good news
this morning.**

But how's the news if we *don't* love Venice?

Prize for clear thinking:

**For many Americans, the biggest problem with having
babies is not having babies.**

Such a problem is inconceivable. But so are all those network scripts.

Illegalese

The best newswriting, or most of the best, is done at the networks. But
some newswriters aren't always at their best. Let's listen to these network
scripts:

Until and unless this citizen is proven guilty, he is, of course, presumed innocent.

You can't call *until and unless* a cliché because the writer has it backward. The correct cliché (if a cliché can be correct) is "unless and until." But either word alone works. A cousin of "unless and until" is "if, as and when." And that, too, is a cliché. Both phrases are legalese, if you please.

Lawyers like to use a string of synonyms or near-synonyms in doublets: "null and void," "do and perform." Or triplets: "cancel, annul and set aside," "give, devise and bequeath," "possession, custody and control." Lawyers use these phrases to be emphatic, to cover all bases and to sound lawyerly. But newswriters should keep from, abstain from and refrain from chewing their cabbage thrice. Even twice.

Next in that excerpt, the word *citizen* is fancy. Why not call him a man? Also, the word *proven* should be *proved*. And *of course* is best avoided. For listeners who know of the long-standing legal presumption of innocence, *of course* doesn't help. And for listeners who don't know, *of course* doesn't help at all. Of course not.

Alcoa was the point-size gainer in the Dow Jones Industrial Average today, rising 2⅜ after several days of losses after being downgraded and having its earnings estimates cut.

After, after! Twice in one sentence is enough to cause *after*shock. And that sentence in the script is too long, too lumpy, too loopy. What's a *point-size gainer?* That lingo is a loser. More to the point, who cut Alcoa's earnings estimates? Management? A newsletter? A brokerage house? "*Having* its earnings estimates cut" sounds as if Alcoa *arranged* to have the estimates cut.

Better: "The biggest gainer among the Dow Jones Industrials today is Alcoa, up two and three-eighths. Recently, earnings estimates for Alcoa were cut—and the stock was downgraded. So Alcoa started slipping—until today." Original: 28 words; rewrite: 31 words. Slightly longer, but definitely clearer.

Since last Tuesday, New Yorkers have been riveted over the fate of a woman brutally attacked in Central Park. As the woman fights for her life in the hospital and the search for her assailant continues, the story has sent shock waves across the country.

The script was broadcast on a Sunday, five days after the crime, so there was no need to say "*last* Tuesday." Instead of *Since last Tuesday,* make it "for five days." Undoubtedly, the attack upset people, but I doubt that shock waves, whatever they are, spread across the country.

"Riveted *over*"? You can be riveted *by* someone's story. Or riveted *to* a spot. Or riveted *at* the sight of a horror. But not riveted *over* anything. If you don't think it over, you may be raked *over* the coals.

Fights for her life is journalese. And *continues* is a weak verb for a lead or lead-in. Better (if you would retain that lead-in's structure—and I wouldn't): ". . . and the police search for her attacker. . . ." Yes, *attacker*, not *assailant*. At least, the writer didn't call it a *senseless* attack—in contrast to a *sensible* attack.

The correspondent went on to echo the anchor and say the victim was

brutally beaten.

The beating *was* brutal, more brutal than most beatings. But one *brutally* is enough. I heard you the first time.

More network work that needs work:

> **Right after Buddy Lazier took the checkered flag to win the 80th running of the Indy 500, three other cars were involved in a spectacular crash just before the finish line. In Brooklyn, Michigan, for a running of the U-S 500, they were delayed by a spectacular crash before the race even got under way. It continues outside of Detroit.**

The first sentence in that excerpt raises several questions. *Involved* is a fuzzy word. Did poor driving by one of the three cars cause the other two to crash? Or what? And what does *just before the finish line* mean? Two *spectacular* crashes? *Spectacular* is a much-overused word. Twice a year it may be bearable, but not in two straight sentences. Or even in two ovals. (Perhaps the writer needs a crash course.)

Got under way = began. Also, the last sentences of that excerpt need straightening out. Those sentences suggest the race was moved from Brooklyn to a track *outside* [no *of*] Detroit. (And better than the two-syllable *outside* is *near*.) But no, the writer was merely slipping in a geographical clue to tell us where Brooklyn is.

Another network excerpt:

> **Now a published report says that to save money the cut-rate airline is offering voluntary unpaid leaves to many of its four-thousand employees.**

What is *a published report?* A thoroughly sourced article in a reliable newspaper? A rumor in a gossip column? (We don't report rumors or gossip, except in highly unusual circumstances.) Why not identify the source? Also: no need for *voluntary.* If the leaves were involuntary, they'd have been *imposed,* not *offered.*

And another network sourcing problem:

> _____ **News has learned the Medicare trustees will report tomorrow that by the year 2001, the Medicare Part A Trust Fund—the part that covers hospital costs—will be 16-billion dollars in the red, according to sources close to the trustees.**

The best sources in the art of writing for the ear agree that one rule in broadcast newswriting is inviolable: Attribution precedes assertion. So never hang "according to" or "she said" on the end of a sentence. But that script opened by crediting the network with *learning* something— then, at the end of the long sentence tagging on a vague attribution. That means the network has learned something according to sources. Absurd! Where were those newsroom eyes that are supposed to eyeball—and, if necessary, blackball—scripts?

Network, too:

> **[L]ater—behind the scenes at Sotheby's for the famous Jackie Kennedy Onassis auction. . . .**

Famous is generally as useless as feathers on a snake. So please don't call the former First Lady or the auction *famous.* If a listener has heard of her— and breathes there a soul with mind so dead who hasn't?—*famous* is silly. As for listeners who don't know the name, *famous* can't fill the void.

No wonder Steve Martin says a writer's best friend is sometimes the delete key.

Writers under the Weather

> "Don't knock the weather; nine-tenths of the people couldn't start a conversation if it didn't change once in a while."
>
> FRANK MCKINNEY (KIN) HUBBARD

Start a *conversation?* If it weren't for the weather, I couldn't even start this column. That's why I don't knock the weather, certainly not in the weather issue; so that leaves me with a few extra knocks for weathercasters and newscasters. But Ed Bliss says an editor should be hard on copy, not on people. So I'll edit myself and say the knocks are for weather *copy*.

The worse the weather, the worse the copy. Instead of telling a dramatic story in a simple, sober style, many writers shift their typewriters into overwrite. But he who overwrites, undermines. Read the simple yet powerful account of the biggest story ever. Here's how a Hebrew rewriteman handled the lead: "In the beginning, God created the heaven and the earth." Period. Big event, simple words, short sentence, great impact.

One of the most objectionable aspects of much weather coverage is what the 19th century British critic John Ruskin called the "pathetic fallacy." When a writer ascribes human behavior, motivation or characteristics to inanimate objects, animals or natural phenomena, he commits what Ruskin calls a "pathetic fallacy." Some poets have made this approach, known as anthropomorphism, work—*the cruel sea, smiling skies, laughing waters*—but in broadcast scripts, it's usually overdone or inappropriate. Here are some broadcast examples:

> **Residents** [better: *people*] **are also waiting, waiting for the fickle but dangerous Hurricane Elena to make up her mind.**

"Fickle"? "Make up her *mind*"? Nonsense. No storm, even one with a name, has a mind to make up, so it can't be fickle. Also: in *fickle but dangerous,* the word *but* is wrong; Elena's "fickleness" helps make the storm dangerous. So *but* should be *and*—and *fickle* should be cast to the winds.

The stylebooks of leading newspapers say that for references to a hurricane, writers should use *it,* not *he* or *she*. And the Associated Press stylebook advises: "Do not use the presence of a woman's name as an excuse to attribute sexist images of women's behavior to a storm."

> **Hurricane Nele has apparently decided not to visit Hawaii.**

If that Nele had any sense, it would have decided to reserve space between a pineapple plantation and a macadamia grove.

> **Hurricane Gloria is still 550 miles out in the Atlantic, but already it's drawing a bead on the Outer Banks of North Carolina.**

"Drawing a bead"? Hurricanes can't aim. They're aimless (but not blameless).

Another script:

Hurricane Gloria first dropped anchor and came ashore overnight across the unprotected Outer Bank islands of North Carolina, almost a worst-possible-case scenario.

Trying to visualize that scene almost blew me away. When a ship drops anchor, it can't go anywhere. Not unless it weighs anchor. So how can a storm drop anchor and come ashore? How can a storm drop anchor at all? *Worst-possible-case scenario* seems to be an effort to pump up "worst-case scenario," which is bureaucratic jargon. But the sly *almost* says it's not the worst. And the weather-beaten word *scenario* is best left for Hollywood.

Hurricane Diana is on a collision course with the coast of North Carolina.

A car can hit a tree, but a car and a tree can't collide. Only moving objects collide. For objects to collide or to be on a collision course, they must both be moving. And to make that script correct, North Carolina would have to be coasting.

A mammoth hurricane in size and scope, but not the killer hurricane forecasters feared it might become.

Mammoth describes its size, so *size* adds nothing. If the writer used *scope* to mean "the area covered by an activity," as the dictionary defines it, then *mammoth* does the job alone. Better: "The hurricane is mammoth but not so mighty as forecasters had feared."

Her threat was more menacing than her power.

Threat = menace, so the sentence is windy double-talk.

This heavy-with-water hurricane dumped as much as 20 inches of rain on Puerto Rico.

Heavy-with-water hurricane? No one else would say it, and no one should write it. *Dumped rain* is journalese. And that's no compliment. So dump it.

Dolly is packing top winds of about 75 miles per [should be *an*] hour.

Packing winds is termed by the UPI stylebook as "low-grade journalese."

> **Those killer tornadoes, reminders that just because records
> are set doesn't mean the news is good.**

Who needs reminding that a record might relate to bad news? But the
writer does need reminding that there's no such thing as a "killer tor-
nado." Or a "killer cyclone" (though sci-fi does have "killer clones").
Storms have the means to kill, but no mind, no motive. Storms don't set
out with a hit list or malice aforethought. Storms *can* kill, but that doesn't
make them "killer storms." Likewise, there is no such thing as a "killer
wind," "killer hurricane," "killer typhoon" or, as a network newscaster
said, a "killer volcano." Just killjoys, killer whales and Kilkenny cats.

> **Vice President Bush will visit the strickened area to let the
> people of this state know the Administration's concern for
> their plight.**

Strickened? The writer meant *stricken.*

> **Officials along the Mississippi and Alabama coasts are
> trying to convince residents in the danger area to leave
> their homes.**

The writer has mistaken "convince" for "persuade." You *convince* someone *that* he should leave or *convince* him *of* the need to leave. But you
persuade him *to* leave.

> **As we said earlier, many people, thousands, have been
> evacuated, and, as we said earlier, the hotels also have been
> closed down. Now this is the first time in the history of
> Atlantic City that something like that has happened. Many
> schools are closed today, and, as we said. . . .**

If you've already said it, why say you've said it? And why keep saying
you've said it? Why, why, why? In the second sentence of the script, *now*
is meaningless. Also in the second sentence: What does *this is the first
time* refer to—the hotel closings? The extent of the evacuation? The magnitude of the storm? The script reminds me of what Abraham Lincoln
said about a long-winded politician: "That blower can compress the most
words in the fewest ideas of any man I ever knew."

> **The path that it's taking now is reminiscent of the storms
> that go way back in time to 1938 or so, the one that would affect
> central Long Island and southern New England. If it had
> gone maybe farther east, it would have missed some of
> those areas. But it's just hugging the coast now until it does
> that.**

That's what the man said, but what *did* he say?

> **Those kind of rains can be moving all the way up to
> northern New England.**

Make it *kinds.* And instead of *can,* make it *may.* We know the rains *can*—
that they have the ability. But *may* indicates a possibility.

"Words still count with me," the writer E. B. White often said. And
his words still count with writers, particularly the words in Strunk and
White's *The Elements of Style.* Even a quick rundown of the handbook's
topic headings is refreshing:

- Use the active voice.

- Put statements in positive form.

- Use definite, specific, concrete language.

- Avoid a succession of loose sentences.

- Express co-ordinate ideas in similar form.

- Keep related words together.

- Place the emphatic words of a sentence at the end.

- Place yourself in the background.

- Write in a way that comes naturally.

- Write with nouns and verbs.

- Revise and rewrite; avoid the use of qualifiers.

- Avoid fancy words.

- Do not inject opinion.

- Use figures of speech sparingly.

- Do not take short cuts at the cost of clarity.

- Avoid foreign languages.
- Prefer the standard to the offbeat.

And four topic headings that are especially apt for the writers and newscasters quoted in this column:

- Be clear.
- Do not overwrite.
- Do not overstate
- Omit needless words.

When we grasp all those points and apply them, *we*'ll have the elements of style.

Going Overboard

We often write too fast, think too slow, or know too little. How else could some of these snippets find their way onto the air?

He's a Soviet seaman who twice jumped ship near New Orleans.

In fact, he jumped overboard, so the best way to put it is, "He jumped *off* his ship." *Jump ship* is slang for "desert"; it also means to go ashore without permission. But some sailors do go ashore with permission, and then *jump ship.*

Ridge Shannon of Shawnee Mission, Kansas, tells me he heard a news report that the Soviet seaman had "*literally* jumped ship." In almost all cases, *literally* adds nothing to a sentence—except length. And *literally* should not be confused with *figuratively.* F'rinstance: "He *literally* hit the ceiling." He hit it *figuratively,* unless you're writing about Michael Jordan or Michelangelo.

How about *virtually?* Ridge asks. Many people use *virtually* to mean *almost.* But most careful writers use *virtually* to mean "in effect although not in fact." An assistant news director filling in for his boss, who's on indefinite leave, is *virtually* the N.D.

The American Museum of Folk Art is actually holding a contest for the best quilt in America. . . .

The sentence means the same without *actually. Literally.*

> **The devastation was so widespread and communications so
> bad that only tonight did it become clear that this is a very
> major disaster. . . .**

"*Very* major" is a solecism—an ungrammatical combination of words; an
intensifier *(very)* can't be used with a comparative. Writers should use
modifiers—reinforcing terms like *very, absolutely, certainly, definitely,
quite*—seldom. If you choose the right nouns and verbs, you probably
won't need modifiers. *Disaster* means large-scale destruction and death.
Is there ever a *minor* disaster?

In *The Penguin Dictionary of Troublesome Words,* Bill Bryson says
the *New York Times* was reporting a *major* initiative, a *major* undertaking,
a *major* speech, two *major* changes, a *major* operation and a *major* cause
on the same day the *Times* of London was reporting a *major* scandal, a
major change, two *major* improvements, two *major* steps, a *major* proposal, a *major* source of profits and a *major* refurbishment. Not to mention Prime Minister John Major.

Bryson, a former *Times* of London editor—born and educated in
Iowa—says: "*Major,* it seems, has become a major word. Generally im-
precise, frequently fatuous and always grossly overworked, it is in almost
every instance better replaced by a more expressive term." As far as I'm
concerned, and I *am* concerned, that's a major pronouncement. A network
evening newscast:

> **Tonight's _____ _____ _____ looks at the
> major overhaul of welfare signed into law today and the
> major questions it raises for recipients.**

Major is a major player in too many scripts. Remember: Where everything is major, nothing is major.

> **It is only possible to understand the enormity of what
> happened here by taking one case, one heartbreaking case
> at a time.**

The writer was talking about an earthquake, but *enormity* = great wick-
edness. He meant *enormousness*. Better: *immensity*.

> **Hospitals were filled to capacity.**

A redundancy. Fortunately, the writer didn't say some patients were "in
guarded condition." *Guarded* = cautious; only a doctor's prognosis can

be *guarded.* A patient can be in guarded condition only when he's a suspect under guard.

Another term we shouldn't borrow, one used by police reporters after an accident: "The two boys were *treated and released."* If they'd been kept in the hospital, we'd say they were *hospitalized.* Ever hear of anyone who has been "treated and hospitalized"? If you say the two boys were *treated,* that implies they were *released.* (The comedian George Carlin complains that whenever *he*'s treated, he's detained.)

> **The *final completion* of I-95 to the airport is a major step in making Philadelphia a modern city.**

Do you think the perpetrator of that redundancy should be *finalized?* And does a stretch of road make a city *modern?*

> **The three armed gunmen who have been holding court officials as hostages left the building and are at a nearby airport.**

Gunmen are men with guns, so those *armed gunmen* should be *dis*armed.

> **The F-B-I says that he's been given a safe haven in Cuba, along with a part of the stolen loot.**

Haven = a place of safety, so *safe* is unnecessary. *Loot* = stolen goods, so *stolen loot,* too, is redundant.

A keen wordwatcher, the former CBS Newsie Emerson Stone, recalls another odd redundancy, a superfluous suffix: A computer expert said her company had simplified its computer's keyboard. And she added, "We wanted to eliminate jargonese."

> **The stock market's been flying higher for months, breaking one new record after another and racking up profits for investors big and small of 201 billion dollars.**

New record is an old redundancy. The total value of all Big Board stocks traded that year was 970 billion dollars, but there's no way of determining what the aggregate profits were. Only the individual investor knows whether the sale of her stock was profitable. If she sold for less than she paid, she wasn't racking up profits. The value of her stock might have increased, but if she didn't sell, she couldn't make a profit. The reporter didn't specify how many days it took to reach that "201 billion," a sum that strikes me as bogus.

He said his personal secretary and her cohorts have left the Rajneesh organization 55 million dollars in debt.

A *cohort* is not a crony, a consort or a colleague; a cohort, originally a large unit of Roman soldiers, is used to describe a group with the same characteristic(s), such as the cohort of people born in 1965.

After months of wrangling over which oxes should be gored on the horns of tax reform, the House Ways and Means Committee, after voting down a G-O-P alternative, approved a Democratic rewrite of the nation's tax code.

Oxes should be *oxen,* and they should be gored no more, especially by *the horns of tax reform*—whatever that is, or they are.

Each player admitted that Strong was not the only source of their drugs and that their cocaine use had been extensive.

Someone can admit his own use of drugs, but he can't *admit* anyone else's. *Each* is singular, so *their* should be changed to *his.*

A devastating fire early this morning swept through a stable at the famed Belmont race track. . . .

The story isn't about the celebrity or obscurity of Belmont. It's about the 45 horses killed in the fire. And scratch *famed.* It's a headline word, not a conversational word. *Famous* is conversational but a good word to avoid in newswriting. *Famous* means "widely known." And if a place is widely known, it needn't be called *famous.* Besides, if a listener never heard of a place, calling it *famous* won't help him or the story.

Something of a royal sendoff today for Prince Charles and Princess Diana as they left swanky Palm Beach, Florida, for London.

Something in me not fond of an incomplete sentence like that one. Something in me not fond of *something of a.* Something else: please, no *swanky-panky. Swanky* smacks of gushy gossip columnists. In the same breathless bag: *posh, pricey, deluxe, ritzy, glitzy, glittery* and *glammy.* Also *chi-chi* (sounds like a panda). A Canadian newsie, John McFadyen, told me, with a wink (I think), that Americans should use *royal sendoff* only when writing about the Boston Tea Party or the American Revolution.

Police in New York City are looking for a trio of thieves who robbed a subway token booth early this morning.

They were not a *trio,* even though they did act in concert.

A pair of U.S. warships is on patrol in the Gulf of Oman, monitoring radio frequencies, ready to escort any cargo vessel that calls for help.

Ships don't come in pairs.

Last week in Congress, a surprise upset for President Reagan.

Sometimes an incomplete sentence or sentence fragment works—but that one doesn't. *Surprise upset* is redundant; an upset *is* a surprise. Also: Did the President score an upset or did someone upset him? The meaning would have been unambiguous if the writer had said "an upset *by,*" instead of "an upset *for.*"

Almost 500 alleged Mafioso are on trial.

The plural is *Mafiosi.* Contrariwise, don't use the plural *graffiti* when you mean only one *graffito.* Or the plural *paparazzi* when you mean one *paparazzo.* And remember that *kudos* exists only in that form. But don't use *kudos* in a script—and never *kudo,* kiddo.

And in Great Britain, the media takes the unofficial holiday quite seriously.

Media is the plural of *medium,* and no matter who says *media is,* and no matter how many say it, it's wrong. The media *are,* data *are* and phenonema *are.* That's the way it is.

13

THE "Ing" THING
(AND OTHER WRONG THINGS)

A reader writes: "A question about a trend I find disturbing in news-writing. I'd like your opinion. I hear more and more stories leading with something like the next couple of examples:

> " 'President Clinton and Russian President Yeltsin signing an important trade deal today. The President saying it's a good deal for the U-S and Russia. . . .'

> " 'British Prime Minister John Major deciding to talk to the I-R-A. Opposition leaders calling the move a disaster. . . .' "

The reader, Cameron Knowles of WSGW-AM, Saginaw, Michigan, goes on to say: "I think the writers are trying to eliminate the use of the conjugated form of the verb 'to be'—*is, are,* etc. I think the use is grammatically incorrect. What's the word, Mr. Block?"

Ungrammatical. Not only ungrammatical, but also unnatural, unconversational, unjournalistic and unjustifiable. Literate adults don't talk like that. Literate children don't, either. But toddlers learning to talk do talk like that: "Mommy going out?" And Mommy or Daddy might reply: "Yes, mommy *is* going out." Without thinking about it, a grownup speaks correctly by inserting *is.* Unless that grownup lapses into baby-talk.

If you take the subway in New York City, you can hear people *ing*ing in the train: "My brother going to that game." When people speak that way, you figure they're new to our country and haven't learned basic English yet. Or else they're school drop-outs—or push-outs.

Literate speakers of English aren't always able to recite the rules of grammar, or parse a sentence (let alone diagram one), or explain why they say what they say the way they say it. But they know, almost instinctively, from speaking English all their lives, from hearing it spoken, from going to school, and from reading books, magazines and newspapers, they know that those examples offered by Cameron are wrong.

In the first example, *signing,* a participle with no helping verb (like *is*) in front of it is an adjective. A verb has three basic tenses: past, present and future. Tense tells us whether an action has already taken place, is now taking place, or will be taking place. If the first example had used *signed,* or *is signing,* or *will sign,* it would help clue in the listener.

A participle is called a verbal, but it's not a verb. So the sentence fragments in Cameron's examples lack the one element that has the power to drive a sentence: a verb. No one can make a sentence go without a verb. No one. Not Hercules, not Houdini, not even Hillary.

Some listeners would assume *signing* in the example is the start of an adjectival phrase set off by commas, and they'd wait for the sentence to be completed by what grammarians call the predicate—and what Paul Niwa of CNBC calls the meat and potatoes. Perhaps those listeners would expect the sentence to end like this: "agreed to meet again tomorrow." Yet the way that example is written, listeners haven't the slightest clue whether the two presidents have already signed, are signing this very moment, or will be signing.

So let's supply verbs and convert those examples into sentences that make sense: "President Clinton and Russian President Yeltsin signed an important trade deal today. Mister Clinton says it's a good deal for the United States and Russia." We should be aware that we need a *where* soon and insert the name of the place where the signing occurred. But at least we've translated that example from *Ing*lish into English. Now let's do the same for the second example: "British Prime Minister John Major has decided to talk to the I-R-A. But opposition leaders call the move a disaster."

The spread of the *ing* thing is what the grammarian H.W. Fowler might have called the survival of the unfittest. What impels writers to *ing* it? Probably a feeling that it makes news sound more newsy, more streamlined, more even-as-I-speak. But as we can see and hear (from the *ing*ing in our ears), *ing* is the wrong thing.

Ing Spots

If you keep hearing an *ing*ing in your ears, it may be because some newscasts carry more Ings than buses in Beijing. (Ng, a common Chinese name, is usually pronounced by Americans as *Ing*.)

> *Raising* clenched fists and *singing* freedom songs,
> 20-thousand blacks are *gathering* for a mass funeral in a
> segregated South African township. Police are out in force,
> but there has been no trouble. 29 victims of racial unrest
> are *being* buried. . . .

Instead of telling us at the outset who or what the story is about, the writer starts with a participial phrase and slides in low gear to another participle. Those preliminary participles conceal the subject and leave us baffled. The weakness of that first sentence is compounded by the lack of a finite verb, one with a tense.

The second sentence is puny because it rests on *are* and *has been;* both are linking verbs and forms of *to be. Are* is in the active voice but expresses no action, so it's static. *But* is incorrect; it implies that what is to follow changes course or is contrary to what might be expected. If police are plentiful, I don't expect trouble. It seems more logical to write, "Police are out in force, *so* there has been no trouble." But we can't use *so* because we can't know for sure the reason there has been no trouble.

The third sentence of the story says *victims of racial unrest* are *being buried*—as if it's being done now. Yet the first sentence said people were *raising* fists, *singing* songs and *gathering* for the funeral. Could all four of those activities be going on simultaneously?

Let's assume the victims were "*going* to be buried" and rewrite the opening: "A mass funeral in South Africa has drawn a crowd of 20-thousand blacks. As they gathered for the burial of 29 blacks, killed in riots [?], the mourners sang freedom songs and raised their fists."

Let's look at another network weakling: It bounces from *ing* to *ing* like the cartoon character Gerald McBoing-Boing:

> A U-S Supreme Court *ruling* today that could affect
> millions of workers nationwide, a *ruling* that states may
> force employers to provide particular kinds of benefits in
> their company insurance plans, for instance, *requiring*
> mental health, alcohol or drug abuse services.

The subject—a ruling that could affect millions—isn't followed by a verb. An incomplete sentence works occasionally, but that sentence, which is the entire item, is too long and confusing. And it needs more than downsizing.

When you were reading *a ruling that states,* didn't you think—for an instant—that *states* was a verb? In that script, the first two *ing* words are nouns, the third is a participle. But whether an *ing* word is a participle (an adjectival form derived from a verb), a gerund (a nounlike form), or a noun, some writers often use them in threes and fours.

Here's a script from the Midwest:

> **U-S Agriculture Secretary Richard Lyng spent the *morning* in Buffalo County, *eating* breakfast in Gibbon and *talking* with community leaders there and *visiting* two Buffalo County farms.**

Is there something in a writer's first *ing* that triggers a mechanism that sends a stream of *ing*s cascading into his copy? Just asking.

This script comes from elsewhere:

> **President Reagan and his wife, Nancy, are *continuing* their August vacation in Southern California, but correspondent _____ _____ is *saying* the president and his wife are *taking* a break from the routine of the presidential ranch near Santa Barbara.**

News reflects change, so I keep saying that *continues* or *continuing* is an unsatisfactory word to use in a lead because it tells the listener that whatever has been going on is still going on.

That lead-in implies that the correspondent is going around saying something. And saying it and saying it. And in the next lead-in, the same writer keeps doing it:

> **Big-city mayors from across the country are *meeting* in New York City *talking* about drug-*trafficking*. And correspondent _____ _____ is *saying* a great deal of attention is *being* paid to the latest drug fad, the *smoking* of crack.**

One possible explanation for writers' *ing*-ing is that they want to tell listeners that events are going on at this very moment, even as we're speaking, and they think *ing* imparts immediacy. An occasional *ing* may add zing, but a cluster cloys. And makes a story soft, ungrammatical, illogical or false.

One of the most disagreeable of all *ing*s is the mistaken use of a participle as the main verb in a sentence, as in this network lead-in:

> **Japan's transport minister today ordering inspections of all Boeing 747's now in use in the country. . . .**

On the same newscast, another leaden lead-in:

Pope John Paul *continuing* **his visit to Africa with a stopover in Zaire.**

Writers who lean on *ing* may not be Ingbats, but they ought to ditch that feeble *Ing*lish.

Put in a Good Word

"Words without thoughts never to heaven go," said Shakespeare. And scripts without thought, or enough thought, barely get off the ground. So let's look at a few scripts whose writers should have had second thoughts:

A Florida man is in custody tonight . . . charged with threatening President Clinton's life. Ronald Gene Barbour . . . an unemployed limousine driver from Orlando was arrested and indicted yesterday. [As soon as we find out he was arrested yesterday, we realize *is in custody tonight* is even weaker than the ordinary *is . . . tonight,* because he has been in custody since last night. The news is: an alleged aspiring assassin has been collared.

[That script was broadcast in California, so why start by mentioning a place (Florida) all the way across the continent? Also, how does the suspect rate three names? And why do so many broadcast writers commit copycat crimes by using middle names for serial killers and Presidential assassins?]

Investigators say Barbour planned to kill the President during one of his jogging runs. And he [*Barbour?*] **went to Washington, D.C., in mid-January, staying in this Virginia motel. But during that same period, Mr. Clinton was on a nine-day European trip. Police say Barbour returned to Florida without ever getting close to the President.**

If the arrest was made public today, it would be better to cut to the catch: "An unemployed limo driver has been charged with threatening the life of President Clinton. Investigators [Secret Service agents?] have arrested Ronald Barbour of Orlando, Florida. He was taken into custody [where?] yesterday. Barbour allegedly intended to kill the President when he was jogging. So, in mid-January, Barbour went to Washington. But the President was in Europe."

How did investigators learn of the alleged plan? If the writer's source material didn't say why the suspect wanted to kill the President, the writer should have added, "No word yet why the suspect allegedly wanted to kill the President." Which leads to another question: How was the suspect allegedly going to do the job? With a gun? A club? An ax? (Just axing.)

Police are investigating the death of of a young man from Brooklyn killed in a spray of gunfire. A gunman opened fire on 17-year-old Dupree Bennett around 10:30 last night at 14-hundred East New York avenue. [*Police are investigating* is one of the weakest leads in creation (you're right; it's not at all creative). If the police do not investigate a fatal shooting, you've got yourself a strong lead. But in this case, the lead is the shooting itself. And if the story is getting a little stale, perhaps: "Police are searching for a (fill in the blank) in the fatal shooting of a Brooklyn man."

[Any wrongdoer who *opened fire* is, by definition, a gunman, so you don't want to say *gunman* there, especially so soon after *gunfire*. Instead of *gunman,* perhaps you could insert a few specifics: "a young man" or "a man in his mid-20s." Or whatever the facts justify.] **Bennett was brought** [should be *taken*] **to Brookdale Hospital suffering from at least four bullet wounds. He died a short time later.** [Better: "He was shot at least four times."] **An unidentified woman, also injured in the incident, was shot in the leg.** [Better: "And a woman was shot in the leg." No need to say she was injured. If she was shot, she was *wounded*. People are *wounded* when they're injured by a weapon—shot, stabbed, hit by shrapnel, or stung by a critic.] **Police are investigating whether the woman knew Bennett or the gunman or whether she was an innocent bystander. Police are still searching for the gunman.**

Bystanders, passersby or victims aren't *innocent*. Describing any of them as innocent is journalese. And no strangers are *perfect*. Why did the shooter shoot? If the writer can't find out, perhaps she can say, "Police say they don't know why the [so-and-so] fired."

Louisiana lawmakers have hit a major stumbling block in the effort to redraw the state's congressional districts. His name is State Senator David Cain of Dry Creek, and he....

His name is David Cain, not Senator David Cain. *Major stumbling block?* Ever hear of a *minor* stumbling block (besides this one)?

> Two Illinois men have been charged with transporting over
> 200 pounds of marijuana after their car was stopped for
> speeding near Joplin.

How could they transport marijuana *after* being stopped?

> Once again today, the situation in Somalia is capturing the
> national spotlight.

The national electrician should pull the plug on *the national spotlight*.
And cart it to the junkyard for rusty clichés.

> Everyone seems to be talking about Japan at the moment.
> Correspondent _____ _____ reports that the
> country really isn't ready for the spotlight.

Have *you* been talking about Japan? Why *at the moment?* How can a
nation be in a spotlight—or under a microscope?

> And January's earthquake caused so much damage to a
> historic Los Angeles church that it went under the wrecking
> ball today.

Sounds as if the church had been jacked up, moved onto rollers, then
pushed along until it passed under a wrecking ball. In any case, *went
under a wrecking ball* is vintage journalese. It's akin to saying that a
surgery patient *went under the knife.* Better: "And January's earthquake
caused so much damage to an old Los Angeles church that today a wrecking crew tore it down."

> A huge winter storm has much of the United States in a
> frozen grip of ice, snow and sub-zero freezing winds. . . .
> Some tough New Yorkers bundled up and braved the brutal
> elements. . . .

The writer deserves an "A" for alliteration and an "I" for illiteration. All
sub-zero winds are freezing. *Frozen* and *freezing* shouldn't be used in the
same sentence, at least not that sentence. *Brutal elements* sounds like more
journalese. And don't credit people who go out in storms for "braving" the
weather. That's not bravery; it's probably either necessity or stupidity.
    And a lead from a city news wire:

> A Los Angeles man was shot and killed today in a fight
> that broke out between two buildings.

Skyscrappers?

As we see from those examples, a script can easily get on air, yet never to heaven go.

Drop Your Weapons

"No man prospers so suddenly as by others' errors," said the 17th century English philosopher Francis Bacon. So prepare to prosper. Just stand back, sit back or lie back, and let prosperity swamp you. But you must pay a price: take a gander at these excerpts from broadcast scripts. Warning: Sensitive readers may find them too graphic.

> **The attorney for defendant Henry Watson dropped a bombshell in his closing argument.**

Don't let anyone drop a bombshell (or a blockbuster), especially in a crowded courtroom. *Drop a bombshell* is a cliché. So is *fired the opening shot*. Even if you're *armed to the teeth,* don't wander into Clichéville. You might set off a *booby trap,* bumble into a *minefield,* or stumble into a *powder keg* or *walking time bomb.* This is no time for you to *bite the dust.* One problem with clichés is, they no longer *pack a wallop.*

While we're at it, let's be on the alert for several clichés that have been worn thinner than a gnat's yawn: *state-of-the-art, the cutting edge* and *pushing the envelope* (unless you're writing about a mail clerk).

> **City officials and union leaders have been burning the midnight oil.**

The only place they *burn midnight oil* is Clichéville.

> **The workers were visibly shaken but not hurt.**

Visibly shaken is journalese. That's the thoughtless, cliché-clotted language of newspeople churning out copy in a race against the clock.

> **Outside, people wait for hours to be treated, and tempers flare when others try to cut in line.**

Don't let *tempers flare;* just write with flair. Sure, we see *tempers flared* (and *tensions mounted*) in print. And we hear on the air that hoary hackspeak all the time. In fact, that's the best argument against it.

> **Lopez was sitting with friends on a courtyard bench at the Marlboro Houses in Coney Island when shots rang out Sunday.**

Resist the cliché *shots rang out.* At least, *give it a shot.*

> **They suggest shaving 33 percent from the paychecks of fire and police department recruits.**

That's not a shave, that's an amputation. Better: *slicing.* Or *chopping.*

> **Inside the city limits . . . in Charlotte's Hidden Valley neighborhood, 23-year-old Thomas Gaddy died after being shot in the head. Police say it happened around midnight following an argument.**

That's the complete script, but it's incomplete. Who shot Gaddy? Who *was* Gaddy? Who was arguing with him? Why? Inside or outside? Clues? And why not use *after* instead of *following?* When you mean *after,* say *after*—if you follow me.

> **She points out that, in her view** [*point out* should be used to point to a fact, not an opinion], **the country is having some difficulty adjusting to a working woman in the role of First Lady. This came up during the presidential campaign between she and Mrs. Bush, as you'll recall.**

Someone should point out to that network anchor that *between* is a preposition. And when a preposition (*about, after, against, at, before, between, by, for, from, in, of, on, over, to, upon, with* and others) precedes a personal pronoun *(she),* the pronoun must be in the objective case *(her).* It's not optional. It's not subject to a vote in the newsroom. It's a must.

Every newscaster can keep a good reference book at his elbow and be an instant grammarian. If you're unsure when to shift from the nominative case to the objective case, try *A Pocket Guide to Correct Grammar.* You can buy it from the publisher, Barron's, at (800) 645-3476. Price: $5.95. You know what they say, "Look it up, you'll remember it longer. Screw it up, and you'll remember it forever."

> **That Bronx couple who allegedly killed their four-year-old daughter has now been charged with murder.**

Has they? Should be "*have* now been charged." A couple is two persons, and they are *they.*

Is it ever correct to use *couple* with a singular verb? Yes, when the two are regarded as a unit: "The couple in the last row is the one we want down front." When you refer to a couple of books or a couple of bucks, *couple* must be joined to the noun with *of.*

> **Texas Rangers are taking over the investigation of a shoot-
> out last night between Rusk County sheriff's deputies and
> an elderly Rusk County man. The deputies were trying
> to serve mental commitment papers to [should be *on*] 62-
> year-old Jarvis Welch when the shooting started. . . .**

Elderly at 62? Most 62-year-olds would resent being called elderly. The 62s probably think of themselves as middle-aged (even though there are few 124-year-olds).

> **Remember those American helicopters shot down by
> friendly fire over Iraq in April? Well, today
> _____ News has confirmed details of a classified
> Pentagon report on the cause of the tragedy, and
> _____'s _____ _____ has more on it tonight.**

Well, I did remember—that morning's *New York Times* with its page 1 piece that broke the story of the Pentagon report. The TV reporter did a fine job of boiling down the main points. And 50 seconds into her package, she said the families of those killed learned about the report from that day's *Times*. And I also remember that Ed Bliss doesn't like *has more*. He says *has more* is uninformative and unimaginative.

So what's wrong with the network's handling of the story? Mainly, the use of the word *confirmed*. That day, when the network confirmed the *Times* story (ascertaining that it was true), the net could then have gone ahead and reported it as fact. No need to credit the *Times*. No need for *confirmed*. Isn't *everything* we broadcast confirmed—verified, validated, authenticated or substantiated? Should be.

Reporting is finding facts and determining whether various bits of information, including rumors, are factual. If we can't confirm an item, we don't broadcast it. Except for unusual circumstances, we don't say on the air that we've confirmed something. Confirmation is a given. If we can't check it out, we chuck it out.

Cleaning up after the Storm

The greatest of faults is to be conscious of none. Thomas Carlyle said it, so you and I can help humanity, or at least a few writers, by looking at this script—reprinted in its entirety—and tagging its faults:

At least 45 people are confirmed dead after a strong earthquake hit the island of Mindoro [*earthquake locator full screen*] in the Philippines.

[As long as those people are *confirmed dead,* they're dead for sure. No need for *confirmed.* But it's not news to say people *are* dead. Billions of people *are* dead. *Are* expresses no action, so it's half dead. If 45 people have been killed, you don't need to describe the quake as strong. That speaks for itself. Rarely do we report foreign quakes that are no great shakes.

[In the first sentence of that script—broadcast on major-market morning television—the elements are presented in the wrong sequence: what's told after *after* should be switched with what's told before *after.* That's usually the case in spot-news stories when you find *after* in the first sentence.

[Also, the writer started with a number, which is a poor way to go. It's preferable to set the scene and tell what caused the deaths so that when you reach the number at the end, you'll reach the high point of the sentence and stop.

[Rather than ending the sentence with words that lack strength or importance, try my version: "An earthquake in the Philippines has killed 45 people." The rewrite tells listeners promptly where the story occurred. The original script might cause listeners to think the quake was in their area, and they wouldn't learn otherwise until the end of the sentence, when they would discover it's far away.]

The quake struck at 3:15 a.m. and had a moment magnitude of seven-point-one. [Was it 3:15 a.m. in the Philippines or in the studio? When we report the time, we use *our* local time. And if we're talking about another time zone, we say so. But why report the time anywhere, unless it has significance? Like the eleventh hour of the eleventh day of the eleventh month—the start of the Armistice in World War I. Or 7:55 a.m., Sunday, December 7, 1941.

[*Moment magnitude?* I've never heard that term. Have you? *Moment magnitude* could be common among seismologists, but it doesn't register with me. And probably not with most listeners.]

The epicenter is 75 miles south of Manila. [*Epicenter* is used so often that it may now be acceptable. But it's more understandable if you say, "The quake was centered 75 miles south of Manila."]

However, no damage or injuries were reported in the capitol city. [*However* isn't a good word to use on the air. *But* is better—and two syllables shorter. Also: report the dead and injured first—people before property!—unless the damage is great and casualties few.

[*Capitol* with a small *c* is a building where a state legislature meets. The writer means *capital*—with two *a*'s. But because a capital *is* a city, it's redundant to refer to a "capital city." (It's also incorrect to refer, as some newscasters do, to "the capital of Manila," as if Manila had its own capital.) The misspelling of *capital* is of no great moment, but when competent editors see a misspelling, they wonder: "Is that writer unlettered or careless? If careless, is he also careless—and couldn't care less—about other facts?"

[When you stop to think about it, which is always a good idea, why report the *absence* of injuries or damage in Manila? Manila is so far from the action—on another island—that I wouldn't expect any effect there.

[It's best to focus on what happened, not what didn't happen. With exceptions. If a prominent bride or bridegroom doesn't show up for the wedding, the no-show is news. And it may be worth mentioning if a dog at the scene of a crime failed to bark.]

The earthquake leveled several villages on Mindoro, destroying nearly 200 homes. [Better: "The quake flattened several villages on Mindoro and destroyed almost 200 homes." Why the rewrite? *Flattened* has more power than *leveled*. And *destroyed,* a verb with a tense, has more impact than *destroying,* which is a participle (not a verb). *Almost,* Ed Bliss once told me, is easier for newscasters to sink their teeth into than *nearly,* which is best used for physical proximity. After you use *earthquake,* you can shift down to *quake*. But don't use the obscure *temblor* or, as some writers mistakenly put it, *trembler.*]

Many of the dead were swept away by a tidal wave. [Does that mean some people were killed by the wave or does it mean that people were already dead when they were swept away? Swept into a paddy? Or swept out to sea?]

Officials say 133 people have been hospitalized with severe injuries. [With all the confusion inherent in a disaster, the number of injured seems too precise. Although officials provided that total, I would modify it: "Officials say more than 130 people have been hurt severely." I'd forget about *hospitalized;* I assume people hurt severely would be hospitalized. Any time the severely injured are *not* hospitalized, you might be able to add, "But hospitals are so crowded, the injured were turned away."]

Mindoro is still recovering from a typhoon last month.
[Wrong tense. It *had been* recovering—until today's quake.]

The storm destroyed most of the island's coconut and rice crops.

This last sentence is interesting, perhaps, but is it newsworthy for *us?* Is Mindoro the world's only source of coconuts? Is it even a major source? Is the crop of any consequence at all? And how important is it for us over here—at least 7,200 miles away—to know about it? When the typhoon hit Mindoro last month, was the loss of crops reported on the air at that station? If so, is there any need to report it again? If it wasn't reported, is there a compelling need to report it now? (Shouldn't the coconut trees have withstood the storm? As William S. Gilbert said, coconuts are husky.)

That quake script should have given an editor bad vibes. The editor should have strolled over to the writer, told him he was on shaky ground, pointed out the script's faults and returned the script for rewriting. All would benefit: writer, editor and listeners.

The actress Lillian Gish said: "I like people to come back and tell me what I did wrong. That's the kindest thing you can do."

Finally

WordWatchers of the world, mount your watchtowers and go on watch. As these broadcast scripts file past us, be alert for faulty copy:

Still to come tonight, a plan to test every student at an unnamed university for the AIDS virus.

Is any university without a name? What the writer means is "an *unidentified* university."

The visit of a foreign dignitary is usually accompanied by much pomp and circumstance [a stale expression] **as well as a mutual exchange of culture, traditions and ideas.** [*Mutual* exchange? In contrast to a unilateral exchange?] **When commentator _____ _____'s first-grade class received such a visitor recently, they rolled out the red carpet in their own special way.**

Rolling out the red carpet is a threadbare cliché.

> **Several law enforcement agencies are forming a joint task force to apprehend fugitives in Minneapolis and throughout the state. The unit is concentrating on apprehending fugitives who are responsible for committing violent crimes such as murder, assault and robbery. Hennepin County Sheriff Don Omodt says since the task force began operating last month, it's apprehended 53 fugitives.**

The writer is infatuated with the verb *apprehend*. But more listeners would comprehend him if he used *find, catch, arrest* or *track down*. The writer is probably the sort who says *altercation* when he means *fight*.

> **In medical news today, a warning from the Food and Drug Administration to an estimated 23-thousand people who may be walking around with defective artificial heart valves.**

The opening phrase—*In medical news*—is typical of many transitions that should be deleted, excised or circumcised. They're a waste of words. No listener would think the item is sports. Better: "A warning to people with artificial heart valves that may be faulty. The government says. . . ." An incomplete sentence like that *is* acceptable on occasion; and this has just been declared an occasion. In the rewrite, why *faulty* instead of the original script's *defective? Faulty* is shorter and more easily understood.

Without hearing *In medical news,* any listener who's at least semi-conscious can tell that network script is medical news. The same for *In business news, In national news, In foreign news.* Some listeners are not interested in medical news, so as soon as they hear that transition, they head elsewhere. They're more likely to listen, though, if the first words are *a warning.*

> **Turning elsewhere now, it happened in Haltom City, Texas. . . .**

Isn't almost every story from elsewhere? (Where else?)

> **Still overseas, Kuwait opened its border with Iraq. . . .**

Still overseas? Hasn't Kuwait *always* been overseas?

> **And back home, one of the Republican party's most prominent senators is trying to put out a political firestorm.**

Not in *my* home. Or in my hometown. Or anywhere near me. Which is why *and back home* is misleading. *Closer to home* is another confusing transition—and a cliché to boot. *Firestorm* is almost always overheated, as is *putting out political fires,* even if they're *spreading like wildfire.* If a writer can cast off all the clichés clogging his cranium, he can start to turn out clear, crisp copy. *She,* too. (And me, too.)

> **In recreation, do you go to Atlantic City only to spend your days and nights in the casinos?**

In recreation? As squirrelly transitions go, that one is nutty.

> **Finally tonight, if you've ever left a movie thinking, 'I could have written a better ending than that,' well, pay attention. High technology is taking moviemaking out of the hands of the** [no need for the second definite article, definitely not] **Hollywood producers and. . . .**

Finally, why do some writers preface the last item in a newscast with *finally?* All it does is signal listeners that the important news has been told and now they're probably going to hear fluff. Which makes it all right for *them* to sign off.

Pay attention? What about listeners afflicted with attention-deficit disorder? Doesn't *pay attention* suggest that listeners have *not* been paying attention? Please don't tell listeners to do this or do that—especially to *pay attention.* It's all right if you're talking to kindergarteners; their attention wanders. But speaking to adults that way is uncalled for—unless you're a drill sergeant. If your scripts are interesting, listeners needn't be told to listen. They *want* to listen. And to pay attention.

As for "Stay with us," it's unbecoming for a newscaster to plead with listeners to stay tuned. Wouldn't you frown if, part-way down this page, I urged readers, "Stay with me." Wouldn't you say to yourself, "This guy has no class. If he were saying something worthwhile, I'd stay with him to the end. Gladly."

> **The Internal Revenue Service is apparently not on top of anyone's popularity list** [*really?*] **as the deadline for filing income taxes fast approaches.**

That's the first sentence of a script reporting the results of a new poll. Well, opinion polls may be new, but they're seldom news. And it isn't news that the IRS isn't overly popular. But the IRS may be at the top of *someone*'s popularity list, perhaps the Commissioner's.

The script says 64 percent of Americans think the IRS abuses its power, at least some of the time. Is 64 percent higher or lower than in the last such poll? Without that information, the raw percentage is almost meaningless. With it, it's barely better. Don't people everywhere think tax collectors abuse their power? In any case, that script had no basis for its assertion about the popularity list; the poll didn't ask people who's on their list—assuming they have one. Besides, who cares?

He was the first black artist to successfully become a national singing star popular with both black and white fans.

Can anyone become a national star *un*successfully?

One person is lucky enough today to say I quit to their boss.

Even if that one person has multiple personalities, *their* should be *his* or *her.*

A network newscast:

As expected [by whom?] **and as we reported he** [who *he?*] **would do last night, Steve Forbes did drop his bid today for the G-O-P presidential nomination and endorsed Bob Dole, but not before delivering one last pitch for his version of a flat tax.**

Yes, network news—and not up to expectations: all in one substandard sentence.

If Forbes's withdrawal *had been* expected, why mention reporting it previously? It certainly wasn't anything to brag about. (Don't brag—unless you lack confidence.) Forbes's name should have been used before the pronoun *he.* And to avoid ambiguity, *last night* should have followed the word *reported.* Otherwise, the sentence could mean the newscast reported the story last night *or* Forbes was expected to withdraw last night. Maybe that serpentine, substandard sentence *can* be justified, because, as they say, "If something is not worth doing, it's not worth doing well."

Having a Word with Writers

"He that loveth correction loveth knowledge."

That motto adorns Mother Teresa's orphanage in Calcutta. But we don't need to be orphans to benefit from the message. That motto should inspire *us:* fair writers who want to become good—and good writers who want to become better. So welcome to the House of Correction.

The first writer who needs correction is this WordWatcher himself. In a recent column, I corrected a flawed script, and Scott Libin of the Poynter Institute pointed out one flaw I had overlooked. The script said that when a first-grade class had received a prominent visitor, "they rolled out the red carpet." I commented that I wouldn't let anyone *roll out a red carpet,* a threadbare cliché.

But Scott noted that the collective noun *class* should take a singular pronoun, *it,* not *they.* A collective noun is singular when all the members of the group are being referred to collectively. But rather than say "*it* rolled out the carpet," I'd put people into the script and substitute *pupils* for *it.* Scott, go to the head of the class.

Now something less painful: *other* people's lapses—and collapses. Two items that ran on a local newscast:

City police say 13-year-old Dominic Lawson was hit by a stray shot last evening [why not *night?* maybe it happened at 5 p.m.] **when an argument between two men resulted in one shooting at the other near the intersection of Fayette and Monroe Streets. Lawson is in stable condition at Johns Hopkins hospital.**

The news in a story like this is not the police. Or what they say or do. If we have confidence in our police sources, we should go ahead and report the news without the opening attribution. Not in every type of crime, but I'd be content to accept the police account of this one.

The news is: "A 13-year-old boy was shot and wounded last evening by a stray shot. . . ." The reference to *Lawson* seems stiff. We usually refer to a child by his first name. Where was he wounded? Arm? Leg? Slightly wounded? Severely? Had he been standing outside his home? What grade is he in? Did he know the two men who were arguing? Arguing about what? Was the shooter arrested? *Near the intersection of Fayette and Monroe Streets* can be reduced to "near Fayette and Monroe Streets."

A common—and wrong—way to start a story like this: "Police are investigating the shooting of a 13-year-old boy." Any time police *refuse* to investigate, you'll have yourself a lead *and* a lead story.

Next in that newscast:

Police also say about 40 rounds were fired from two cars in a drive-by shooting in East Baltimore around 10 p.m. Three

**people were hit, and one of them, who witnesses say was
only 15 years old, was pronounced dead where he fell at
North Avenue and Hope Street.**

The number of rounds fired is not the news. Nor is the number of
people shot. The news is the boy shot dead. And that should precede the
previous item about a boy wounded. Another pronouncement: Avoid
writing that people were *pronounced dead.*

Not only did the writer bury the lead, but he also wrote his scripts
poorly. His scripts have too many holes. If the police know the number of
shots fired, they should know whether the victim was a boy or girl. And
they should know the name. Where was the teen standing, on the side-
walk? What about the other two victims? What's the extent of their
wounds? Were the three people who were shot together? Were the people
in the cars firing at the same person(s), or were they firing at each other?

Still another target for correction has been suggested by Scott Libin:
scripts that say the police are searching for a suspect. Scott reminds writers that when someone commits a crime, the police are *not* looking for a
"suspect"; they're looking for the person who did it, the culprit.

Next case, from Boston:

Remember Shawn Eckardt? [Why ask a question that
probably gets a "no" answer? Why ask a question at all?
Huh?] **The would-be bodyguard of Stoneham**
[Massachusetts] **figure skater Nancy Kerrigan? Well, he got
out of prison today** [where?]. **He was the last of those
convicted of plotting the knee-whacking** [if you're going to
be word-making, you've got to create something that fills a
need and isn't headshaking-making] **to be set free. The assault
was designed** [*intended*] **to remove Kerrigan from the 1994
U-S figure skating championships. Eckhardt** [I don't know
how Shawn, or Shaun, or Sean, spells his first name, but I
do know that his last name shouldn't be spelled *two* ways in
one script; spelling does matter: If the name has an "h," it may
affect pronunciation. And the writer shouldn't try to defend
himself by quoting Mark Twain: "I never trust a man who can
spell a word only one way."] **was asked if he'd learned**
[learned what?] **while in stir** [*in stir* is too slangy for
broadcast]. **Upon release, the 300-pound Eckardt's first
priority** [a dangling modifier: his *priority* wasn't released] **was
'to get something to eat.' He called prison food 'indescribable**
[shocking!],**' so he went to a restaurant and ordered
biscuits and gravy** [fascinating; yeah, right]. **He'd spent
15 months in the Oregon State penitentiary for racketeering.**

But the deadliest sin is that the writer made a factual error: In the second sentence, he refers to the man as a would-be (why *would-be?*) bodyguard to Nancy Kerrigan. Correct: Tonya Harding.

Whoever put—or allowed—those scripts on the air (writers, editors, producers, anchors) should be sentenced to one to three years in journalism school—without possibility of early release. Or else serve an indefinite sentence in the House of Correction. With me.

A Script Fit for a Crypt

This script ran on a morning newscast:

> **Circus crowds watched in horror as a nine-thousand-pound elephant crushed her trainer to death, then took off thru the streets of Hawaii.**
>
> **The 21-year-old elephant was shot, then given a lethal injection.**
>
> **Officials say she was probably spooked by a new circus worker.**

If you were news director at that major-market television station, how would you react to the script?

1. Would you be so pleased that you'd toss the writer a luau?
2. Would *you* get spooked and rush through the newsroom like a rogue elephant in *musth,* and smash everything in your path?
3. Would you give the writer a lethal injection?
4. Would you inject the script with some life by rewriting it?

If you chose 4, why not rewrite it now and see what you come up with. Stick with the same few facts that appear in the original. But you're authorized to add a few plausible factlets. For example, instead of merely echoing the original script and saying *the elephant was shot,* you may want to use the active voice and say a policeman, a zookeeper, or a humane society officer shot the elephant. A few inventions like that, nothing fancy or far-fetched. And don't try to top Groucho's Marxmanship: "I shot an elephant in my pajamas. How he got in my pajamas, I don't know." (That may seem irrelevant, but as Groucho said, "Irrelevant never forgets.")

I'll wait while you write. . . . Zzzz. . . . Time's up. Now that you've completed your rewrite, let's look at the original script. If I were telling a friend about the rampage, I wouldn't start by saying, "Circus crowds looked on in horror." (Besides, wasn't it *a* crowd, not *crowds?*) And I would zero in on the action, not the *re*action:

"A circus elephant crushed her trainer to death. . . ." I'd want to tell *where* early in the sentence, not at the end. The original says the elephant "took off through the streets of Hawaii." Hawaii is the name of the state *and* the state's largest island. In any case, we don't refer to the streets of a *state* (nor the state of its streets).

The accident occurred in Honolulu, but the story is not *about* Honolulu, so we certainly wouldn't want to spotlight the place-name. We want to use it early in the script. But don't start, "In Honolulu today. . . ." We don't start a story with "In [place-name]." An excellent network editor once chided me for doing that. He said that it's "a lazy man's way" of starting a story. Every story originates somewhere. There's nothing arresting about a place-name, nothing that stops listeners in their tracks.

Often, broadcast newswriters pick up a piece of wire copy, glance at the dateline (the place where the news service obtained the basic information) at the top and forget that listeners can't see the dateline. So usually we must insert the place-name. And if we don't insert it high up, listeners may presume the story is local. In most cases, we can work in the place-name at or near the beginning of the first sentence: "Honolulu police shot a wild elephant. . . ." Or "Police in Honolulu shot. . . ." But the news isn't the death of an elephant, it's the death of a human. How about "A Hawaiian circus elephant crushed her trainer. . . ."? Perhaps, but we wouldn't want listeners to think *Hawaiian* modifies circus or elephant: Hawaii isn't known for growing elephants or producing circuses.

Better: "A circus elephant in Honolulu has crushed her trainer to death. The elephant then bolted out of the circus grounds and charged through the streets."

The first sentence in the original mentioned *a nine-thousand-pound elephant.* I wouldn't highlight the elephant's weight, especially before mentioning *elephant* the first time. A half-tonner can crush someone just as dead as a four-and-a-half tonner. As soon as you hear that an elephant has killed someone, you don't ask yourself, "I wonder how much that critter weighs." That's because our mind's eye already sees a jumbo.

The second paragraph of that script begins with the age of the elephant. Who cares about its age? I'd use the age if it had been one day old. Or 100 years old. Or if I had a lot more air time. But every elephant has an age. I'm concerned about people, not pachyderms. Don't worry: I wouldn't call an elephant a pachyderm any more than I'd call a spade an entrenching implement. What about the trainer? I'd certainly use the trainer's sex and age before the animal's.

An Associated Press story that moved the day *before* that script was broadcast identified the trainer as a 37-year-old man. The AP story said the elephant went berserk the *previous* day, at the Saturday matinee. Which means that when the TV station broadcast the story, it was almost two days old. No wonder the script has no time element, like *today* or *yesterday*. Which raises another question: Haven't many listeners read the story in their Sunday papers or heard it on the air already, before the Monday newscast? But perhaps the video—noted on the script—was compelling, at least for the producer.

The AP story, 560 words, says that when the elephant broke away, a dozen people were hurt. But the story doesn't say whether the elephant hurt them, or whether they hurt themselves in their panic to get away. Nor does the story say how badly they were hurt. Even so, the injured are worth including in the script.

The original script's last sentence is acceptable, although *officials* is vague. Was it city, county, state or federal officials—or circus officials— who said the elephant had been spooked by a new worker? The attribution would be improved by another word or two. The AP story *is* specific.

Now that we've examined the script in the ICU with an ECU (extreme close-up), we see that it's too scrawny to ride the airwaves. Let's hope your script is sturdy, though not elephantine.

14

NOOSEPAPERS
(AND WHEN THEY EAT THEIR WORDS)

Do you ever fish frantically for a fast fact to plug a hole in your script? If you fish in newspapers or magazines, you fish in hazardous waters. Though many publications do a remarkable job in gathering, writing and printing tens of thousands of facts in each edition, they do make mistakes. Real whoppers. Which leaves us fishermen not knowing whether a detail in an article is a firm fact, or a fishy fact—or a false fact, which is, in fact, a non-fact. If you use just one assumed fact that turns out to be a non-fact, you may be heading for deep discomfort—or dismissal.

You get an idea of how risky fishing for facts can be by looking at some mistakes newspapers have owned up to. (There's no telling how many they don't own up to.) The *New York Times,* for instance, ran this Editors' Note Feb. 17, 1995:

"A front-page article on Feb. 5 about drinking on college campuses included a description of a University of Virginia student, Brett Sanders, who was quoted as saying he had moderated his drinking after a trespassing conviction involving alcohol.

"In fact, Mr. Sanders was not convicted, nor was he ever involved in such an incident. The account came from a member of Mr. Sanders's campus fraternity who identified himself to a reporter as Mr. Sanders, whom he otherwise described accurately. The reporter visited the campus again yesterday and verified that Mr. Sanders was not the student he had interviewed."

That sobering correction came from one of newspaperdom's best. The *Times* also stumbled in another front-page article Sept. 25, 1994. It said the treasurer of Sandusky County, Ohio, had placed $6.5 billion in an interest-rate investment. The correct amount was $6.5 million—a difference of $6.4935 *billion.* The paper also acknowledged misplacing Portage County, Ohio. It's east of Akron, not near Toledo. Similarly, on Nov. 24, 1991, a

Times travel column placed Biloxi and Gulfport in Louisiana instead of Mississippi. Imagine, if you had borrowed bum dope from that Ohio story in the *Times:* you might have been dismissed, deported and doomed to gather guano on Guam. Or to sell seashells in Seychelles.

But *Smart Money* topped the *Times*'s $6.5 billion error. The monthly magazine co-published by Hearst and Dow Jones acknowledged in June 1996 that it had said franchising accounts for $800 million in annual U.S. sales—but that "the figure is actually $800 billion," an error of $799,200,000,000.

The *New York Times* also misplaced 200 million *years.* It ran this correction Nov. 20, 1996: "A front-page article yesterday about the discovery of a 2.33-million-year-old jaw, described as the earliest definitively dated fossil of the genus Homo, which includes humans, misstated the period during which anatomically modern humans are thought to have arisen. It was 200,000 to 100,000 years ago, not 200 million to 100 million years ago."

Most corrections seem minor, except for the people affected—including broadcasters who misappropriate a fact that's not a fact. *Wall Street Journal,* Feb. 3, 1997: "Citizens Against Government Waste is being audited by the Internal Revenue Service. The organization was misidentified as Citizens for Government Waste. . . ." *New York Times,* Feb. 5, 1997: "An obituary of the painter Theodore Stamos yesterday misidentified a survivor. Kostas Stamastelos is his brother, not a sister. And the same day, a *Times* columnist said, "Maryland's governor was misdescribed here on Monday as a 'gutsy Republican'; Parris N. Glendening is a rock-ribbed Democrat."

Errors even creep into long-settled historical facts. The *Times* said (Aug. 10, 1993) Benjamin Franklin watched the first American balloon flight in 1793. That would have been an out-of-grave experience; Franklin died in 1790.

A *Times* article said (Oct. 14, 1994) Lt. Col. George Armstrong Custer and his troops killed 300 Sioux at Wounded Knee Creek, South Dakota, in 1890. Wrong battle, wrong state, wrong victor, wrong year: Custer and his men were killed by Sioux in the Battle of Little Big Horn River, Montana, in 1876. A *Chicago Tribune* column (Aug. 2, 1991) placed Custer's last stand in Wyoming. And the *Trib* told (Nov. 2, 1994) of a pioneer who reached California in 1864 by way of the Panama Canal; the canal wasn't completed until 1914.

Connoisseurs of corrections may also appreciate this string of corrections from the *New York Times* of Sept. 29, 1993:

"The obituary of Lieut. Gen. James H. Doolittle in late editions yesterday misidentified his college. He was at the University of California at Berkeley when the United States entered World War I; the University of California at Los Angeles did not exist then.

"The obituary also misstated the history of the Richtofen Flying Circus, the squadron of German pilots that plagued the Allies. It fought in World War I, not World War II.

"A picture caption with the obituary misstated the year the general accepted the Medal of Honor from President Franklin D. Roosevelt. It was 1942, not 1945. . . ."

Some newspaper mistakes can be fatal: The *Times* acknowledged (Aug. 6, 1996): "An article on Sunday about endangered plants in Hawaii described castor beans erroneously. While castor beans are used to produce an oil that functions as a laxative, the beans themselves contain a protein, ricin, that is highly poisonous. They are not 'edible.' "

Time magazine even misplaced Elvis Presley. It reported (Feb. 12, 1996) that he was in "permanent residence" at Forest Hill Cemetery, Memphis. But a reader pointed out that Elvis had been moved to the grounds of Graceland Mansion in 1977. And *Time* also acknowledged (Jan. 27, 1997) an erroneous time-shift: "In our review of Walter Mosley's *Gone Fishin'*, the original in his series featuring black hero Easy Rawlins [Books, Jan. 20], we said the publication of Mosley's *Devil in a Blue Dress* had been aided by the commercial success of Terry McMillan's novel *Waiting to Exhale. Waiting to Exhale* was published in 1992, two years after *Devil in a Blue Dress* appeared."

They say doctors bury their mistakes; so do newsweeklies. *Time's* correction about Mosley's book ran at the end of its Letters section. And *Newsweek* ran this correction (Jan. 27, 1997) at the end of *its* Letters section: "Our article 'The Trials of Silicone' (Society, Dec. 16) reported that Dow Corning's 1996 sales were $250 billion. In fact, its sales were projected at $2.5 billion. Newsweek regrets the error." The *Economist* often runs letters as correctives (Jan. 25, 1997): "You say that the Caribbean hurricane season begins in September. Actually, it officially begins on June 1st and ends November 30th." But the *Economist* usually runs corrections in tiny type at the bottom of a column. On Feb. 1, 1997: "Our piece on gambling last week incorrectly stated that the industry earned $44.4 billion in profits in 1995. This figure was for revenues. Our apologies to all those who have scrambled to set up or invest in casinos since our story appeared."

If a reporter or writer doesn't make a mistake in an article, an editor can. *The Washington Monthly* conceded (November 1994): "Someone must have spiked our water cooler the night we edited Chalmers Roberts' review of Doris Kearns Goodwin's *No Ordinary Time* [September 1994]. (1) Joseph Lash, not Eleanor Roosevelt, was the author of six books. (2) It was Missy LeHand's suffering a stroke, not FDR, that prompted the president to change his will to leave her half his estate. (3) FDR depended on two of his unmarried cousins, not married cousins, for company. (4) FDR's mistress and longtime friend is Lucy Rutherfurd [*is?* she died in 1948], not Lucy Rutherford. These errors were ours, not Roberts'. . . ."

In another mixup, the playwright Edward Albee was wronged. The author of "Who's Afraid of Virginia Woolf?" wrote to the *Washington Post,* which printed his letter Dec. 11, 1996, under the head "Distressing Mistake": "While I was delighted that The Post photographed me at the Kennedy Center, I was shocked that the newspaper had given me a wife, and that her name is Percy ["Star-Studded Praise for Hard-Earned Achievements," Style, Dec. 9]. This kind of sloppy journalism is deeply distressing, for two people are with me in the photograph: Mrs. John Steinbeck—widow of the Nobel laureate, who is a dear friend, though to whom I am not married, and whose name is not Percy—and Mr. Jonathan Thomas, with whom I have been living happily for 27 years."

Even a journal published by the Smithsonian Institution, *Wilson Quarterly,* can slip. In spring 1991, for example, it said Aristotle had refined a theory first proposed by the Greek anatomist Galen. The next *WQ* admitted, "The review should have stated the opposite; Aristotle died in 322 B.C., some 450 years before Galen was born."

A *Chicago Sun-Times* columnist wrote (Dec. 17, 1992): "Scoopsville. It's a done deal. Bill Daley, brother of Mayor Daley is President-elect Bill Clinton's ABSOLUTE DEFINITE [her emphasis] pick to become the next transportation secretary." Wrong. Four years later, the columnist said (Dec. 6, 1996) Bill Daley was "expected" to be appointed U.S. Secretary of Transportation. One week later, Daley was appointed Secretary of Commerce.

In 1992, that *Sun-Times* columnist also said she deserved "the dumber-than-a-crate-of-tombstones award for wishing happy birthday Wednesday to actress Colleen Dewhurst. Wish you were still here, Colleen." Miss Dewhurst had died in 1988.

The *New York Observer* reported (Aug. 12, 1996) that a young couple had bought an apartment in a Manhattan condominium where "they will now have as neighbors Fran Warren, a singer from the big-band era, and comedian-actor Ted *(The Mary Tyler Moore Show, Caddyshack)* Knight." That's not such a pleasant prospect when you consider that Ted Knight died in 1986.

A magazine that covers the newspaper industry, *Editor & Publisher,* admitted (Nov. 2, 1996) what it called "an honest blunder": *E&P* had run an obituary of a journalism professor, Terry Clark, but it was Dr. Clark who wrote the obit (of a colleague). In its editing process, *E&P* said, "the writer mistakenly became the subject."

USA Today acknowledged (Dec. 13, 1996) another kind of mistake: "Cardinal John O'Connor did not ask the pope to excommunicate Madonna from the Catholic Church. A story Wednesday in USA Today was incorrect."

The New York *Daily News* ran this correction Jan. 18, 1995: "A profile of retiring Patrolmen's Benevolent Association president Phil Caruso on Jan. 11 should have made clear that a statement about his 1988 grand jury testimony regarding a PBA escrow fund was based on a story in another newspaper and had not been verified independently by The News. Caruso denies authorizing a withdrawal from the fund." *Not verified independently!*

Corrections, too, sometimes need correction. The *New Republic* admitted (Feb. 3, 1997): "The correction we ran in this spot one week ago was itself incorrect. . . ."

The *New York Times* conceded (Oct. 31, 1995) that a film review four days earlier had misquoted a young mother. The correction quoted her as saying, "I gave birth to an endangered species"—not "a dangerous species." And the *New York Times* Sunday Magazine (Aug. 25, 1996) identified U.S. Representative Henry Hyde as "head of the *Senate* Judiciary Committee."

The *Times* occasionally runs a quarter-page ad that says "to err is human." The head over the ad reads, "We Mean to Be Right. But Sometimes We're Wrong." ("What one reads in the newspaper," Bismarck said, "can also be true.")

Don't rely on a newspaper or magazine for correct spelling for a super. Misspellings crop up in print often. On its cover for May/June 1996, *Ms.* misspelled "feminism" as "feminisim." A founding editor of *Ms.,* Gloria Steinem, has said, "Writing . . . keeps me from believing everything I read."

We all make mistakes. Who needs to borrow mistakes from other people? Mistakes to the left of us, mistakes to the right of us, mistakes in front of us, printed and perpetuated. (Tennyson, anyone?) When we want to borrow something from the *Times*—or any other publication—how do we know whether what we're appropriating is 100 percent accurate? Which word or words, which assertion, which implication, may be wrong? And which word may be terribly (but not noticeably) wrong? The best course is to follow these guidelines:

1. Don't steal stories from newspapers, even if it's only petty larceny.

2. Don't accept everything you read as fact. No matter how respected the paper, or how prominent the byline, or how well written the story, newspapers are bedeviled by mistakes. (I hope you don't find any of mine—or too many of mine.)

3. Proceed with extreme caution.

4. If you don't have the time or resources to confirm a story, go ahead: rewrite it. But be sure to credit the newspaper (in broadcast style). One prudent reason: you won't be sticking your neck out; you'll be sharing—or shifting—responsibility. When the *Daily Herald* says the mayor told it something or other, and you need that story, write it warily: "The Daily Herald *quoted* Mayor Molehill as saying. . . ." That way you're protecting yourself because you don't know whether the newspaper quoted the mayor accurately, or whether anyone at the paper even talked to him.

A writer who lifts a word or a story from a newspaper without determining whether it's correct risks trouble. So the best policy in a newsroom is to use newspapers merely as tip sheets, not as the truth, the whole truth and nothing but the truth, so help me FCC. As the Italian proverb has it, "To trust is good; not to trust is better."

The English writer Samuel Butler has put the problem of print's plausibility into perspective: "The most important service rendered by the press is that of educating people to approach printed matter with distrust."

So keep your nose in the news but your neck out of the noose.

Words to the Wise

What's wrong with this lead-in?

> **One person is hospitalized and another is headed to Lynn district court after an alleged home invasion in Lynn.**
> **_____ _____ is live from Lynn district court with the latest.**

Let us count the ways:

1. Is that *person* a man, woman or child? If we know, let's say so.

2. Saying that someone is hospitalized—or that many people are hospitalized—is not news, newsy, or newsworthy. Tens of thousands of people are in hospitals.

3. An *alleged* home invasion? Do the police suspect that the homeowner wants to file a false insurance claim? Does the writer mean an *alleged* home-invader? Or an invader of an *alleged* home (what the police used to call a disorderly house)?

4. *Invasion:* The writer has buried *invade,* a good action verb, in a vapid noun, *invasion.* Halfway down that lead-in, the underplayed noun *invasion* gives off the first whiff of action in the story. And what follows *after* in that lead should precede *after.* After all, if you phoned a friend about the story, you wouldn't say, "One person is hospitalized and another is headed. . . ." You'd start with the action—not the reaction. You'd talk about the thug(s) who stormed into a home. (We speak of a *home invasion,* but not a *home-invader.*)

5. Why call the reporter *live?* We wouldn't switch to a dead reporter. Some reporters may seem dead, but if they're standing by, they should be alive. They'd better be alive. ("Live at Five," they say of some newscasts, "Dead by Six.")

6. While we're counting, let us count the *Lynn*s: three in that script. Too many.

7. The *latest?* Presenting the latest is what newscasts are all about. Remember, news is what's new. And what's new is the latest. (So what else is new?)

Who edited that script? *Was* there an editor? Did a newsroom-invader (a Darth Vader) abduct the *editor?* Unfortunately (perhaps fortunately), that leaden lead-in is the only part of the script that fell into my clammy claws. I have only a few facts to work with, so my rewrite is a product of speculation, interpolation, extrapolation and desperation:

"Two men with guns forced their way into a Lynn home today and beat a woman guest. A passerby who saw the break-in called the police, and they caught one intruder. The injured woman is in the hospital, and the suspect is on his way to Lynn District Court. Jane Jones has the story."

If the invasion of the booty-snatchers had previously been broadcast, I might have written the lead-in this way: "Police are searching for a gunman who broke into a Lynn home and beat a woman guest. Another gunman was caught by the police at the scene, and he's now on his way to Lynn District Court. Jane Jones has the story." Or, depending on the extent of previous coverage and the time elapsed since the crime, I'd write this: "A suspect arrested in a home-invasion is now being taken to Lynn

District Court, and Jane Jones has the story." To which many an anchor would add, under her breath: "We hope."

Another script from the same major-market television station is an anchor's tag:

> **That's it for the weather. Just one reminder. Sunday is**
> **Daylight Savings Time. Don't forget to turn your clocks**
> **forward one hour on Sunday.**

The first two sentence are a waste of time. When the weathercaster stops talking about the weather, everyone knows that's it for the weather. No need for the anchor to proclaim the obvious. In fact, there is a need for the anchor *not* to do so. And no need to say, "Just one reminder."

Better: "Daylight Saving [not *Savings*] Time starts Sunday. Remember (more emphatic than *Don't forget*), at two ayem, Sunday, set your clock ahead one hour."

Let's look at another snippet:

> **Investigators are trying to find out what caused**
> **Wednesday's deadly helicopter crash.**

Instead of *deadly,* make it *fatal. Deadly* can mean either "causing death" or "capable of causing death." But *fatal* is unambiguous; it describes something that has already caused death or dire consequences, or will do so—inevitably. But writers *are* correct in referring to a *deadly* disease, a *deadly* enemy and a *deadly* weapon.

> **The probe into Monday's deadly gas attack on a Tokyo**
> **subway has lead to an arrest and a second dramatic raid on**
> **a Japanese religious cult.**

Probe is a newspaper-headline word. Print editors use *probe* as a synonym for *investigation* because *probe* can be squeezed into a one-column head. But *probe* is not a spoken word, not unless you're speaking about a doctor who probes a wound. And did the writer mean an attack with deadly gas or an attack that caused death? *On* a subway? The writer was on the wrong track. Either an event occurs *in* the subway, which is the underground tunnel, or *on* a subway train. Riders say they *take the subway,* but they don't say they take *a* subway. And the writer should get the *lead* out and make it *led.*

Dramatic? Aren't most raids dramatic? Writing coaches say, "Show, don't tell." So, instead of calling something dramatic, tell us what happened that makes it dramatic.

The script about the Tokyo story goes on:

> **In a full** [as opposed to *partial?*] **military-type mission today, specialists seized more containers of potentially noxious chemicals.**

What exactly is a *military-type* mission? One with air cover? *Noxious* chemicals? *Noxious* means harmful to living things. The writer might have meant *toxic,* which means capable of causing injury or death. But many listeners (and writers) are unsure of the meanings of *noxious* and *toxic.* A better word for those chemicals, closer to the tone of the terror in Tokyo, is *poisonous* or *deadly.* And no need for *potentially.*

In our line of work—and it *is* work—words count. So let's work on being deadly accurate.

Babbledygook

> **Good evening. Gangsters and gunfire, a breaking story at this hour.**

The hour: 11 p.m.; the place: New York City; the story: the lead on a television network flagship. The first word of the shooting reached a 911 operator at 7:21 p.m.—more than 3½ hours before the newscast. (Is that a *breaking* story? Give me a break.) The co-anchor picks up the intro:

> **Well, it looks very much like a mob hit tonight outside Lenox Hill Hospital. Police say a member of John Gotti's Gambino crime family was gunned down. He is now inside that hospital as doctors work to save him. Tim Thomas** [I've changed his name] **is at the scene now with more for us. Tim.**

Tim:

> **Well** [another *well?* a good, folksy word, but don't go to the well too often], **it's an incredible story.** [If it's incredible, how can we believe it? But what's so incredible about a shooting? And in the Big Bagel? Instead of wasting our time, go ahead, tell the news. And calm down.] **It's reminiscent of the** [should be *a*] **Chicago gangland hit circa 1920.** [Mr. Reporter, tell

us what the story is all about before telling us what you think it's reminiscent of. Better yet, don't tell us what it's reminiscent of. Especially in another city. Hasn't New York had enough of its own gangland shootings? And why use a Latin word, *circa,* instead of *around?*]

This is the victim's car behind me. Again, you hear that he is an alleged member of the Gambino crime family. ["*You hear*"? Is it hearsay? In fact, Anchor Number Two had already quoted the police as saying the guy *is* a Gambino bambino.] **What we have, police are telling us** [who's *us?*], **is that somebody** [better: *someone*] **was driving down this street, apparently waiting for the victims to walk out of Lenox Hill Hospital. Driving down the street** [again?] **when they saw their intended victims, they pulled their car up, got out of the car and opened fire.**

And perhaps [a weak word for this scene, and I don't mean maybe] **you can see that the window of this car, several windows of this car, were actually** [unneeded] **shot out.** [Q: What connection did that car have with the shooting? A: The wounded man had been getting into the parked car. Tim should have told us.] **We have tape shot here shortly after this happened at 7:30 tonight** [no, it didn't], **and perhaps** [again!] **you can see that Police Commissioner Bratton was one of the first people to arrive and try to figure out exactly what happened here.**

[*One of the first?* One of the first fifty? If the Commish *was* one of the first on the scene, how did he get there so fast? Who cares? The next day, the *New York Times* ran a full column on the shooting, about 750 words, but didn't mention him at all. A better opening line than the vague and vapid "Gangsters and gunfire": "A Gotti henchman shot on the Upper East Side." Reference to that area classes it up a little.]

Again [*again* again?], **the person, the victim** [previously, we were told of *victims*] **is, we're told, Handsome Jack Giordano** [in fact, this is the *first* mention of him; better: "Jack Giordano, known as Handsome Jack"; another question: known to *whom* as Handsome Jack? most such nicknames are bestowed by newsies], **allegedly a capo in the Gambino crime family.** [For the Gambino family, that's a threepeat.] **We also spoke to someone who witnessed** [better: *saw*] **it.** [What's *it?* And what's Giordano's condition? His age? Was he armed? Where does he live? Is he an ex-con? (Yes.)]

Witness:

Just I heard gunshot, just people were running out. [Some witness! That's the entire soundbite. His name and speech suggest he's a foreigner. (This verbatim text was recorded by a commercial transcription service.) Next, we hear from a police captain, four unidentified people, none of them witnesses, then Tim again.]

Police are telling us [better: "Police say"; leave *us* out of it; most information comes from someone's telling us] **that Giordano and his driver were inside Lenox Hill Hospital visiting someone, and they came out of the hospital, and what you were just looking at was a live picture of bullet holes in the doors in** [*to* or *of*] **the emergency room of the hospital, so apparently who was firing, whoever was firing that gun, really** [unneeded; really!] **didn't care about anybody** [better: *anyone*] **else** [no kidding!], **except hitting his intended victims.** [*Victims?* Who was targeted besides Giordano?]

Now police are telling us [our ears are telling us that we're hearing too much of that locution] **they have one person in custody. They're not releasing his name at this point** [instead of saying *at this point,* why not *yet?*] **Again** [yet *again*], **this happened at 7:30 at night** [again, no it didn't!]. **There were a lot of people out on the street here on 77th Street.** [*There were* and *there is* are dead phrases. Better: "Many people were on 77th Street." Were they in danger? Did they provide descriptions or spot a license number?]

We [*I?*] **also hear** [from whom? a police official? a hospital official? a busybody?] **that Giordano is in very serious condition, in critical condition, I should say, with three bullet wounds to the neck and to the back.** [Should be "wounds *in* his neck and back."] **We are also told** [by whom?] **it's possible that he has been paralyzed. That's the latest here at** [*on!*] **77th Street. I'm Tim Thomas. Bill** [also a pseudonym], **back to you.**

Bill:

All right, Tim, thank you.

(Who says that being a reporter is a thankless job? Thank him? Bill oughta spank 'im.)

In defense of the reporter, he might have arrived at the scene late, and he might have been new to reporting and new to our language. And apparently he was so pressed for time he had to ad lib. Whatever the excuses, the explanations and the perhapses, we're left with a news report that's wordy, jumbled, repetitious, uninformative—unsatisfactory.

And the television critic Marvin Kitman, a Newsday hitman, would probably call all that hash (and rehash) babbledygook.

Sources Say

If someone in your newsroom whispered, "They say you're resigning," wouldn't you ask, "Who are *they?*" And wouldn't you want to know whether *they* is one person or several? And, if only one person, is she the news director? Or an intern? Wouldn't you want to find out who has been bad-mouthing you? Or, worse yet, true-mouthing you? If you can learn who they *is* (or are), perhaps you can gauge the weight of the assertion. Or whether your informant is making it up. Making it up, perhaps, to get your goat, or to make himself seem knowledgeable. And did *they* say *resign* or *re-sign?*

Those questions—and more—come to mind whenever newscasters present news sourced so vaguely it's not sourced at all. So vaguely that listeners are left up in the air.

On a network newcast, a U.S. general in Bosnia commented about a U.S. colonel who was quoted in a newspaper. The colonel had spoken bluntly about the U.S. mission there. The general's on-camera reaction: He said he was disappointed in the colonel's comments, and he said he was looking into them.

In the next scene, in a follow-up to the flap, the television correspondent said,

> **But sources say the U.S. government is embarrassed and concerned.**

Sources is too vague. All news comes from sources. Was *sources* the general? He knows better than to go on record with that comment. So if he *was* the source, perhaps the correspondent could have attributed the remark to *a high-ranking U.S. officer.* Or if that would put the general on the spot, then perhaps *a U.S. officer.* But the correspondent said *sources,* plural. Two generals? Other reporters? A high-level U.S. official? A foreign official? A grave-digger? All of them?

The remark attributed to *sources* is such an obvious conclusion that you wonder whether it's the correspondent's own assertion, one he decided to pin on the ubiquitous and suspicious *sources.* But putting words in other people's mouths is unhygienic—and unsavory. The remark about the U.S. government sounds plausible. But the best news organizations ban the practice of quoting *sources* and ban the plural *sources* when a reporter has only one source. "When quoting one person," the *Broadcast News Style Guide* says, "don't manufacture others to make a point." Broadcast News (a part of the Canadian Press news agency), goes on to tell its staff, "After interviewing a fire investigator, for example, it's misleading to write: *Fire officials say. . . .*"

When you attribute a fact or a remark to a *source,* you raise several questions: Was the source a piece of paper or a human? Did someone really say that? And say it like that? If a listener believes you're honest *and* accurate, still another question arises: Is that unidentified someone in a position to know what he's talking about? Is he someone whose word we can take, someone whose opinion is worth listening to?

Another sore spot: using the passive voice to say a news organization *has been told.* This type of non-sourcing is as uninformative as *sources.* A television network script:

> _____ **News has been told that this is the critical weekend for retired General Colin Powell. Powell** [should be *he*] **is known to want to run for President, but his family is known to have deep reservations about that. He reportedly will finish weighing all considerations and decide this weekend whether he will or won't run. . . .**

_____ *News has been told?* By whom? Powell? Someone in Powell's camp? Someone in a rival camp who wants to push Powell into declaring himself? A pollster? A consultant? A mischief-maker? The reporter himself?

If, for valid reasons, reporters can't identify a source, they should at least give us a sense of who their sources are. But the best sources say that *sources say* should go:

The *Wall Street Journal Stylebook* tells the WSJ's staff: "The word *source* itself is usually best avoided. It often conveys the idea of either more or less authority than the person deserves. *Sources say* may suggest to the reader that we are uncertain that we have the facts straight, so we are putting the onus on an unnamed *source.* In other cases, *sources say* carries the connotation of *inside knowledge. . . .*

"If a negative quotation isn't involved and the person's identity isn't confidential, there may seem to be no specific objection to calling a source a source: *a police source, a White House source.* But *spokesman* or *representative* is much preferred if the information is provided on the record."

The *New York Times Manual of Style and Usage* says: "The best news source . . . is the source that is identified by name. But it is also true that a newspaper, to give its readers information vital to them, must sometimes obtain it from sources not in a position to identify themselves.

"The decision to permit anonymity of a source must first of all be justified by the conviction of reporter and editor not only that there is no other way to obtain the information, but also that the information is both factual and important.

"When it is established that anonymity of the source cannot be avoided, the nature of the source must be specified as closely as possible. The bald and meaningless *sources said* will not do, and *reliable sources* is not much better. *'United States diplomat* is better than *Western diplomat,* which is better than *diplomat.* And better still is *a United States diplomat who took part in the meeting'.*"

Canada's national news service, the Canadian Press, says in its stylebook: "News sources given anonymity should be identified as specifically as possible. *Sources said* is bare bones and lacks credibility. Also don't use the hackneyed or meaningless phrases *political observers* and *senior officials* and adjectives like *key, informed, veteran.*" The Canadian Press also says: "Don't use others' unnamed sources as if they were CP's. Unnamed sources in stories picked up from newspapers or broadcast should be [tied to the specific] paper or broadcaster. . . ."

And the *Reuters Handbook for Journalists* says, "Avoid the vague *reliable sources, well-informed sources, sources, quarters, circles* or *observers.*"

So be as specific as possible. That way, listeners can consider the source. Feel free to quote me (by name, please): What's a *source* for the goose isn't fit for the editor who takes a good gander.

Name Drop-kicking

Warning. Reader discretion advised: adult content, adult language and excessive violence—to good taste and good writing.

Let's go right to the script:

> **Barry Switzer, that emotional, errogant** [the sportscaster probably meant "arrogant," not "error-prone"] **idiot who coaches the Dallas Cowboys, has done it again.**

Voice-over:

**Yes, that's the man I'm talking about. He blew today's
game with the Philadelphia Eagles. We pick it up with
game tied at 17 on a 4th and one, and Switzer goes for it,
and Emmitt Smith is stopped. . . .**

The super identified Switzer as "Bonehead Coach." Yes, *bonehead.* And
idiot is what the man said. Not in a bar. Not in a car. But *over the air.* In
a major market. (If the questionable play had worked, Joe Durso Jr. asks,
would the sportscaster have called Switzer a genius? And Prof. Durso, of
the University of Montana, also wonders whether the sportscaster would
have used the same words if he'd been broadcasting in Dallas.)

Sportscasters *are* allowed considerable latitude—and attitude. But the
writer of that script has gone out of bounds. There are certain norms we
don't overstep. We don't insult people. And we don't call people nasty
names. Especially in front of the whole world—or whatever share we have.

If Oscar Wilde had been watching that sports segment, he might
have said, as he once did: "There is much to be said in favor of modern
journalism. By giving us the opinions of the uneducated, it keeps us in
touch with the ignorance of the community."

The sportscaster who wrote that script may not be uneducated (or
undereducated), just untrained—and unrestrained. In any case, he's not
the person responsible for letting that script go on the air. The person at
fault is the editor (if any). Or the producer. But, ultimately, the news
director.

The writer might have been doing the best he knows how. But super-
visors must supervise. And impose norms: norms of fairness, impartiality
and civility. And even broadcasters allowed to express opinions on the air
shouldn't abuse that privilege by name-calling. Ben Bradlee, the former
executive editor of the *Washington Post,* urges reporters and editors to ask
themselves at the end of every story, "Have I been as fair as I can be?"

"Good sports writing," says *The Associated Press Stylebook and Libel Manual,* "depends on the same writing and reporting tools as any
other story. A stylebook . . . is an aid in reaching that goal."

For style *and* class, we also might look to *The Economist.* It, too,
looks down on that sportscaster's kind of name-calling. And every other
kind. The style guide of the British newsweekly cautions: "Do not be
hectoring or arrogant. Those who disagree with you are not necessarily
stupid or insane. Nobody needs to be described as silly: let your analysis
prove that he is."

While we're at it, let's look at some more good advice in *The Economist Style Guide:* "Do not be too pleased with yourself. Don't boast of your own cleverness by telling readers that you correctly predicted something or that you have a scoop. You are more likely to bore or irritate them than to impress them. So keep references to *The Economist* to a minimum, particularly those of the we-told-you-so variety. References to 'this correspondent' or 'your correspondent' are always self-conscious and often self-congratulatory."

Another script:

> **We all know by now that Saint Ignatius is going for football championship number five!**
>
> **And on the other side of the field, Brunswick is looking to be the spoiler!**
>
> **_____'s got [should be "_____ *has*"] a preview of tomorrow's big matchup [delete *matchup,* make it *game*], coming up next!**

Delete *coming up; next* says it all.

All those exclamation points, one after each sentence, exceed the quota good writers impose on themselves for a whole year. Viewers can't see the bangs, of course, but they can *hear* them. And that story isn't worth shouting about. In fact, no story is. If it's big, you don't need to raise your voice. What you need to do is write it right—tight and bright. And we should all know that we never start a story by saying, *We all know.* Because we *don't* all know.

As for *looking to be* in the second sentence of that script, that's not English, even in Sportsville. It's substandard. Remember, we must maintain our norms. (No, not Norm Crosby, Norman Bates, or Norman Oklahoma.)

Next up to bat, another sports story that also was broadcast in a major market:

> **A former high school baseball star was arrested for stealing a uniform worn by Babe Ruth, plus 200-thousand dollars' worth of baseball cards.**
>
> **William W_____ the Third stole the uniform Ruth wore in the 1942 movie "Pride of the Yankees."**
>
> **The uniform was first stolen from a Hollywood costume company in 1952, another owner was killed in a mob hit,**

and it spent much of the early 1990's in a police property room.

Ruth's uniform was size 44 pants and size 50 shirt.

That script tosses out far more questions than it even takes a swing at: Where was the uniform stolen? How? When? Did the Babe ever wear it in a game? Or did he wear it only in a movie? Were the uniform and the baseball cards stolen from the same place? How many cards? Were they in a display case? A vault? A closet?

Was any of the loot recovered? When the latest thief stole it, was it already stolen property? Was it in the police property room when it was stolen? Where? Who was the owner killed in a mob hit? (Was he a heavy hitter?) Where was the arrest made? How? Was the alleged thief trying to fence the stuff? Pawn it?

The script's second sentence says "William W_____ " *stole* the uniform. Excuuuse me: Was he *convicted* of stealing it? Where? What's his sentence? And who cares what sizes Ruth wore? Except his tailor, his biographer and baseball fans who cherish stats.

Even if we could get answers to all those questions, we couldn't—and wouldn't, and shouldn't—use them. But if we had answers to just a few, we could do a better job.

All in all, those scripts should have been sent to the shredders. And the writers to the showers. Not so incidentally, Barry Switzer's team, the Dallas Cowboys, went on to win the Super Bowl. Not bad for a *bonehead!* So the sportscaster who maligned him violated several rules, including a basic rule in broadcasting: "Never kick a man when he's up."

15

AFTER MATH

Getting the words right is hard. But getting the numbers right can be still harder. Even when the numbers are small, writers can fall. And when they're wrong, they should get the gong.

Let's look at an excerpt from a network newsmagazine:

> **He** [an economist] **says the average French citizen hands over fully 46 percent of all his income to the government in all kinds of taxes. The average American, he says, hands over just 30 percent. That's more than 15 percent less.**

Whoa! *More than 15 percent less?* The *more* and *less* are baffling, more or less. And woe unto those who trip over simple numbers. What Americans pay is 16 *percentage points* less.

According to the script's basic figures on taxation, the French payment exceeds the American payment by 53 percent. To calculate how much *more* the French pay: subtract the American payment (30) from the French (46) and divide the result (16) by the first number (30). When you divide 16 by 30, you get .5333. That's $^{53}/_{100}$. *Voilà:* 53 percent.

How much *less* is the American payment? Divide 16 by 46. The answer: 35 percent.

But the numbers in that script aren't the only problem. The words need work, too. The correspondent said the average American hands the government *just 30 percent* of his income. *Just* 30 percent? Just or unjust, leave out *just;* let the number speak for itself: 30 percent will do. As for the French, who hand over *fully 46 percent,* that number doesn't need a modifier either.

The correspondent also reports that the director of a French orchestra says the government provides "a full 20 percent" of his budget. If the correspondent calls 20 percent "full," what would he call 100 percent? I don't want to fulminate about *full* and *fully*, but they suggest that the writer is huffing and puffing.

Another *faux pas:* The correspondent calls the Champs-Elysees "noisy and fume-filled." Noisy it is. But "fume-filled" isn't conversational. "Filled with fumes" is conversational, but as far as an observer can see—and smell—not true.

The correspondent goes on to say that a French actress in the 60-percent-tax category must pay an extra "wealth tax" that boosts her tax rate to 70 percent. He calls the jump to 70 percent from 60 percent an increase of "10 percent." Wrong again. It's an increase of 10 *percentage points.* When we follow the formula for figuring percentages, we subtract the smaller number (60) from the larger (70) and divide the result (10) by the first number (60). The result: an increase of .1666—16 percent.

If you, too, are an innumerate, welcome to the club. Many of us need to review a high school textbook that deals with percentages. And we all need to keep in mind some advice in the newsletter *Copy Editor.* It offers five rules from Edward MacNeal, author of *Mathsemantics: Making Numbers Talk Sense.* He says:

- Mistrust all percentages over 100.

- Don't use the word *times* with comparative modifiers, such as *more, larger, better, less, fewer, smaller* and *worse.* [The *Wall Street Journal*'s in-house gazette, "Style & Substance" says: *Three times greater than* is the same as *four times as great as,* but the latter is less confusing. The *WSJ* also says we should write *times as high* or *times as fast* or whatever, to avoid the ambiguity of "times higher" or "times faster."]

- Double-check comparisons containing words like *tripling* and *threefold.*

- Avoid mixing fractions, percentages and decimals . . . and never mix them within a single comparison.

- Mistrust percentages added to other percentages.

Copy Editor also passes along a passel of other tips on percents. Two of them:

- A tripling is an increase of 200 percent, not 300 percent. An increase of 300 percent is a quadrupling. [Doubling is a 100 percent increase.]

- A phrase like *six times fewer than* is absurd.

To see that your math doesn't do a number on you, ask someone in your newsroom who's good at figures to check your math. (No, it isn't called *aftermath*.)

Some writers are so taken with numbers that they plug them into scripts in the belief numbers make scripts impressively factual. But they don't.

Let's listen to this network anchor lead-in:

> **It took the six-man, six-woman jury just over eight hours to reach and deliver today's verdict in the trial of John Salvi. The defense said Salvi was insane when he stormed two abortion clinics and pumped out deadly rifle fire. Correspondent _____ _____ reports what the jury said.**

When a jury returns a verdict, our first question is, "Guilty or not guilty?" We don't ask, "How many men on the jury?" "How many women?" After all, or before all, we knew the composition of the jury from the outset, so it's not news. The length of the jury's deliberations may be worth mentioning, but it's not more important than the verdict. Nothing is. *Just over eight hours?* We round off numbers, so if we needed to use that number, we'd say merely "eight hours."

And *pumped out deadly rifle fire* doesn't sound like anything that should be said on a newscast. Or anywhere. People don't talk that way. What Salvi did was, he shot two people dead.

After the anchor's lead-in, the correspondent said,

> **John Salvi stood without emotion as a visibly shaken jury delivered its verdict.**

As for Salvi's showing no emotion, people's emotions are often not discernible. *Visibly shaken* is journalese. The next words on the air came when the forewoman of the jury spoke, and we finally learned that the defendant had been found guilty—of murder. No matter what arguments someone might advance for delaying the news so long—*Salvi found guilty*—it's not sound journalism. If it makes sense to delay the news to hold the audience, why not tease the verdict and save it for the last item in the newscast?

Another network newsmagazine has been found guilty (by me) of committing first-degree attempted thought control:

> **Finally tonight, a look ahead to a story you'll be talking about this week: a comet that hasn't passed this way in, oh, about 10-thousand years. Could be the brightest in decades. . . .**

We don't know what's in anyone else's mind, and often not even in our own, so how can an anchor tell us what we're going to be talking about? Did *you* go around talking about that comet? Or was your conversation like mine: comet-free—even *comet*ose?

They say more listeners can name the Three Stooges than can name three justices on the U.S. Supreme Court. As if to confirm that assertion, an anchor in the Midwest broadcast this tease about the remake of the $100 bill:

Coming up, a facelift for former President Ben Franklin.

Former President? We don't refer to a person long dead as a *former* President, especially when he was *never* President.

Wanted: News, Not Views

More and more, newscasts tell us less and less. That's not true of all newscasts, but it's too true of too many. The problem is newscasters who misspend time by telling us what they think. Or what they think *we* think. Or, even worse, how to think. Here are some network excerpts we should think about.

Good evening. We begin tonight with news that millions of people throughout the world will think is long overdue.

Whatever that is, it's not news. Much of what we hear on newscasts may strike millions of people as long overdue. But the population of the world exceeds five billion, so those *millions* (whether two million or 200 million) are only a small fraction of the total. If it makes sense to describe the expected reaction to news not yet reported, why not use even bigger numbers to beef up a script: "Billions of people in the world will be indifferent to this news. Or will think it premature. Or right on time. Or somewhat overdue."

What *is* long overdue in that script is the delivery of news. It's best to just tell what happened today, the *facts*. Don't try to describe how people *will think*. Or might react. The news is the action, not the presumed reaction. Also, the anchor needn't announce that he's beginning. As soon as he says "Good evening," we know he has begun.

Same newscast:

Here's a sad piece of news from overseas about health. At a meeting in Malawi, in Africa today, the news for Africa's

**senior defense officials must have been devastating.
International health officials have told** [why not the simple
past tense *told?*] **them that in some African armies one of
every two soldiers is infected with the AIDS virus.**

Much of the news we hear is sad, but an anchor shouldn't tell us a
story is sad. We can figure that out for ourselves. We don't have to be
cued. The script said the news *must have been devastating,* a tense you
might call the past-presumptive. But who needs speculation? Or devas-
tation? Or characterization of news? What we need is news—unadorned,
unadulterated, unadumbrated. (Of that last word, Emily Dickinson might
have said, Now, there's a word you can tip your hat to!)
Next in the newscast came this:

**In California, the horror caused by children. An attack so
brutal that authorities are groping for an explanation.**

No light. Just fright. And *authorities?* Authorities in child behavior?
Medical authorities? Police? In his lead-in, the anchor told of

an infant victim and the suspects who are not much older.

Not much older? The correspondent went on to say the victim was one
month old and the suspects in his beating were three boys—one six years
old and two eight years old. Figure it out: the six-year-old was 72 times
as old as the victim, and the eight-year-olds were 96 times as old.
The correspondent said the boys had walked into a home "to steal a
bicycle." Did the boys break in? Or did they find the door unlocked? And
did they steal a bicycle?
The next night, the newscast carried another piece on the beating but
for the second time didn't mention that the two eight-year-olds were
brothers. Twins. The anchor tagged the piece:

Violence and sadness in California.

That's no help to listeners who aren't aware that the beating of an infant
is both violent and sad.
Another network's evening newscast introduced a package:

**This is not the kind of story the world wants to see or hear,
but it is important.**

Don't worry; the *world* won't see or hear it—just the audience. But why tell listeners it's not what they want? And why call the story important? Aren't all network stories important? Shouldn't they be? Our job is to report the news, not to tell folks that they don't want to hear what we're going to tell them.

Nor is there any point in telling people they may not know what they're about to be told. Yet one network correspondent said,

> **You may not know this, but a brave new world of medical records is upon us.**

You can begin most news stories, "You may not know this. . . ." But you should know enough not to. Unfortunately, the correspondent's assertion— about patients' medical records not being so confidential—has been widely known for a long time. Further, his tired allusion to the 1932 novel *Brave New World* has gone flat.

And a third network's newsmagazine on another subject:

> **When we come back, new discoveries about what really happened that night. And what we found out, many doctors and hospitals may not want you to see.**

Sounds like one of those ads for an insider's newsletter: "What your dentist doesn't want you to know." Or "Bagels! What's *really* in them."

Some network scripts have other holes:

> **Then the doctor gave her the terrible news, but at first, she didn't understand his meaning.**

She didn't understand his meaning? That passeth all understanding. Perhaps the anchor meant "she didn't understand what the doctor told her."

> **For companies, domestic violence also hits the bottom line hard, up to five billion dollars lost annually. . . .**

That *up to* makes the total as elastic as a bungee cord. How was that sum arrived at? In fact, it's an *unk-unk:* unknown and unknowable.

> **On Capitol Hill, it's now a six-pack of Senate Democrats calling it quits for re-election—six and counting.**

A *six-pack* of Senators? And a *twelve-pack* of Representatives?

> **Captain Tony, who ran for mayor here as a self-confessed**
> **gambler, adulterer and gun smuggler and won, says a clean,**
> **orderly themed Key West is no Key West at all.**

Self-confessed? Who can confess for you but you? So *self* should go on the shelf. Also, many lawyers consider a confession a *written* instrument. In any case, that excerpt needs rehabilitation: "Captain Tony ran for mayor here as an admitted gambler, smuggler and adulterer—and won. He says a clean, orderly theme-park Key West is <u>not</u> Key West." (Yes, things are seldom what they theme.)

> **For travelers trying to get home for the holidays, it's been**
> **nothing short of frustrating.**

If it's *nothing short of frustrating,* it's frustrating.

> **The accused in this case is a Georgia man named Ellis**
> **Wayne Felker, who was to have died** [better: *was to have*
> *been executed*] **last month for the murder 15 years ago of**
> **Evelyn Ludlum.**

An inmate on death row is no longer labeled *the accused.* Right after the crime, he's a *suspect,* later the *accused.* But when the accusation is proved in court, he's found guilty—and thus *convicted.* So he's no longer merely *the accused.*

Also: Why give the murderer a middle name—but not the victim? Broadcast style calls for the elimination of middle names, except when there's a possibility of confusion with someone else. Or when someone of substance has long been identified with a middle name: Harriet Beecher Stowe, Henry Wadsworth Longfellow, George Washington Carver. All of them made their name in a more leisurely time. But nowadays we have less time and can't afford to misspend time—while telling listeners less.

A Thinkless Job

We'd all like every broadcast think-piece to be a masterpiece, a mini-masterpiece. But as the comedian Phil Silvers told a young beauty when she said she'd do *anything* to get into television, "It's not that easy." So let's listen to this network think-piece and see what we think:

> **Summer is supposed to be a season of escape and renewal.**
> [Tell me something I don't know.] **This year, summer has**
> **turned into the season of sorrow.** [For whom? Not for

everyone. Not for most. Not even for one-tenth of one percent.] **Fear and mourning have suddenly become our new national pastimes.** [Nonsense.]

The vast majority of us don't know any of the people killed in this summer's tragedies, yet we hang on the coverage of these horrid events because the people who were harmed were innocents. [We followed those events because they were so unusual and so many people were killed—not because the *harmed* were "innocents" (whatever that means).] **They never had a chance.** [A maudlin cliché.]

From the barracks bombing in Saudi Arabia, where Americans were slaughtered [better: *killed;* animals are *slaughtered,* people are *massacred*] **as they slept, we learned that our military is never safe anywhere, even in a country not at war, even in a place where opposition is practically illegal.** [We've long known that military people are never safe anywhere in peacetime, not even aboard warships and warplanes. *Especially* aboard warships and warplanes.] **From the crash of TWA Flight 800, we're afraid we'll learn that a determined terrorist can strike virtually at will, that what happened overseas in places like Lockerbie can happen here, too.** [We've also long known that terrorists can strike anywhere at any time: Terrorists tried to assassinate President Truman in 1950. And in 1954 they shot five congressmen.] **And from the attack at the Olympics in Atlanta, we learn that the place that was said to be the most secure place was not.** [Who ever said Centennial Olympic Park was the *most* secure place? And what's to learn?] **It's what makes terrorism so sinister: Everyone is a target.** [*Everyone* is not a target. But anyone might be.]

Sometimes we take for granted that which is most important. [Platitude: "a flat, dull or trite remark, especially one uttered as if it were fresh or profound."] **Freedom is a good example. Until a week or two ago, who of us gave a second thought to the basic privileges we enjoy every day, our comings and goings?** [Our *comings and goings* are basic rights, not *basic privileges.*] **Freedom, it turns out, is fragile. A blow against it anywhere injures us all.** [More banalities imparted as profundities.]

During this summer of sorrow, most of us will try to maintain a demeanor of normalcy, but underneath the facade of everyday life, we share fear. [Our everyday life is not a *facade.* And polls tell us the dominant fear is of crime.

Besides, we share much more than fear.] **Terrorism is what we talk about now.** [We talk about everything under the sun.] **Terrorism is what we don't want our kids to look at on TV.** [How about not watching criminality? Barbarity? Obscenity? Vulgarity? Vacuity?] **Terrorism is what hangs in the air like the heat of a hot summer's day that no breeze can blow away.** [More hot air.]

That's it, folks, word for word: a plenitude of platitudes. Nothing new, insightful, engaging, original or interesting. When you think about it, what's missing from that so-called think-piece is thought. (Please don't accuse me of textual harrassment, but that think-piece was more than twice as long as Washington's second Inaugural Address.)

Next, another network correspondent:

Today, Hurricane Bertha focused its fury on the fragile Bahamas island chain. [Storms don't focus on anything.] **Storm-force winds raked Nassau early this afternoon.** [*Storm-force winds?* Try "windstorms."] ... **Not a single cruise ship remained in port. All left early to escape the potentially treacherous seas.** Delete *potentially.*

The next correspondent on that newscast reported from Savannah, Georgia, that 50,000 people had been told to leave the Outer Banks:

And, in fact [delete *in fact*], **the U-S Navy has taken some extra** [delete *some* and *extra*] **precautions as well, ordering its sailors to remove 45 ships and submarines to safer ground.**

Safer ground? Sailors don't *remove* ships. And they can't move ships ashore—or to *safer ground.* (If a ship goes aground, the captain will land in hot water.) When Navy ships are in port—anchored, moored to buoys or tied up to a pier—and a big storm is approaching, the ships sail away lickety-split—to take less of a licking.

Another network storm:

The reason why so much rain fell here in Puerto Rico was because the storm was moving at only six miles an hour.

A multiple redundancy: *reason why* and *reason . . . was because.* More net's work:

An incredible scene in Quebec. Take a look at this. [Please, don't tell viewers to view—or listeners to listen.] **Rivers**

armed [*armed* rivers?] **with nearly a foot of rain over the weekend turned into an invasion force.** [That military metaphor should be scuttled.] **Floodwaters took over the streets, sent thousands of people running for their lives and wrecked many of their houses. . . .**

A family buys a *house,* then turns it into a *home.* Better: "wrecked many homes."

A network non-storm:

Spiver Gordon is the leading civil rights leader in Alabama who believes this racial division is fueling the fires of hate.

A *leading leader?* Whoever let that get by was not a leading reader. *Fueling the fires of hate* is journalese. Don't fuel fears, fuel controversy, or fuel speculation. In short: Don't fuel around.

Another network nugget:

And so the senator leaves the place he has loved with the most fulsome praise ringing in his ears. . . .

Fulsome does not mean "abundant." It means excessive or insincere. The anchor went on to ask the senator,

You will miss it [the senate], **won't you?**

But that short question violated two basic rules of interviewing: Don't suggest an answer. And (with few exceptions) don't ask a yes-or-no question. Instead, let's hear the interviewee think and speak for himself.

And let's see more proof that writers, reporters, editors, producers and anchors are thinking.

When Words Fail You

An unemployed poet,

an anchor said on the air,

held a two-hour siege at the altar of St. Patrick's Cathedral in New York last night.

An *un*employed poet? Ever hear of anyone employed to write poetry? (As the poet Robert Graves told a banker, "There's no money in poetry—and no poetry in money.") And have you ever heard of one man, alone—particularly a poet—laying siege to anything? Especially when he's *in* the place under siege?

A siege is "the surrounding and blocking of a town or fortress by an army bent on capturing it." And police can lay siege to a building. But the intruder in the cathedral pretended to have a bomb, took control of the altar and held off the police. No matter what he did, he did not lay siege to the altar or to the cathedral. And he certainly didn't "hold" a siege. One can hold a grudge, or an audience, or a winning hand, but no number of people, even an army, can "hold" a siege. Police probably *besieged* him (and *beseeched* him). So, chances are, he himself was *under* siege. Whatever was happening, the poet was far too busy to commit any new rhymes.

If the anchor or someone else on the script-assembly line had checked a dictionary for *siege,* he would have learned—or been reminded—that the word used in the script was being misused. Handy thing, a dictionary. If we take a minute to check, a dictionary can keep us out of trouble. I usually turn first to my *American Heritage,* 3d ed. It's liftable—and occasionally uplifting. Its Usage Panel of writers, editors and educators provides help with simple notes on hundreds of words. Among these notes is one on the word *behalf.* When should we say "*in* behalf of someone"? And when should we say "*on* behalf"? The *American Heritage Dictionary* also discusses synonyms for many words, spelling out the nuances of words that may seem similar. For instance: *continual, continuous, constant, ceaseless, incessant, perpetual, eternal, perennial, interminable.*

For a larger collection of synonyms, every newsroom needs a good thesaurus. The one I find most helpful is *Roget's International,* 5th ed. Other thesauruses named Roget are not so good. Likewise, *Webster's New International Dictionary*—the second edition is best—is not to be confused with any old Webster's, a name available to anyone.

Another reference book that I find invaluable is *American Usage and Style: The Consensus* by Roy Copperud. An expert, he offers the views of other experts, as well as his own views, on disputed points.

When I can't find what I'm looking for in Copperud (or if I want a second—or third—opinion (or if I can't find anyone who agrees with me), I turn to one of the other leading guides on usage:

The American Heritage Book of English Usage. This book has assembled the opinions of the usage panel that are scattered throughout the *American Heritage Dictionary.*

The Careful Writer by Theodore M. Bernstein.

The New York Times Manual of Style and Usage, edited by Lewis Jordan.

Modern American Usage by Wilson Follett.

Harper Dictionary of Contemporary Usage by William and Mary Morris.

A Dictionary of Contemporary American Usage by Bergen Evans and Cornelia Evans.

Practical English Usage by Michael Swan.

The Writer's Hotline Handbook by Michael Montgomery and John Stratton, now out of print, is based on a phone-in grammar service sponsored by the University of Arkansas at Little Rock. This campus doesn't have a football team, but a member of the English faculty will tackle any question on usage free. All you have to do is phone (501) 569-3161. An expert is scheduled to be on hand from 9 a.m. to 2:30 p.m., Central time, Monday through Friday.

The hotbed of hotlines, with six grammar services, is Ohio. They're among 70 hotlines—listed in the back of this book—that have sprung up across this country and Canada. The hotlines answer short questions about writing—by phone, fax or E-mail—free (not *for* free).

You can get a copy of the annual directory of hotlines free by sending a note to Grammar Hotline Directory, Tidewater Community College Writing Center, 1700 College Crescent, Virginia Beach, VA 23456. Enclose a stamped, addressed envelope (no. 10).

A newswriter can't pick up a phone every time he's stumped, but he can pick up a usage book. The slimmest work on usage I've run across, 60 pages, is the *Goof/Proofer.* It focuses on two dozen of the most common goofs: misuse of *like;* misuse of *and* after *try* [as in "I'll try and go"]; misuses of *I, me, myself* and other personal pronouns; confusion of *good* and *well;* confusion of *fewer* and *less;* confusion of *can* and *may;* use of verbs and pronouns that don't agree in number with their subjects.

Goof/Proofer also lists more than 300 homonyms, words that sound the same but have different meanings. Any broadcaster will benefit from the reminder that when he delivers one word, a listener may hear another word. A copy of *Goof/Proofer* can be obtained by joining SPELL (Society for the Preservation of English Language and Literature), POB 118, Waleska, GA 30183. Membership is $20 for the first year; after that, $15 a year. Members of that non-profit organization get a copy of *Goof/Proofer* free, plus a newsletter on language six times a year. (For the record, I'm a member.)

Anyone who has read this far deserves a small reward, an observation by Mark Twain: "The difference between the almost right word and the right word is really a large matter—'tis the difference between the lightning bug and the lightning."

As I continue to say, one of the not-at-all-right words for the first sentence of a story is *continues. Continues* lacks newness and newsiness, which are especially desirable for the start of a story. Action verbs make sentences move, but *continues* is unmoving. So this lackluster lead is a loser:

> **The stalemate in Beirut *continues*. Shiite terrorists *continue* to hold some 40 American hostages, and the terrorists *continue* to demand freedom for some 700 Moslems held in northern Israel. . . .**

Three *continues* in seven seconds! Dull, duller, dullissimo. The writer should have searched for the latest development in that story or taken a new approach and led with that. Almost any verb would be preferable to *continues*. For a subsequent sentence, *continues* may be acceptable, but for the crucial first sentence, it's inapt. So let offenders be warned about this thoughtless habit: It should be discontinued.

And for those who have made it this far, we offer another bonus, more of Mark Twain: "A powerful agent is the right word; it lights the reader's way and makes it plain. . . . Whenever we come upon one of these intensely right words in a book or a newspaper, the resulting effect is physical as well as spiritual, and electrically prompt. It tingles exquisitely around through the walls of the mouth and tastes as tart and crisp and good as the autumn butter that creams the sumac berry."

WWW. (Watching and Weighing Words)

The word is out that in many newsrooms the word is in. Surveys show that almost all news directors say the skill they prize most is writing. And news directors tell me they're paying closer attention to what's being written. So I'm going to join them in their wordwatching and their quest for better writing. You have my word.

As someone who lives by the word, I listen to newscasts carefully. And when I need a quick news fix, I turn to radio. For the past few days (this was my first column in *Communicator,* May 1984), I've been turning it on to give New York City's top news stations a once-over. To make sure I'd be able to quote them word for word, I've taped them. Here's some of what they broadcast:

> **An ocean liner has made an unscheduled stop in the
> Caribbean—atop a coral reef.**

I like that line. I traced it to the writer, Greg Johnson of the AP in Washington, D.C. Take a bow, Greg, but not the whole ship.

> **Some residents outside Hilo, Hawaii, had to hot-foot it to
> safety after authorities told them lava was threatening their
> homes.**

I like *hot-foot*, but in the middle of the sentence it loses its kick. The sentence would have been stronger if the writer had built up to the key word or key idea: "Hawaii's Kilauea volcano is threatening homes near Hilo, as lava flows closer, so some residents have had to hot-foot it to safety."

> **Today the question of aid to El Salvador became a lot more
> heated because House Speaker Tip O'Neill, the ranking
> Democrat in Congress, called for a full-scale investigation
> into whether the War Powers Act is being violated by the
> Reagan administration.**

Don't start a story with *today,* except as a transition; listeners assume the news is today's. Also: question*ers* and question*ing* get heated—but not questions. And why describe an investigation as *full-scale?* Did O'Neill or any officeholder ever call for a half-scale investigation? The sentence, 40 words, is over-long. And overheated.

> **Mayor Koch is now a Knight of the French Legion of
> Honor. It was bestowed upon him today at City Hall
> ceremonies. French President François Mitterand paid
> Koch the visit and gave him the award.**

That item is weakly written: The first sentence lacks an action verb and the second sentence lacks the active voice. *Is* is a linking verb, not a verb of action. Better: "France has made Mayor Koch a Knight of the French Legion of Honor. President Mitterand himself presented the award today at City Hall." The overhaul is shorter by one-third. And stronger.

> **Police in Strasbourg, France, don't think the shooting of
> the American consul there was a political act.**

You could improve the news item by moving "not" from before *think* to after *was:* "Police in Strasbourg, France, say they think the shooting of the

American consul there was not a political act." Although the original script used the word *think,* I rewrote it to *"say* they think." No one knows what anyone else is thinking; all we know is what someone *says* he thinks.

[Gunmen] robbed 21 million dollars from a security vault in Rome.

The verb should be "stole." You can rob a bank, but you can't rob money. "Rob" means "to steal *from."*

Security was tight for NATO defense ministers who began arriving in Turkey today for a ministerial-level meeting this week on nuclear planning.

And on another newscast:

Queen Elizabeth is to arrive in Jordan today, and security is tight.

When you write about tight security, your script is just about as newsy as if you wrote, "The sun rose in the east today." If you find a meeting of NATO defense ministers that lacks security or has lax security, then you'd have news. If tight security is the most important fact that you have to write about, you don't have much of a story. Also, in that first excerpt: with *today,* you don't need *this week.*

[It] was the second hijacking in as many days.

A common error. When you highlight the order of events and start with an ordinal number, like *second,* the construction in that sentence requires you to follow with a cardinal number: *two.* That would make your sentence read: "[It] was the second hijacking in two days."

According to the indictment, Castellano conspired in three murders personally.

Personally should be rubbed out.

The Reagan administration is putting on the full-court press now on behalf of the President's aid proposals for El Salvador.

Overuse of *full-court press* has made it a cliché. Some writers use it to mean an all-out attack, but a "full-court press" is a basketball tactic. (And if you write about a courtroom filled with newspeople, don't call it "a full-press court.")

> **International finance is a tangled web, and it's likely to get**
> **a good bit more complicated as we approach the weekend**
> **and the threatened default by Argentina on interest**
> **payments on its massive foreign debt.**

That script is a tangled web, but don't get entangled yourself, webster. Many stories *are* complex; it's our job to simplify them, not tanglify them. That broadcast sentence is too long. Imagine a newscaster reading it aloud, and imagine a listener trying to disentangle it. There's no need to tell listeners that international finance is complex.

> **He's been taking a controversial position on Central**
> **America.**

The *New York Times*'s in-house critique, "Winners & Sinners," calls *controversial* an "empty word." W&S says it would be "hard pressed to cite a word that tells less yet appears more often."

> **Jesse Jackson wasn't in New York this morning, but he'll**
> **return for tonight's TV debate among the three candidates.**

I may be interested in where someone was, or where he is, or where he's going, but please don't tell me where he is not.

> **With suspensions of the distribution of Girl Scout cookies**
> **spreading because pins and other harmful debris have been**
> **found in a few of the cookies, the Food and Drug**
> **Administration says the F-B-I wants to find out who**
> **planted pins and other harmful objects in some cookies.**

The lead is long and busy, so it de-emphasizes the core of the news, which is that the F-B-I has entered the case. And the sentence has many other faults. It brings to mind Mark Twain's criticism of asserted defects in less than one page of *The Deerslayer:* "[James Fenimore] Cooper has scored 114 offenses against literary art out of a possible 115. It breaks the record."

Twain went on to urge that a writer "say what he is proposing to say, not merely come near it; use the right word, not its second cousin; eschew surplusage . . .; avoid slovenliness of form; use good grammar; employ a simple and straightforward style." Amen.

Whaaat?

Let's face FAQs—and Internetniks know FAQ stands for Frequently Asked Questions. One of the FAQs is that thoughtful people who listen to network news often ask, "Whaaat? How did *that* get on the air?" So in the interest of upgrading writing (without degrading writers), let's look at the kinds of scripts from evening newscasts that puzzle listeners and raise questions:

> **First, it was a successful clone** [should be *cloning*] **of a sheep in Scotland. Now researchers in this country have upped the ante and the fear.**

Concern, maybe, but *fear*? Who expressed fear other than the anchor? And how can fear be *upped*? *Up* is a newspaper headline verb, not a verb used in conversation. Sounds like journalese, not journalism.

When you raise the ante in a poker game, you raise the stakes. Also: when someone raises the ante, everyone has to pay more for a share in a venture or a share of total expenses. In that news story, what stakes were raised? By whom? How? Why? (If someone clones a cow, I'd wonder who raised the steaks.)

> **More news in context now in our headline story. We're trying to give you in-depth coverage of this evidence of life on Mars. . . . This is really mind-provoking stuff that we're dealing with.**

All right, give us context—but without using the word *context*. Scrap all that talky *stuff*. And stop *trying*. Just give us the news.

> **New developments tonight in the Whitewater and Democratic campaign fund-raising investigations.**

Anchors who speak of *new developments* aren't telling us anything new. We already know that newscasts present what's new. Anchors should go ahead and tell us the developments. (Who reports *old* developments?)

> **In California, fresh details today give new context and perspective to that deadly shoot-out between police and**

**bank robbery suspects captured live on television last
Friday.**

Sounds as if the two bad guys were *captured live.* But they were shot
dead. Were they still only *suspects*? After that anchor lead-in, the correspondent said:

Local [delete] **police are investigating** [better: *trying to find
out*] **whether the pair** [better: *the two men*] **are** [*were;* they're
dead] **the notorious A-K-47 bandits who nabbed more than
a million dollars from two L-A banks last year.**

Nabbed money? *Nab* is a headline word. They grabbed the money, but
they weren't nabbed.

She bore a child to [*had a child by*] **Randolph Churchill.** . . .
**The Harriman home in Washington became like a think
tank-cum-cocktail party, where ideas were raised, money
rained down and power was grown.**

How many listeners know that *cum* is Latin for "with"? Questions are
raised, but *ideas*? Someone's power can grow, but power is not *grown*.
Another problem: abrupt, inconsistent shifts in construction from the passive *(were raised)* to the active *(rained down)* and back to the passive
(was grown).

**The Supreme Court is expected to officially issue its ruling
on doctor-assisted suicide in July.**

When does the court issue a ruling *un*officially?

It is a town gripped in grief.

Good grief! A town can't be gripped *in*—or even *by*—grief.

**It's the videotape that exposed disturbing revelations about
a correction system in deep trouble.** . . .

Exposed revelations? How's that again? A revelation is a disclosure, so
how can something already public be exposed? That broadcast sentence is
disturbing and *in deep trouble.*

We start tonight [an anchor who starts by telling you he's
starting is off to a bad start] **with the latest** [isn't the latest

what newscasts are all about?] **on a still-developing story. . . .
Last night the read was it** [a hurricane] **probably would hit
the U-S mainland. What's the read tonight?**

The read from here, pal, is that your script needs rereading—and rewriting. *Read* is a term used by newspeople so pressed for time they rely on insiders' language—among themselves. But for careful writers, *read* is still a verb.

Now some points to mention here.

May I point out, yet again, the need to proceed with dispatch and not to tell us what you're going to tell us without telling us anything new.

**Our lead story tonight centers around new technology, new
definitions of theft and accused citizens' rights to a fair trial.**

Centers around should be *centers on.* The center is at the center; it can't be *around* anything. And nothing can *center on* three subjects. Lead with the lead story. With time so short, why take time to sketch a snapshot?

**Hers was one of 150 houses decimated by 14 tornadoes
that ripped across Arkansas, cutting a 260-mile path of
destruction. They touched down 37 times into homes and
lives.**

Too many numbers jammed together. *Decimated* is misused; what's needed is "destroyed." Do tornadoes *cut* a path? (Sounds like a shortcut.) Or do they plow, punch, trample or steamroller a path? Oh, well, at least no one said, "It sounded like a freight train coming through."

**The sheriff's department in Pasco County, Florida, believes
it has a remedy for this so-called disease** ['mad cop disease']:
**a new training program, unlike any other, that teaches
officers how to remain calm during a chase.**

Unlike any other? How can a reporter know that the program's technique is unique?

**Rap music star Tupac Shakur is recovering tonight after
being shot several times last night in Las Vegas.**

Recovering? He died. Failure to attribute that assertion puts an anchor in the position of practicing medicine without a license.

And no one, the F-B-I's inclined to believe, has taken credit for [the bombing].

Inclined to believe is fuzzy; the FBI either knows or doesn't know. And a terrorist doesn't get *credit;* we should write that he takes responsibility.

The weather's making news again tonight in the South and in the West. Northern California still reeling [should be *is still reeling*] **from massive flooding, and we've just learned tonight** [every item carried on a newscast is something the newsroom has *learned;* and *just learned tonight* sounds like razzle-dazzle] **the late word is the early estimate** [*late/early?*] **of the damage, one-point-five billion dollars. That will grow, but it** [the estimate?] **makes this the worst flood in the state's history** [an *estimate* can't make it the worst], **left behind** [better: *caused*] **by ten straight days of powerful winter storms** [delete *winter:* ever hear of a summer storm in January?]. **Valuable farmland north of Sacramento still completely submerged** [should be *is still submerged;* no need for *completely;* better: *under water*], **and damage is expected to top, again, one-point-five billion dollars.** [Why tell us again? And why tell us you're telling us again?] **That's the first estimate.** [But not the first time you've told us.]

Someone should have placed a storm watch on that windy script. It starts by saying *the weather's making news.* Silly. Everything on a newscast is *making news.* There's no need to say it; there's a need *not* to say it. And to say that the weather is making news *again* detracts from whatever newsiness it might have.

As for the damage estimate, who made it? Property owners who tend to fear (or fake) the worst? Insurance companies, which tend to minimize losses? Or an impartial party? Also: in conversation, people don't say *one-point-five billion dollars.* They say, "a billion and a half dollars."

The repetition in that torrent of words in the script makes it seem as if it was written by someone whose memory is leaky. Which results in a script that's eminently forgettable—and regrettable.

For a time today, at high noon, it was more like the movie "High Noon" on the floor of the House chamber.

Did Grace Kelly and Gary Cooper make a House call? What did they or their 1952 movie have to do with what occurred that day, 45 years later, in the House? How many viewers remember the movie? Or the plot? Or even saw the movie? To listeners familiar with the plot, mention of the movie suggests a showdown between a heroic figure and the forces of evil. Who took those roles in the House? The writer of the news script should have set the scene in her or his own words without dragging in an old movie title.

> **While in Eastern Europe today, first lady Hillary Rodham Clinton visited Auschwitz, the Polish death camp. . . .**

The death camp was not Polish. It was on Polish soil, but at that time Poland was under the heel of Nazi Germany, which ran the camp.

> **Friday, the Air Force will park its planes for a national safety review. Billy Ogston's family wants to know why, after decades of improvements, their son was a victim of such a fatal year.**

No one is killed by a year.

> **The known situation is that these Games are now being run under a cloud of security and fear.**

Known situation? Try that again, please—in English. P.S. What is a *cloud of security?*

The next story followed a piece on the Persian Gulf:

> **Congressional findings are out today** [*are out* can mean the findings have been out for an hour or a month] **on another Persian Gulf controversy** [this item followed a Gulf story]. **Remember those videos of laser-guided, so-called smart bombs pumped out by the Defense Department during the war against Iraq?** [A story shouldn't hinge on a listener's memory. What if a listener doesn't remember those videos of five years earlier?] **Here's what these pictures don't show. Congressional investigators say these so-called smart bombs, as well as stealth fighters and Tomahawk cruise missiles, were affected** [favorably? adversely?] **by rain and clouds. They performed, it said** [*it?*], **no better than conventional, cheaper weapons. And post-war claims of success by the manufacturers were, and I quote the Congressional finding now, 'overstated and misleading,' end of quotation.**

The words *quote, unquote, end quote* and *end of quotation* should be quarantined. They're not conversational: they're intrusive, irruptive and inelegant. Here's a way to write the script without queering it with *quote* and *unquote:* "The investigators say the claims of success by manufacturers were 'overstated and misleading.'"

The quotation marks around "overstated and misleading" signal the anchor to deliver those three words so they *sound* like quoted matter. But even without special delivery, whether read as a quotation or not, those three words mean the same. (See pages 145-148.)

In a world that's declared similarity to be the key to success, Lynn dares to be different.

If similarity is the key to success, why do so many products and services trumpet their differences and supposedly unique qualities? It would be daring if Lynn did the *same* as competitors.

Bomb number eight turned up today at the post office in Leavenworth, Kansas, addressed to the federal prison, where two letter bombs were delivered yesterday. All of them, say officials, were rigged to maim or kill, which makes something of a hero out of Dana Sanadurusi, a reporter who yesterday spotted the first of the suspicious-looking letters sent to his newspaper's office in Washington, D.C.

Something of a hero? He was nothing of a hero. If you call someone who spots a suspicious object and calls the police a hero (or *something of a hero,* whatever that means), what do you call someone who goes into a burning building and, despite the smoke and flames, rescues an unconscious news director?

Under a plea bargain deal, he could spend as little as 20 years in prison.

Deal is redundant: a plea bargain *is* a deal. And 20 years is not so *little.* As Oscar Wilde put it, in prison "each day is like a year, a year whose days are long."

When Hurricane Fran hit the coast just south of here, the brunt of this storm swept across this area, literally cutting away 10 to 15 feet of the beach and. . . .

Can a *brunt* sweep? Trash one *this,* and dispose of *literally,* which is only litter.

The anchor introduced a correspondent on another story by saying he

**has been on top of this story since it broke. He's been
digging, checking and re-checking with his sources and now
has the latest.**

That's not news; that's impropaganda. Don't all reporters dig, check and
re-check—and produce the latest?

Next, the reporter:

**They've got a lot of leads, but they're not all panning out
down in Atlanta.** [For listeners south of Atlanta, it's *up.*] **Over
the weekend, agents questioned several militia members
across the South. And while that is still going on, we're told**
[by whom?], **it's** [what's *it?*] **not showing as much promise
as first thought** [by whom?]. **Secondly, the composite
drawings are receiving less emphasis from agents. . . .**

You can't have a *second* (not *secondly*) without a *first.*

Say, how *did* all that shoddy material get on the air? In network
newsrooms, it seems, that's a SAQ—seldom-asked question.

Soup of the Month

If Broadcast Newswriting were a company on the Big Board, I'd be bullish:
Its sources are inexhaustible, its products indispensable, its consumers in-
satiable. But some of the Company's products are faulty, with words misused, language abused, stories confused. Yet most of the faults are
preventable or correctable. And executives say they're bearing down on the
assembly lines. The Company's shares may be attractive because its assets,
especially its workers, are undervalued. So the outlook could be favorable.

I was asked to evaluate the Company by Joe Tiernan, the former
editor of the *Communicator.* He asked me because I hold newswriting
workshops at radio and TV stations. In my travails across the country,
here is what I found in the Company's plants:

1. Most of the products are serviceable and many are commendable;
but some are deplorable.

2. News directors have so many responsibilities that most N.D.s
lack time to oversee their writers.

3. Some N.D.s who do have the time lack the writing and teaching
experience necessary to train their writers.

4. Quality control is inadequate. In many cases, the missing link is a good editor. Unless a script is edited skillfully along the way, the assembly line is no better than a bucket brigade: The product arrives at the end of the line no better than it started out.

Yet those minuses are offset somewhat by pluses that indicate a hunger for improvement: 1) News directors tell me how highly they rate newswriting. And how they'd like to have more newswriting that's first-rate. 2) Writers—including reporters, producers and anchors—tell me how much *they* value good writing. Many acknowledge shortcomings and say they want to write better.

If the quality of broadcast newswriting has been declining, it may be due partly to those newcomers whose goal is to become anchors, not writers. Most of them have an uneasy acquaintance with English, and are short on journalistic basics and street smarts. One script I read after it was broadcast illustrates several common problems in writing, reporting and editing:

> **And, [name of co-anchor], in case you didn't know it, [name of city] Mayor _____ _____ has proclaimed January as National Soup Month. In honor of the event, the Campbell's Soup Company brought their Soupmobile here to _____ . One of the three stops they made today was here at the Salvation Army. _____ city employees as well as some of _____'s needy stood in line to warm up. The Soupmobile is making a ten-city tour of the country. It will be here for two more days before the chefs on board pack up and move on to _____ for a three-day stop.**

The lead-in and voice-over are riddled with flaws from start to finish: Why should an anchor deliver the news to a co-anchor? And why suggest the co-anchor may be unaware of that item? Why use the mayor's first name? And why not get the company's name right—Campbell, not Campbell's? (The soup itself is called Campbell's.) Also, *their* soupmobile should be *its*. And why does an anchor say *here* (unless the Salvation Army is encamped in the studio)? Who cares where the Soupmobile is going next (especially when it'll be hundreds of miles away)? And who cares how long it'll park there?

The biggest problem, though, is the naive (yet souped up) approach. The event has all the earmarks of a press-agent stunt—commercialism but with no commercials. A Campbell press agent probably drafted the proclamation and arranged for the mayor to sign it. The script implies that Campbell was responding to the mayor's proclamation, but any reporter who has ever covered mayors or governors knows they sign proclamations at the drop of a hint or a contribution. Or a hint of a contribution. Why would a mayor spontaneously proclaim a National Soup Month? And how could a local official make it *national?* What a crock! No one was hurt, I suppose. And some poor people were helped. Not to mention the press agent (and good press agents seldom want to be mentioned).

In a small town on a slow news day, it may be news when the Campbells are coming. But the news should be written with some savvy. If a writer needs seasoning, then it's up to an editor or producer or anchor or news director to set the writer straight. No matter what size the town or the newsroom, every script should be read by other eyes so another Company product doesn't go bad—and another writer doesn't wind up in the soup.

As writers, our goal is to do more than stay out of the soup, even alphabet soup. Our goal is to write better scripts—shorter, sharper, stronger. Writing requires far more than simply putting words down. Writers must think clearly, understand language thoroughly and watch what they say, intently. You can improve your writing skills, but only through writing and writing and, when time permits, rewriting.

16

ALL ELSE

Q. What else can be said about broadcast newswriting?

A. Plenty else.

Q. O.K., let's start with one else: What are the tricks to writing news?

A. The only trick is to know how to write and to understand what you're writing about. And the secret is to make it seem as if it's not a trick.

Q. Huh?

A. We don't engage in tricks or trickery. The writer H. Jackson Brown, Jr., put it: "Don't waste time learning the 'tricks of the trade.' Instead, learn the trade."

Q. But how?

A. They say, "We always learn from others and end up teaching ourselves."

Q. How can you teach yourself?

A. "Teach yourself by your own mistakes," said the novelist William Faulkner. "People learn only by error."

Q. What about shortcuts?

A. There are no shortcuts, no gimmicks, no quick fixes, no simple steps, no easy answers, no magical cures, no cut-rate, can't-miss techniques, no one-fits-all solutions. "There are no shortcuts to any place worth going," according to the singer Beverly Sills. And you can't become a better writer overnight—even if you work the overnight. As a CD developer said, "ROM wasn't built in a day." And as Nero noted, "Rome wasn't burned in a day."

If there ever could be one single answer on how to become a better newswriter, it would be: write, write, write, work, work, work. Work *works*. The more you write, the more you *can* write. The more you can write, the more you can learn. And the better you'll write.

Q. Learn from whom?

A. From someone who's better.

Q. What if I'm the best in my shop?

A. "Best in my shop" may be a modest boast: The best may be not much better than the rest. Many newcomers—and oldtimers—regard themselves as masters. That's why there are so few masters. The critic Robert Hughes said, "The greater the artist the greater the doubt; perfect confidence is granted to the less talented as a consolation prize."

Q. What about getting *outside* help?

A. Most newsrooms don't get outside help. And newspeople, like most other people, find it hard to improve when they have no one to learn from but themselves.

Q. What about learning from writers with more experience?

A. Learn from anyone who knows more than you. The best writers know how much more *they* have to learn. (At the age of 70, an accomplished French writer said, "Every day I am learning to write.")

Q. So what's the answer?

A. Whether you become a writer or a Writer depends on you.

Q. How so?

A. If you want to improve, and apparently you do, you'll have to do it yourself.

Q. Please explain.

A. Experts say good writing can't be taught but can be learned. I disagree with Oscar Wilde's epigram: "Nothing that is worth knowing can be taught."

Q. What do *you* say?

A. I say writing *can* be taught and *can* be learned.

Q. How?

A. By you, as part-time teacher and full-time learner. The author Jacques Barzun says all good writing is self-taught: "Almost any professional writer will tell you that nobody can teach another person to write. . . . But all writers admit that they were helped by criticism; somebody showed them the effect of what they had written—the unintended bad effect. In doing so, the critic pointed out where the trouble lay and perhaps what its cause was. . . . The truth remains that the would-be writer, using a book or a critic, must teach himself. He must learn to spot his own errors and work out his own ways of removing them." You don't learn from success, you learn from failure—examining failure. The billionaire stock trader George Soros says: "To others, being wrong is a source of shame; to me, recognizing my mistakes is a source of pride. Once we realize that imperfect understanding is the human condition, there is no shame in being wrong, only in failing to correct our mistakes."

Q. Any other advice?

A. The author John Ciardi says: "A writer can develop only as rapidly as he learns to recognize what is bad in his writing. . . . [The bad writer] never sees what he has actually written. . . . He does not see because, in plain fact, he cares nothing about it. He is out for release, not containment. He is a self-expressor, not a maker. . . ." And as for the good writer: "His progress toward good writing and his recognition of bad writing are bound to unfold at something like the same rate."

Q. Anyone else?

A. For the beginner who asks, "How can I learn to write?" Prof. David L. Grey says the right response is: "Do you care enough to work at it? Or, rephrased: How are your motivation and willingness to accept criticism? Are you willing, literally, to sweat over words? And is your primary purpose random self-expression, or is it to communicate something systematically to someone else? Such a philosophy for writing requires practice and self-discipline, as well as corraling the ego. It demands . . . a willingness to 'grope' relentlessly for the best word and set of words. And it demands active seeking out of the best library and human sources of information and insight."

Q. What else?

A. Listen to the best newscasters and the best reporters, even if it means (sob!) turning to another station or network. Listen carefully. Tape newscasts that have the best writing. Play them back. Replay them. Analyze them. And suss out what makes the best writing the best. But don't try to follow the footsteps of a writer you admire. "Find your own voice," says the broadcaster Jeff Greenfield. "Don't be Hemingway, Oscar Wilde, Tom Wolfe; they are taken."

Read some of the books on writing mentioned throughout these pages. Read other good books to deepen your appreciation of good writing and to build up the vast fund of general knowledge needed by newswriters. Read widely, read copiously, read unceasingly. You are what you read, so read, read, read.

Keep in mind an observation by the actress Glenda Jackson: "The only lesson you ever learn is how very difficult it is to act well and how very easy it is to act badly." The same is true about writing.

Q. Why haven't you mentioned humor?

A. Funny, thought I had. Humor is hard to write and harder to write about. In news scripts, it's especially fragile. Most news stories don't lend themselves to humor.

Too much of what's intended as humor in newscasts is contrived and clunky. Most often, the best humor in a newscast depends on humorous aspects of the event itself, not in the newswriter's effort to get a laugh. In fact, most real humor in newscasts produces a smile or a glint of appreciation, not a guffaw. We hear too much on the air that's intended to be humorous but sounds as if it has been pounded out with a sledgehammer. What's needed is the delicate touch of a watercolorist.

"Everything is funny as long as it happens to someone else," Will Rogers said. We might have fun *with* someone else, but we never should make fun *of* people. Misfortune isn't a matter for jest. We don't make fun of those who've just lost a game, a home or an election.

One last thought about humor: If you write something that's humorous, don't apologize for it. Don't tell your listeners, by word or gesture, that you're uncomfortable with something that's supposed to be humorous. If you're uncomfortable with it, rewrite it. Or, better yet, kill it.

Q. What about puns?

A. As a recovering punster, I'm in no position to puntificate. In scripts, I use them infrequently. They're harder to put across on air than on paper. In print, wordplay sometimes works. But broadcasting is a different playing field. That's because many listeners usually need time to catch on, and we can't call a timeout. A gazette issued by pundits, the *New York Times*'s in-house monitor, "Winners & Sinners," set down two good rules on puns: "If in doubt, don't. If anybody nearby winces, definitely don't." The trouble with so many puns we hear and see is that they're obvious or ham-handed, unless, of course, they're our own. So when in doubt, toss it out.

Q. You haven't mentioned pronunciation.

A. Pronunciation! It's important in broadcasting because mistakes mean a loss in an anchor's (or reporter's) authority and credibility. The columnist Sydney J. Harris says the 10 words mispronounced most often are: *nuclear, realtor, conversant, chaise-longue, harass, lingerie, frequent* (as a verb), *forte, monstrous* and *disastrous.* Several other words that I hear kicked around: *cellulite* (should be pronounced cell-you-light), *covert* (the preferred pronunciation is like *cover* with a final *t*), *dour* (do-er, not dow-er), *lambasting* (as in baste), *onerous* (as in *honor*), *patently* (pay-tently), *schism* (the *sch* is pronounced like *s*), and *long-lived (lived* rhymes with *dived).*

Q. What can be done for writing blocks?

A. For some newswriters, blocks (including this Block) are a recurring problem. A freelance writer sitting at home can afford the luxury of having a writing block. But broadcast newswriters can't. We have to produce a lot of copy in a short time, often in frantic haste. We can't permit ourselves any hangups. So we have to develop inner strength, self-control and devout determination.

If you're stymied by a block and can't get past it, here are several ways to deal with it: Do whatever worked for you the last time you were blocked. Or put your story aside—assuming you're not on deadline—and work on something else while your subconscious works on the original story. Or get up and get a cold drink. Or a hot drink. Or eat early. Or walk around in the newsroom. Or leave the newsroom and take a stroll. Or leave the station and take a run. Splash water on your face. Then go back to your original story and get a move on. Discipline yourself. Tell yourself, "I can do it. I will do it. I must do it, I'm going to do it." Then do it. If you're still drawing a blank, think of your paycheck—blank. If that doesn't work, lower your standards. Or run away and join the circus.

Q. How do you deal with the blahs?

A. Don't be blasé. Develop P.M.A. (positive mental attitude). But if newswriting becomes dull for you, if it's no longer interesting or challenging, or never was, maybe you need a change of scenery. Or a new line of work.

Q. How can I learn to write faster?

A. Write more. Speed comes with experience. Meeting deadlines is imperative, but writing fast isn't necessarily a virtue. We're hired as writers, not typists. I can't write without thinking first. So I'm suspicious of speed demons, whose fingers fly across the keyboard. Don't *they* need time to think? Don't *they* need time to come up with the right word? Don't *they* need time to figure out how to say it the best way possible? (Do I sound envious?) Warning: Beware of writers who type faster than they think.

Q. What's the best way to avoid mistakes?

A. Write nothing. Usually, the person who makes no mistakes makes nothing. Mistakes are inevitable when writing in a hurry in the hurly-burly. "The greatest mistake you can make in life," the early 20th century author Elbert Hubbard said, "is to be continually fearing you will make one." Don't let anxiety about mistakes spook you. Your goal should be to turn in copy with zero defects. But if writers always succeeded in doing that, editors could be deleted. Even when writers have someone else checking their copy—editors, producers or anchors—writers mustn't relax their guard against those pesky errors that try to sneak into copy.

Q. How do you deal with deadlines?

A. Dutifully. How else?

Q. Is there a question you were hoping I'd ask?

A. Yes: "Why bother learning to write well when many superiors, so to speak, don't recognize good writing—and reward bad writing?" My answer is: people who are serious about writing want to write as well as they can. Even the uncommitted don't say, "I want to write just so-so." If you're in the news biz (or any business), you have no business hanging around unless you want to do your best. And who knows? You might wind up working for someone who *does* know—and require—good writing. In any case, who not be the best you can be? If you're content with mediocrity, you've bought, borrowed or boosted the wrong book.

Q. Why did you call this chapter All Else?

A. What else? It's a catchall for odds and ends that didn't fit elsewhere, or that deserved different treatment, or that I forgot to put in earlier.

Q. So why didn't you call it Odds & Ends?

A. I was going to, but then I ran across another book using that title for a chapter.

Q. How did you happen to think of "All Else"?

A. On the "CBS Evening News with Walter Cronkite," the three writers were assigned to stories by category: National, International and

All Else. Everything that didn't fit into the first two categories—storms, space, disasters, features, plus the other writers' overflow—went into All Else. As a former All Else writer, I thought it would be an apt heading.

Q. What about "zip"? The title of this book suggests that the book will tell how to write with "zip." Yet you haven't touched on "zip."

A. I might not have been writing with zip, but most of what I've been saying makes for zip. This book's main lesson is that good broadcast newswriting produces copy that's clean, clear and crisp. So if you practice what I've been preaching, you'll write with zip.

Q. Any afterthoughts?

A. One thought about "after"—a thought that deserves repeating. If you find "after" in a lead sentence, you should probably rewrite the sentence: Put what comes after "after" *before* "after." For instance, you first write, "Police are searching for a man in a Santa Claus suit after he robbed a downtown bank." But then you realize that you've put the cart before the reindeer. So you rewrite it: "A man in a Santa Claus suit has robbed a downtown bank." But I wouldn't add "today." If it had occurred yesterday, we would have reported it yesterday. Besides, my use of the present perfect tense—*has robbed*—rules out the need for "today." Also: I wouldn't say the police are searching for him. I probably wouldn't mention the police, unless they're deliberately *not* searching for him.

Q. Anything else?

A. Yes. If you apply all these tips and rules—and if you apply yourself—*you* can have the last word.

APPENDIX A

Further Reading and Reference

BROADCAST NEWSWRITING

Beginning Broadcast Newswriting, 3d ed., by Tim Wulfemeyer (Iowa State University Press, 1993).

Broadcast Journalism: An Introduction to News Writing, 3d ed., by Mark Hall (Hastings House, 1986).*

Broadcast Journalism: Techniques of Radio and TV News, 3rd ed., by Andrew Boyd (Butterworth-Heinemann, 1994).*

Broadcast News, 3d ed., by Mitchell Stephens (Harcourt Brace Jovanovich, 1993).*

Broadcast Newswriting: The RTNDA Reference Guide by Mervin Block (Bonus Books/RTNDA, 1994).

Rewriting Network News: WordWatching Tips from 345 TV and Radio Scripts by Mervin Block (Bonus Books, 1990).

Television Newswriting: Captivating an Audience by Frederick Shook (Longman, 1994).*

Writing News for Broadcast, 3d ed., by Edward Bliss, Jr., and James L. Hoyt (Columbia University Press, 1994).*

WRITING (General)

On Writing Well, 5th ed., by William Zinsser (Harper & Row, 1994).*

*Softcover

Style: Ten Lessons in Clarity & Grace, 4th ed., by Joseph M. Williams (Scott, Foresman, 1994).*

The Associated Press Guide to News Writing, 2d ed., by René Cappon (Arco, 1991).* [Sold by the AP as *The Word.**]

The Elements of Style, 3d ed., by William Strunk Jr. and E. B. White (Macmillan, 1995).*

The Golden Book on Writing by David Lambuth (Viking Press, 1984).*

The Practical Stylist, 7th ed., by Sheridan Baker (Harper & Row, 1990).*

The Suspended Sentence: A Guide For Writers by Roscoe C. Born (Scribners, 1993).

The Use and Abuse of the English Language, 2d ed., by Robert Graves and Alan Hodge (Paragon House, 1990).*

Write Tight by William Brohaugh (Writer's Digest Books, 1993).

Writing with Style: Conversations on the Art of Writing by John R. Trimble (Prentice-Hall, 1975).*

WRITING/REPORTING

Basic Media Writing, 5th ed., by Melvin Mencher (Brown & Benchmark, 1996).*

Broadcast News Writing and Reporting, 2d ed., by Peter E. Mayeux (Brown & Benchmark, 1996).*

Crafting the News for Electronic Media by Carl Hausman (Wadsworth, 1992).

ENG: Television News by Charles F. Cremer, Phillip O. Keirstead and Richard D. Yoakam (McGraw-Hill, 1996).*

News Reporting and Writing, 7th ed., by Melvin Mencher (Brown & Benchmark, 1997).*

Professional TV News Handbook by Charles Coates (Bonus Books, 1994).

Radio and Television Reporting by Roy Gibson (Allyn & Bacon, 1991).

Reporting for Radio by Chuck Crouse (RTNDA/Bonus Books, 1992).

The New News Business: A Guide to Writing and Reporting by John Chancellor and Walter R. Mears (HarperCollins, 1995).*

Television News, Radio News, 4th ed., by Irving Fang (Rada Press, 1985).

Writing, Reporting, and Producing, 2d ed., by Ted White (Focal Press, 1996).

EDITING

Getting the Words Right: How to Revise, Edit & Rewrite by Theodore A. Rees Cheney (Writers Digest Books, 1990).*

Line by Line: How to Edit Your Own Writing by Claire Kehrwald Cook (Houghton Mifflin, 1985).*

GRAMMAR/USAGE

A Pocket Guide to Correct Grammar, 2d ed., by Vincent F. Hopper, Cedric Gale and Ronald C. Foote: revised by Benjamin W. Griffith (Barron's, 1990).*

American Usage and Style: The Consensus by Roy Copperud (Van Nostrand, 1980).

Dictionary of Contemporary Usage, 2d ed., by William and Mary Morris (Harper & Row, 1992).*

Handbook of Good English by Edward D. Johnson (Facts on File, 1991).*

Modern American Usage by Wilson Follett (Hill and Wang, 1980).*

Modern English Usage, 2d ed., by H.W. Fowler, revised and edited by Sir Ernest Gowers (Oxford University Press, 1987).*

Modern English Usage, 3d ed., by H.W. Fowler, edited by R. W. Burchfield (Oxford University Press, 1996).

Painless Perfect Grammar: The National Grammar Hotline's Most Frequently Asked Questions by Michael Strumpf and Auriel Douglas (Bandanna Books, 1997).*

Practical English Usage by Michael Swan (Oxford University Press, 1995).

The American Heritage Book of English Usage (Houghton Mifflin, 1996).*

The Borzoi Handbook for Writers by Frederick Crews and Sandra Schor (Knopf, 1985).

The Careful Writer: A Modern Guide to English Usage by Theodore M. Bernstein (Atheneum, 1965).*

The Good English Guide by Godfrey Howard (Macmillan Reference Books, 1993).*

The Language of News: A Journalist's Pocket Reference by Jack Botts (Iowa State University Press, 1994).

The Oxford English Grammar by Sidney Greenbaum (Oxford University Press, 1996).

Webster's Dictionary of English Usage (Merriam-Webster, 1989).

Webster's New World Guide to Current American Usage by Bernice Randall (Simon & Shuster, 1988).

Woe is I: The Grammarphobe's Guide to Better English in Plain English by Patricia T. O'Conner (G. P. Putnam's Sons, 1996).

Working with Words: A Concise Handbook for Media Writers and Editors, 3d ed., by Brian S. Brooks and James L. Pinson (St. Martin's Press, 1996).*

STYLEBOOKS

The Associated Press Broadcast News Handbook, compiled and edited by James R. Hood and Brad Kalbfeld (The Associated Press, 1982).*

The Associated Press Stylebook and Libel Manual, 31st ed., edited by Norm Goldstein (The Associated Press, 1996).*

Broadcast News Style Guide, edited by Keith Leslie (Broadcast News, 1997). [Broadcast News is a unit of The Canadian Press.]

Broadcast News Writing Stylebook by Robert A. Papper (Allyn & Bacon, 1995).

Los Angeles Times Style and Usage Guide, compiled by Kathy Gosnell (Times Mirror, 1995).

The Economist Style Guide (The Economist Books, 1991).

Reuters Handbook for Journalists by Ian Macdowell (Butterworth-Heinemann, 1992).

The New York Times Manual of Style and Usage edited by Lewis Jordan (Times Books, 1976).*

The UPI Stylebook, 3d ed. (United Press International, 1992).*

U.S. News & World Report Stylebook for Writers and Editors, 7th ed. (U.S. News & World Report, Inc., 1994).*

Wall Street Journal Stylebook, 4th ed. (Dow Jones, 1995).*

Washington Post Deskbook on Style, 2d ed., compiled and edited by Thomas W. Lippman (McGraw-Hill, 1989).*

REFERENCE

American Heritage Dictionary, 3d ed. (Houghton Mifflin, 1992).

Dictionary of Concise Writing by Robert Hartwell Fiske (Writer's Digest Books, 1996).

Merriam-Webster's Collegiate Dictionary, 10th ed. (Merriam-Webster, 1994).

Random House Unabridged Dictionary, 2d ed. (Random House, 1993).

Roget's International Thesaurus, 5th ed. (HarperCollins, 1992).

Webster's New International Dictionary, 2d ed. (G. & C. Merriam, 1961).

Webster's New World Dictionary, 3d college ed. (Simon and Schuster, 1994).

HISTORY

Now the News: The Story of Broadcast Journalism by Edward Bliss, Jr. (Columbia University Press, 1991).*

APPENDIX B

Grammar Hotline Directory

ALABAMA

JACKSONVILLE 36265
  (205) 782-5409—Grammar
  Hotline
  Monday through Friday,
    8:00 a.m. to 4:00 p.m.
  Jacksonville State University

TUSCALOOSA 35487-0244
  (205) 348-5049—Grammar
  Hotline
  Monday through Friday,
    8:30 a.m. to 5 p.m.;
  Tuesday through Thursday,
    6 p.m. to 9 p.m.
  University of Alabama

ARKANSAS

LITTLE ROCK 72204
  (501) 569-3161—Grammar
  Hotline
  Monday through Friday,
    9 a.m. to 2:30 p.m.
  University of Arkansas
    at Little Rock

CALIFORNIA

MOORPARK 93021-1695
  (805) 378-1494—National
    Grammar Hotline
  Monday through Friday,
    8 a.m. to 1 p.m.
  Moorpark College

SACRAMENTO 95823-5799
  (916) 688-7444—English
  Help Line
  Fax (916) 688-7443
  Monday, Wednesday, Friday,
    7 a.m. to 8 a.m.;
  Tuesday and Thursday,
    7 a.m. to 9 a.m.; 24-hour
  answering machine
  Cosumnes River College

SAN JOSE 95120
  (408) 997-1142—
    Karen Gentrup CPS
  Fax (408) 997-2546
  Monday through Sunday,
    8 a.m. to 9 p.m.
  Letter Perfect

COLORADO

PUEBLO 81001-4901
  (719) 549-2787—Grammar
    Hotline
    24-hour answering machine
    —leave message and calls will
  be returned.
  University of Southern Colorado

DELAWARE

NEWARK 19716
  (302) 831-1890—Grammar
    Hotline
  Monday through Friday,
    9 a.m. to noon and
    1 p.m. to 5 p.m.
  University of Delaware

FLORIDA
CORAL GABLES 33124
(305) 284-2956—Grammar
Hotline
Monday, Wednesday,
Thursday and Friday,
9:30 a.m. to 5 p.m.;
Tuesday, 11 a.m. to 7 p.m.
University of Miami

FT. LAUDERDALE 33314
(954) 475-6596—Grammar
Hotline
Monday through Friday,
8 a.m. to 4 p.m.
Broward Community College

PENSACOLA 32514-5751
(904) 474-2129—Grammar
Hotline and Writing Center
Monday through Friday,
8 a.m. to 5 p.m.; some evenings
5 p.m. to 9 p.m., and
Saturday 9 a.m. to noon
University of West Florida

WINTER PARK 32789
(407) 646-2191—Writing Center
and Grammar Hotline
Monday through Friday,
10 a.m. to 7 p.m.; evening
and weekend hours vary.
Rollins College

GEORGIA
ATLANTA 30303-3083
(404) 651-2906—Grammar
Hotline
Monday, 8 a.m. to 7 p.m.;
Tuesday through Thursday,
8 a.m. to 6:30 p.m.;
Friday, 8 a.m. to 4 p.m.;
Saturday, 10 a.m. to 1 p.m.
Georgia State University

ROME 30162-1864
(706) 295-6312—Grammar
Hotline
E-mail JoAnne_Starnes
@floyd.fc.peachnet.edu
Monday through Friday,
9 a.m. to 5 p.m.
Floyd College

ILLINOIS
CHARLESTON 61920-3099
(217) 581-5921—Grammar
Hotline
Monday through Thursday,
9 a.m. to 3 p.m. and
6 p.m. to 9 p.m.;
Friday, 9 a.m. to 1 p.m.
Eastern Illinois University

DES PLAINES 60016-1268
(847) 635-1948—The Writeline:
Dr. Grammar
E-mail richard@oakton.edu
Monday through Friday,
10 a.m. to 2 p.m.
Oakton Community College

NORMAL 61790-4240
(309) 438-2345—Grammar
Hotline
Fax (309) 438-5414
E-mail jvisor@ilstu.edu
Monday through Friday,
9 a.m. to 4 p.m.
Illinois State University

OGLESBY 61348-9691
(815) 224-2720, ext. 491
—Grammar Line
Monday through Friday,
8 a.m. to 4:30 p.m.
Illinois Valley Community College

INDIANA

INDIANAPOLIS 46202-5140
  (317) 274-3000—Writing
  Center Hotline
  Monday though Thursday,
  8:30 a.m. to 6 p.m.;
  Friday, 9 a.m. to 2 p.m.;
  Saturday, 10 a.m. to 3 p.m.
Indiana University

WEST LAFAYETTE 47907
  (317) 494-3723—Grammar
  Hotline
  Fax (317) 494-3780
  E-mail owl@cc.purdue.edu
  WWW http://
  owl.english.purdue.edu/
  Monday through Thursday,
  9 a.m. to 4 p.m.;
  Friday, 9 a.m. to 1 p.m.
Purdue University

KANSAS

EMPORIA 66801-5087
  (316) 341-5380—Grammar
  Hotline
  Monday through Thursday,
  10 a.m. to 4 p.m.;
  Friday, 10 a.m. to 2 p.m.;
  Monday, Tuesday, Thursday,
  7 p.m. to 9 p.m.
Emporia State University

OVERLAND PARK 66210-1299
  (913) 469-4413—Grammar
  Hotline
  Monday through Thursday,
  8 a.m. to 8 p.m.;
  Friday, 8 a.m. to 2 p.m.;
  Saturday, 9 a.m. to 1 p.m.
Johnson County
  Community College

LOUISIANA

LAFAYETTE 70504-4691
  (318) 482-5224—Grammar
  Hotline
  Monday through Friday,
  8 a.m. to 4 p.m.
University of
  Southwestern Louisiana

MARYLAND

BALTIMORE 21250
  (410) 455-6304—Grammar
  Hotline
  Fax (410) 455-1030
  E-mail lharris@umbc.edu
  Monday through Friday,
  1 p.m. to 3 p.m.
University of Maryland
  Baltimore County

COLLEGE PARK 20742
  (301) 405-3787—Grammar
  Hotline
  Monday through Thursday,
  9 a.m. to 4 p.m.;
  Friday, 9 a.m. to 2 p.m.
University of Maryland
  College Park

EMMITSBURG 21727
  (301) 447-5367—Grammar
  Hotline
  Monday through Friday,
  9 a.m. to 5 p.m.
Mount St. Mary's College

MASSACHUSETTS

BOSTON 02115-5096
  (617) 373-2512—Grammar
  Hotline
  Monday through Friday,
  8:30 a.m. to 4:30 p.m.
Northeastern University

LYNN 01901-4093
(617) 593-7284—Grammar
Hotline
Monday through Friday,
9 a.m. to 4 p.m.
North Shore Community College

MICHIGAN
FLINT 48503-2383
(810) 762-0229—Grammar
Hotline
Monday through Thursday,
8:30 a.m. to 3:30 p.m.;
Wednesday and Thursday,
5:30 p.m. to 8 p.m.;
Friday, 8:30 a.m. to 12:30 p.m.
Mott Community College

KALAMAZOO 49008-5031
(616) 387-4442—Writer's Hotline
E-mail ASC_LAB@wmich.edu
Monday through Friday,
9 a.m. to 5 p.m.
Western Michigan University

MINNESOTA
ST. CLOUD 56301-4498
(320) 255-3109—Grammar
Hotline
WWW http://
leo.stcloud.msus.edu
Monday through Thursday,
9 a.m. to 6 p.m.;
Friday, 9 a.m. to 3 p.m.
St. Cloud State University

MISSOURI
JOPLIN 64801-1595
(417) 624-0171—Grammar
Hotline
E-mail dsimpson@clandjop.com
Monday through Friday,
8:30 a.m. to 5 p.m.
Missouri Southern State College

KANSAS CITY 64110-2499
(816) 235-2244—Writer's Hotline
Monday through Friday,
9 a.m. to 4 p.m.
University of Missouri-
Kansas City

SPRINGFIELD 65804-0089
(417) 836-6398—Writer's Hotline
Monday and Thursday,
9 a.m. to 7 p.m.;
Tuesday and Wednesday,
11 a.m. to 9 p.m.;
Friday, 9 a.m. to 1 p.m.
Southern Missouri
State University

ST. LOUIS 63110-1088
(314) 367-8700, ext. 1740
—Writer's Hotline
Fax (314) 367-2784
E-mail tzlatic@slcop.stlcop.edu
Monday through Friday,
9 a.m. to 4 p.m.
St. Louis College of Pharmacy

NEW JERSEY
JERSEY CITY 07305-1597
(201) 200-3337
(201) 200-3338
—Grammar Hotline
Monday through Friday,
9 a.m. to 5 p.m.;
Monday through Thursday,
8 a.m. to 4 p.m. (summer).
Jersey City State College

NORTH CAROLINA
GREENVILLE 27858-4353
(919) 328-6728—Grammar
Hotline
Monday through Wednesday,
9 a.m. to 8 p.m.;
Thursday, 11 a.m. to 5 p.m.;
Friday, 9 a.m. to 2 p.m.
East Carolina University

RALEIGH 27695
ON-LINE ONLY
—On-Line Writing Lab
E-mail grammar@ncsu.edu
WWW http://
www2.ncsu.edu/ncsu/grammar
Daily
North Carolina State University

OHIO
ASHLAND 44805
(419) 289-5110
(419) 289-5156
—Writing Advice
E-mail shuff@ashland.edu
Monday through Thursday,
10 a.m. to 9 p.m.;
Friday, 10 a.m. to 4 p.m.
Ashland University

CINCINNATI 45236
(513) 745-5731—Grammar
Hotline
Fax (513) 745-5771
Monday through Friday,
9 a.m. to 5 p.m.

CLEVELAND 44122-6195
(216) 987-2050—Grammar
Hotline
Monday through Thursday,
9 a.m. to 3 p.m.;
Saturday, 10 a.m. to 2 p.m.
Cuyahoga Community College

DELAWARE 43015
(614) 368-3925—Writing
Resource Center's Hotline
Fax (614) 368-3299
Monday through Friday,
9 a.m. to noon and
1 p.m. to 4 p.m.,
September through April.
Ohio Wesleyan University

ORRVILLE 44667
(216) 683-2010—Grammar
Hotline
Monday through Thursday,
9 a.m. to 5 p.m.;
Friday, 9 a.m. to noon
University of Akron
Wayne College

TOLEDO 43606-3390
(419) 530-4939—Writing Center
Monday through Friday,
9 a.m. to 5 p.m.
University of Toledo

OKLAHOMA
BETHANY 73008
(405) 491-6328—Grammar
Hotline
Fax (405) 491-6659
Monday through Friday,
9 a.m. to 5 p.m.
Southern Nazarene University

CHICKASHA 73018
(405) 224-8622—Grammar
Hotline
Monday through Friday,
9 a.m. to 5 p.m.
Mrs. Underwood,
retired teacher and editor

STILLWATER 74075
(405) 744-6671—Grammar
Hotline
E-mail
write-i@vml.ucc.okstate.com
Monday and Thursday,
11:30 a.m. to 7:30 p.m.;
Wednesday and Friday,
9 a.m. to 5 p.m.

OREGON

PORTLAND 97207-0751
  (503) 725-3570—Writing Helpline
  E-mail wrcenter@irn.pdx.edu
  Monday through Friday,
    9 a.m. to 5 p.m.
  Portland State University

PENNSYLVANIA

GLEN MILLS 19342
  (610) 399-1130
  Monday through Friday,
    9 a.m. to 5 p.m.
  Burger Associates

PHILADELPHIA 19122
  (215) 204-5612—Writer's
    Helpline
  Fax (215) 204-7083
  E-mail
    lsalem@nimbus.ocis.temple.edu
  Monday through Friday,
    8:30 a.m. to 3:30 p.m.;
    24-hour answering machine.
  Temple University

PITTSBURGH 15232
  (412) 344-9759—Grammar
    Hotline
  Monday through Friday,
    9 a.m. to 5 p.m.;
    24-hour answering machine.
  Chatham College

SOUTH CAROLINA

CHARLESTON 29409
  (803) 953-3194—Writing Hotline
  Fax (803) 953-7084
  E-mail williamsa@citadel.edu
  Monday through Friday,
    8 a.m. to 5 p.m.;
    Sunday through Thursday,
    7 p.m. to 10 p.m.
  The Citadel

CHARLESTON 29401
  (803) 792-6390—Grammar
    Hotline
  Fax (803) 792-9179
  E-mail waldrept@musc.edu
  Monday through Friday,
    8:30 a.m. to 5 p.m.
  Medical University
    of South Carolina

COLUMBIA 29208
  (803) 777-7020—Writer's Hotline
  Monday through Friday,
    9 a.m. to 5 p.m.
  University of South Carolina

SPARTANBURG 29302
  (864) 596-9186—Grammar
    Hotline
  Monday through Friday,
    9 a.m. to noon;
    Monday through Thursday,
    1:15 p.m. to 6 p.m.
  Converse College

TENNESSEE

NASHVILLE 37209-4515
  (615) 353-3349—The Grammar
    Doctor
  Fax (615) 353-3558
  E-mail
    grammar_dr@nsti.tec.tn.usnsti
  Monday through Friday,
    8 a.m. to 4:30 p.m.
  Nashville State Technical Institute

TEXAS

AMARILLO 79178-0001
  (806) 374-4726—Grammar
    Hotline
  Monday through Thursday,
    8 a.m. to 9 p.m.;
    Friday, 8 a.m. to 3 p.m.
  Amarillo College

AUSTIN 78712
  (512) 475-8372—Grammar
  Hotline
  E-mail writing@uts.cc.utexas.edu
  Monday through Thursday,
  9 a.m. to 7 p.m.;
  Friday, 9 a.m. to 3 p.m.
  University of Texas

HOUSTON 77002
  (713) 221-8670—Grammarline
  Monday through Thursday,
  7:30 a.m. to 9 p.m.;
  Friday, 7:30 a.m. to 2 p.m.;
  Saturday, 11 a.m. to 4 p.m.
  University of Houston Downtown

SAN ANTONIO 78212-4299
  (210) 733-2503—Grammar
  Hotline
  Monday through Thursday,
  8 a.m. to 8 p.m.;
  Friday, 8 a.m. to 3 p.m.
  San Antonio College

VIRGINIA

BLACKSBURG 24061-0112
  (540) 231-5436—Grammar
  Hotline
  E-mail gram@vt.edu
  Monday through Friday,
  8 a.m. to 5 p.m.

STERLING 20164
  (703) 450-2511—Grammar
  Hotline
  Monday through Thursday,
  9 a.m. to 3 p.m.;
  Friday, 9 a.m. to 1 p.m.
  Northern Virginia Community
  College - Loudoun Campus

VIRGINIA BEACH 23456
  (757) 427-7170—Grammar
  Hotline
  E-mail writcent@vblrc2.tc.cc.va.us
  Monday through Friday,
  10 a.m. to noon;
  additional day and evening
  hours vary.
  Tidewater Community College

WEST VIRGINIA

CHARLESTON 25302
  (304) 343-2644
  Daily, 8 a.m. to 6 p.m.;
  24-hour answering machine,
  7 days a week.
  Mrs. Cardea

WISCONSIN

MILWAUKEE 53211
  (414) 229-2260—Grammar
  Hotline
  E-mail tarc@csd.uwm.edu
  Monday through Thursday,
  9:30 a.m. to 2:30 p.m.;
  Friday, 9:30 a.m. to 1:30 p.m.
  University of Wisconsin
  Milwaukee

PLATTEVILLE 53818-3099
  (608) 342-1615—Grammar
  Hotline
  E-mail grammar@uwplatt.edu
  Monday through Thursday,
  9 a.m. to 4 p.m.;
  Friday, 9 a.m. to noon.
  University of Wisconsin
  Platteville

STEVENS POINT 54481-3897
  (715) 346-3568—Tutoring
    Writing Lab Hotline
  E-mail drucinsk@uwsp.edu
  Monday through Thursday,
    9 a.m. to 4 p.m.;
    Friday, 9 a.m. to noon
  University of Wisconsin
    Stevens Point

CANADA

EDMONTON, ALBERTA T6J 2B7
  (403) 497-5663—Grammar
    Hotline
  Fax (403) 497-5347
  Monday through Friday,
    9 a.m. to 11:30 a.m.
  Grant MacEwan
    Community College

INDEX

A

Absolutes, 109
Accidents, 202, 203, 207, 218, 240
Accuracy, 130, 196-97, 199, 201
Action, 8, 9, 39, 40, 47, 129, 131, 134, 151, 152, 196, 206, 271, 272
vs. reaction, 104, 197, 240, 248, 262
Action verbs, 8-9, 39
Active voice, 8, 73, 128, 130
Adjectives, 131, 180
Adverbs, 46
After, 231, 290
Ages, 101, 200, 240-41
Albee, Edward, 245
Alliteration, 60, 227
Ambiguity, 199-201, 206-7, 208
American Heritage Book of English Usage, 269
American Heritage Dictionary, 179-80, 188, 269
American Usage and Style: The Consensus, 86, 186, 269
Amiel, Henri Frédéric, 71
Amis, Martin, 70
Angell, Roger, 188-89
Animal Farm, 128
Anthropomorphism, 212
Are, 8, 36, 40
Aristotle, 61, 65, 245
Arnold, Matthew, 61
Ascham, Roger, 63
Associated Press Broadcast News Style Book, The, 145, 146

Associated Press Guide to News Writing, The, 130, 170
Associated Press Radio-Television News Style Book, The, 146
Associated Press Stylebook and Libel Manual, The, 25, 212, 256
Attribution, 7, 15, 37-38, 41-42, 15, 109, 112, 142-45, 211, 277
Audience, 135, 143, 179

B

Bacon, Francis, 228
Baker, Sheridan, 164
Barzun, Jacques, 68, 132-33, 285
Basic News Writing, 33
Bates, Jefferson D., 134-35
Bates, Norman, 257
BBC Style Guide, 21, 194
Beginning Broadcast Newswriting, 135, 147
Bell Labs, 44
Belloc, Hilaire, 61
Berle, Milton, 166
Bernstein, Theodore M., 28, 85, 172, 192, 269
Berriochoa, Mike, 173
Bismarck, Chancellor Otto von, 246
Bliss, Jr., Edward, 143, 147, 153, 212, 232
Bohnen, Jerry, 155
Boileau, Nicholas, 61
Bostian, Prof. Lloyd, 129
Brave New World, 264

Brecht, Bertholt, 64
Brevity, 128, 130-31
Brinkley, Christie, 15
Brinkley, David, 15
Brix, Dale, 22, 144
Broadcast Newswriting as Process, 146
Broadcast Journalism, 143, 146
Broadcast News, 32, 144, 147, 154
Broadcast News Manual of Style, A, 147
Broadcast News Process, The, 144 146
Broadcast News Style Guide, 254
Broadcast News Writing, 144, 146
Broadcast Newswriting, 143, 145
Broadcast Newswriting as Process, 144
Broadcast News Wriiting, Reporting and Production, 144, 154
Broadcast News Writing & Reporting, 144, 147
Broadcast News Writing Stylebook, 144
Broadcast Writing, 147
Broadcast Writing Style Guide, 146
Brooks, Brian S., 144
Broussard, E. Joseph, 143, 146
Brown, Jr., H. Jackson, 284
Browning, Robert, 159
Bryson, Bill, 217
Buffon, Georges de, 65
Bundy, McGeorge, 185
Bunyan, John, 71
Burns, George, 29
Butler, Samuel, 247
Buttafuoco, Joseph, 12

C

Caldwell, John, 186
Callihan, E.L., 169, 171
Camus, Albert, 62
Canadian Press, 255
Canby, Henry Seidel, 65
Capote, Truman, 65
Cappon, René J., 130, 163
Careful Writer, The, 28, 85, 192, 269
Carlin, George, 218
Carlyle, Thomas, 230
Carver, George Washington, 265
Catchphrases, 28

"CBS Evening News with Walter Cronkite," 153, 289-90
CBS News, 145, 153, 164-65
Champollion, Jean François, 180
Charles, Prince of Wales, 196-97
Charnley, Mitchell V., 146
Chekhov, Anton, 131
Cheney, Theodore A. Rees, 43, 133, 151
Chesterfield, Lord (Philip Dormer Stanhope), 62
Chicago Sun-Times, 245
Chicago Tribune, 243
Chronological order, 202-4
Ciardi, John, 28, 286
Clarity, 35, 43, 59-71, 130-31, 203-5, 208, 210, 279
Clark, Roy Peter, 135-36
Clark, Terry, 246
Clichés, 19-20, 27-29, 148-50, 156-58, 166-71, 185-86, 227-28, 234-35, 274
Clinton, Hillary Rodham, 279
Clinton, President William, 222, 225
Coates, Charles, 143
Cohler, David Keith, 143
Cohn, Alan, 192
Coleridge, Samuel Taylor, 65, 67, 68
Collective nouns, 229-30, 237
Colton, Charles Caleb, 61
Commands, 55, 235
Communicator, 128, 186, 271, 281
Complete Stylist and Handbook, The, 164
Confucius, 18, 61
Connectives, 42-43
Content, 68, 70
Contractions, 45
Conversational language, 7, 10, 11, 12, 17, 30, 33, 36, 38, 42, 45, 48, 64, 69, 132, 142, 143, 144, 145
Cooper, Gary, 278
Cooper, James Fenimore, 274
Copperud, Roy, 86, 186, 269
Copy
    faulty, 233-36
    humanizing, 39
    reading aloud, 48-49
Copy Editor, 260-61

Courtesy titles, 142, 186-88 (See also *Miss, Mr., Mrs., Ms.*)
Crafting News for the Electronic Media, 143, 147-48
Cremer, Charles F., 56
Crews, Frederick, 151-52
Cronkite, Walter, 2
Crosby, Norm, 257
Cumulative sentence, 43
Custer, George Armstrong, 243

D

Daily News (New York), 246
Daley, Bill, 245
Daley, Mayor Richard J., 139
Dangling modifier, 238
Datelines, 21, 120, 240
Deadlines, 289
Deerslayer, The, 274
Degas, Edgar, 199
Dependent clauses, 5-6
Dewhurst, Colleen, 245
Diana, Princess of Wales, 196-97
Dickinson, Emily, 263
Dictionary, use of, 193-94
Dictionary of Americanisms, 191
Dictionary of Clichés, 185
Dictionary of Word and Phrase Origins, 185
Disasters, 217, 230-33
Don'ts, 1-18
Doolittle, James H., 244
Dryden, John, 63
Dunsany, Lord, 61

E

Ear
   writing for, 15, 34, 35, 47, 76, 131, 139, 143, 146, 147, 202, 211
Echo-chamber effect, 52
Eckert, Allan W., 96
Economist, The, 244, 256-57
Editor & Publisher, 246
Einstein, Albert, 189

Elements of Legal Style, The, 44
Elements of Style, The, 14, 43, 167, 174, 215-16
Elgar, Sir Edward, 185
Eliot, T.S., 18, 186, 202
Elizabeth, Queen, 196, 273
Emerson, Ralph Waldo, 64
Emphasis, 43-45, 70, 131, 133, 137, 138, 151, 274
Encyclopedia Britannica, 190
ENG: Television News, 56
Espy, William R., 187
Euphemisms, 24
Euripides, 32
Evans, Bergen, 174, 270
Evans, Cornelia, 270
Evans, Harold, 46, 167
Exercises, 97-127

F

Facts, overuse of, 15
Factual errors, 18, 242-47
Falstaff, 93
Fang, Irving E., 143
Faulkner, William, 284
Fénelon, François, 66
Fenollosa, Ernest, 40
Ferguson, Charles W., 68
Figures of speech, 167
Fishlock, Trevor, 187
Follett, Wilson, 70, 270
Forbes, Steve, 236
Ford, Ford Madox, 67
Foreign words/phrases, 128, 174
Fowler, Francis G., 132
Fowler, Henry W., 28-29, 67, 132, 222
Fox, Michael J., 11
France, Anatole, 60, 65
Francis of Assisi, Saint, 185
Franklin, Benjamin, 186, 243
Freeman, Douglas Southall, 137-38
Frequently asked questions (FAQ), 275-81
Fry, Don, 50

G

Galen, 245
Garner, Bryan A., 44
Garvey, Daniel E., 143
Gass, William, 63
Gerunds, 223-24
Getting the Words Right: How to Revise, Edit & Rewrite, 43, 133, 151
Gibbon, Edward, 67, 70
Gibbs, Wolcott, 30
Gibson, Roy, 143
Gilbert, William S., 30, 233
Glenn, John, 22
Glubok, Norman, 191
Godard, Jean-Luc, 68
Goethe, Johann Wolfgang von, 61
Goetz, Bernhard, 172, 191-92
Golden Book on Writing, The, 43, 151
Goldwyn, Sam, 162
Goodwin, Doris Kearns, 245
Goof/Proofer, 270
Gorbachev, Mikhail, 142, 145, 148
Gossip, 211, 219
Grammar, 136, 139, 221, 222, 229, 270, 275
Grammar for Journalists, 169
Grammar Hotline Directory, 270, 297-304
Grammar, Rhetoric and Composition, 169
Grand jury, 16
Graves, Robert, 41, 268
Greenfield, Jeff, 286
Grey, Prof. David L., 286
Grimm, Baron Friedrich Melchior, 65
Gunning, Robert, 134

H

Hall, Mark W., 143, 146
Halley's Comet, 162
Harding, Tonya, 238
Hare, August W., 63
Harper Dictionary of Contemporary Usage, 270
Harris, Sydney J., 288
Hart, Sen. Gary, 148
Hausman, Carl, 143, 147-48

Hawthorne, Nathaniel, 66
Hazlitt, William, 64, 69
Hearst, Patty, 188, 189
Hemingway, Ernest, 48-50, 62, 67, 286
Hill, Benny, 202
Hoaxes, 47
Hohenberg, Prof. John, 99
Holgate, Jack F., 143 146
Homophones, 201-2
Hoover, J. Edgar, 11
Hotaling, Burton L., 145-46
Hoyt, James L., 143, 147
Hubbard, Elbert, 289
Hubbard, Frank McKinney, 211
Hughes, Robert, 285
Hugo, Victor, 149
Humor, 287

I

I, 45, 142, 270
Inging, 221-25
Interpretative Reporting, 168-69
Interviews, 268
Irony, 194
Irving, Washington, 69
Is, 8, 40
It is, 8, 151-52
Ives, Mitchell, 62

J

Jackson, Allan, 153
Jackson, Glenda, 287
Jackson, Jesse, 274
Jail/prison, 12
Jargon, 128, 171-72, 204-5, 216, 218
Johnson, Greg, 272
Johnson, Samuel, 64, 166
Jones, John Paul, 11
Jonson, Ben, 64, 67, 68
Jordan, Lewis, 270
Joubert, Joseph, 61, 68
Journalese, 34, 169, 197, 210, 213, 214, 226, 227, 228, 268, 275
Journalism Quarterly, 129

Journalist's Notebook of Live Radio-TV News, 144
Jury, 16

K

Keach, Stacy, 159
Keirstead, Phillip O., 56, 144
Kelly, Grace, 278
Kennedy, Sen. Edward, 184
Kerrigan, Nancy, 237-38
Kilpatrick, James J., 70, 139-40
King, Martin Luther, 11
King's English, The, 132
Kitman, Marvin, 253
Knight, Ted, 246
Koch, Mayor, 272

L

Lambuth, David, 43, 44, 151
Landor, Walter Savage, 61
Lash, Joseph, 245
Last Hurrah, The, 148
Last word, 43-45
Latimore, Dan, 144, 146
Lazarus, Emma, 91
Leads, 3, 4, 5, 6, 8, 9, 10, 11, 12, 13, 15, 21, 24, 32, 34, 36, 40, 41, 42, 44, 50, 52, 154, 155, 158, 165
Lead-ins, 28, 51-54, 56, 73, 77, 78, 79, 80, 82, 83, 85, 88, 89, 90, 124, 186, 190, 191, 205, 206, 207, 210, 247, 248, 261
Lead-outs, 51, 56
Lee, Robert E., 138
Legalese, 209-11
LeHand, Missy, 245
Lewis, Carolyn Diana, 144
Libin, Scott, 237
Lincoln, Abraham, 214
Listeners, 2, 3, 4, 5, 6, 7, 9, 10, 11, 12, 13, 14, 15, 16, 17, 20, 23, 25, 26, 27, 30, 32, 34, 35, 36, 37, 38, 39, 42, 45, 46, 47, 48, 50, 51, 52, 54, 55, 60
Longfellow, Henry Wadsworth, 265
Los Angeles Times, 25

Lucas, F.L., 43
Luce, Henry, 30

M

McBoing-Boing, Gerald, 223
McCarthy, Colman, 28
Macaulay, Thomas Babington, 69
MacDonald, R. H., 147
MacDougall, Curtis D., 168-69
McFadyen, John, 196, 220
McNamara, Robert S., 185
MacNeal, Edward, 260
McQuain, Jeffrey, 188-89
Major, Prime Minister John, 222
Mallery, Richard D., 169
Manual of Radio News Writing, A, 145-46
Martin, Steve, 211
Marx, Groucho, 239
Mason, James, 178
Math, 159, 259-61
Mathsemantics: Making Numbers Talk Sense, 260
Matthews, Mitford M., 191
Maugham, W. Somerset, 63, 65
Maurois, André, 70
Mayeux, Peter E., 144, 147
Meador, Ron, 21
Meanwhile, 21
Mencher, Melvin, 33, 144, 189
Meppen, Adrian J., 146, 154
Metaphors, 128, 166-67, 169, 172
Middle initials, 11
Middle names, 11, 225, 265
Mies van der Rohe, Ludwig, 15
Mill, John Stuart, 66
Miss, 187, 188
Missouri Group, The, 144
Misspellings, 232, 246, 249
Mitterand, Francois, 272
Mixed metaphors, 172
Modern American Usage, 270
Modern English Usage, 28-29
Modifiers, 217
Moen, Daryl R., 144
Montaigne, Michel de, 69
Montgomery, Michael, 270

Moore, Mary Tyler, 11
Morley, Christopher, 62-63, 66
Morris, William and Mary, 185
Moses, 179
Mosley, Walter, 244
Mosse, Baskett, 146
Mount St. Helens, 189-90
Mr., 142, 187, 188
Mrs., 187, 188
Ms., 186-88
Ms. magazine, 246
Murrow, Edward R., 11, 35
Murry, J. Middleton, 62, 65

N

Names, 10, 11
Natural sound, 55-56
Naval Terms Dictionary, 174
Navratilova, Martina, 175
"NBC News Update," 96
Nelson, Admiral Horatio, 204
Nelson, Dick, 191
Nero, 284
New Republic, 246
New Yorker, 26, 27, 30, 188-89
New York Observer, 245-46
New York Times, 26, 28, 37, 185, 188,
    217, 230, 242-44, 246, 274, 287
*New York Times Manual of Style and
    Usage,* 187, 255, 270
News, 12, 13, 33, 248
    characterization of, 5, 110, 178, 179,
    262, 263
News on the Air, 146
News by Radio, 146
News Reporting and Writing, 144
News releases, 11, 47
Newscasts, one-minute, 57-58
Newsman's English, 46, 167
Newspapers, 15, 16, 17, 242-47
Newswriting for the Electronic Media,
    143
Nicknames, 11
1984, 128
Niwa, Paul, 222
Nixon, President Richard, 148

Nominal style, 129-30
Nominative case, 229
Numbers, 9, 15, 16, 81, 120, 136, 206,
    231, 232, 238

O

Obituaries, 48, 188
O'Connor, Cardinal John, 246
O'Connor, Edwin, 148
O'Connor, Martin J., 48
O'Neill, Thomas "Tip," 272
100 Ways to Improve Your Writing, 136
Orwell, George, 128-29, 167, 175
Othello, 185
Oxford English Dictionary, 166

P

Papper, Robert A., 144
Paraphrasing, 45, 147
Paris Review, 49-50
Participial phrases, 5-6, 137, 223
Participle, 5, 191, 232
    vs. verbs, 221-25
Partridge, Eric, 185
Pascal, Blaise, 66
Passive voice, 73, 39-40, 128, 130, 164
Past tense, 25
Pauses, 43, 55, 114, 148
*Penguin Dictionary of Troublesome
    Words,* 217
Percentages, 260-61
Periodic sentence, 43-44
Personal pronouns, 11-12
Peterson, Prof. Ted, 186
Philip, Prince, 196
Picasso, Pablo, 10
Place-name, 164-65, 176, 196, 202-3,
    240
Plimpton, George, 49
Pocket Guide to Correct Grammar, A,
    229
Politics and the English Language, 129
Polya, George, 66
Pope, Alexander, 63, 65, 166, 167
Porter, Katherine Anne, 66, 67

Power Language, 188-89
Poynter Institute for Media Studies, 135-36, 237
Practical English Usage, 270
Prepositions, 43, 164
  personal pronouns and, 229
Present perfect tense, 92, 158-59
Present tense, 41, 161
Presley, Elvis, 244
Press releases, 47
Print newswriting, 15-16
Prison/jail, 12
Professional's TV News Handbook, 143
Pronouns, 11, 45-46, 229
Pronunciation, 288
Provost, Gary, 136
Pulitzer Prize, 137, 138
Punctuation, 114-15
Puns, 148, 287
Python, Monty, 23

Q

Quality control, 282-83
Questions, 7, 42, 48, 75, 160-63, 207
Quill, 187-88
Quintilian, 61, 64, 66
Quotations, 7, 42, 45, 142-48
Quote, unquote, 145-48, 279

R

Radio News Handbook, 146
Radio News Writing and Editing, 144
Radio and Television Reporting, 143
Radio-Television News Directors Association, 128
Random House Handbook, The, 151-52
Ranly, Don, 144
Reader's Digest, 17
Reading aloud, 48-49
Reagan, President Ronald, 145, 148
Redundancies, 172-77, 198-200, 207, 209, 213, 217-20, 267, 280
Report, 166, 211
Reporting for Television, 144
Reuters Handbook for Journalists, 255

Rewriting, 5, 13, 48-50, 163, 164, 165; 166, 247, 283, 290
  Amtrak funding (script), 125-27
  coffee and lung cancer (script), 110-12
  construction crane collapse (script), 117-20
  elephant rampage (script), 239-41
  gorilla's rescue of boy (script), 98-99
  library fire (script), 112-15
  Pope's visit (script), 120-23
  Princess Diana's second child (script), 104-7
  prisoner's escape from plane (script), 99-104
  Redskins tickets to capture fugitives (script), 115-17
  Sakharov's smuggled letters (script), 107-110
  sinkhole (script), 123-25
Richmond News Leader, 138-39
Rivers, William L., 143
Roberts, Chalmers, 245
Rogers, Roy, 166
Rogers, Will, 287
Romance languages, 132
Ronstadt, Linda, 185
Roosevelt, Eleanor, 245
Roosevelt, President Franklin D., 244, 245
Rosetta stone, 180
Royko, Mike, 27
Rules for writing, 128-40
Rumors, 166, 211
Ruskin, John, 212
Ruth, George Herman "Babe," 257-58
Rutherfurd, Lucy, 245

S

Safire, William, 67, 68, 69, 188, 195, 204
Sain, Johnny (pitcher), 3
Salvi, John, 261
Saussure, Albertine Adrienne Necker de, 65
Says, 29, 45, 99, 112

Schiller, Friedrich von, 64
Schopenhauer, Arthur, 71
Scientific words, 128
Sentences
  cumulative, 43
  emphasis in, 43-45
  incomplete, 200, 219-20, 223, 234
  linking, 42-43
  loose, 43
  periodic, 43-44
  positive form, 41, 175
  short, 38
  subject-verb-object pattern in, 6, 7, 12, 38, 114
Sequence, 138, 139, 231
Shakespeare, William, 28, 40-41, 71, 225
Shakur, Tupac, 277
Shannon, Ridge, 195, 216
Shaw, George Bernard, 63, 70, 71
Sheridan, Richard Brimsley, 64
Shook, Frederick, 144, 146
Silence, 55-56
Siller, Bob, 164
Sills, Beverly, 284
Silvers, Phil, 265
Similes, 128, 166-67
Simple & Direct, 132-33
Sins, 19-31
Smart Money, 243
Smeyak, G. Paul, 144
Smith, Sydney, 64
Smithsonian Institution, 245
Society for the Preservation of English Language and Literature (SPELL), 270
Source copy, 32, 33, 46-47, 49, 50
Sources, 7, 37, 142, 143, 144, 145, 146, 211, 253-55
Sportswriters, 171-72, 255-58
Stein, M.L., 134
Steinem, Gloria, 187, 246
Stendhal, Marie Henri Beyle, 63
Stephens, Mitchell, 32, 144, 147, 154
Sterne, Laurence, 64
Stevens, Wallace, 62
Stevenson, Robert Louis, 64, 70

Stone, Emerson, 200, 218
Stone, Lucy, 185
Stowe, Harriet Beecher, 265
Stratton, John, 270
Strunk, Jr., William, 2, 14, 35, 43, 46, 66, 167, 174-76, 192, 215
Style, 43
Style, 59-71
Styron, William, 71
Subject-verb-object (s-v-o), 6, 7, 12, 38, 114
Subordinate clauses, 38
Superlatives, 190
Surmelian, Leon, 68
Swan, Michael, 270
Swift, Jonathan, 64
Switzer, Barry, 255-56, 258
Synonyms, 29-30, 269
Syntax, 207-8, 219, 229-30, 236

T

Tags, 52, 56, 81, 90
Tease(r)s, 51, 57, 91, 262
Technique of Clear Writing, The, 134
Television News, Radio News, 143
Television News Reporting, 145
Television Newswriting: Captivating an Audience, 144
Ten Commandments, 2, 179
Tennyson, Alfred Lord, 247
Thaw, Evelyn Nesbitt, 189
Thaw, Harry K., 189
There is, there are, 8, 150-52
Thesaurus, 269
Thompson, Emma, 10
Thoreau, Henry David, 67
Tiernan, Joe, 281
Time, references to, 156, 181-84
Time, 154, 155, 156, 158, 181, 182
Timeliness, 33
Times, (London), 187-88, 217
Tips
  news, 48, 247, 290
  writing, 1, 2, 9, 32-50, 54, 130
Tobin, Richard L., 187
Today, 153-57

"Today" show, 92-93
Toner, Albert, 169-70
Tonight, 157-59
Transitions, 21, 22, 110, 155, 191, 234, 235, 272
Trimble, John R., 133, 151
Trollope, Anthony, 63
TV News Off-Camera, 145
Twain, Mark, 25, 67, 128, 271, 274-75

U

Umbrella leads, 80, 165
United Press International Broadcast Stylebook, The, 145, 214
Updike, John, 10
USA Today, 246
Usage, 62, 140, 179, 180, 187, 188, 195, 269, 270
Ustinov, Dmitri, 185

V

Vague words, 166
Vanderbilt, Gloria, 189
Verbs
  intransitive, 40
  transitive, 40, 41
Voice
  active, 8, 39, 73, 128, 130
  passive, 39-40, 73, 128, 130, 164
Voice-overs, 51, 54-56, 84, 85
Volcanoes, 189-90
Voltaire, François Marie Arouet, 65
von Bülow, Claus, 189

W

Waite, Terry, 206
Wall Street Journal, 189, 243
Wall Street Journal Stylebook, 254-55
Walters, Roger L., 147
Warren, Carl, 144
Warren, Fran, 246
Washington, George, 138, 267
Washington Monthly, The, 245
Washington Post, 245
Waste Land, The, 186

Way with Words, A, 43
We, 45
Weather, 22-23, 211-16, 278
Weaver, J. Clark, 144, 146
Webber, Andrew Lloyd, 11
Webster's New International Dictionary, 269
Webster's New World Dictionary, 188
Webster's Unabridged Dictionary, 34
Weinbaum, William, 171-72
Wesley, Rev. Samuel, 62
Whissen, Thomas, 43
White, E.B., 2, 14, 35, 43, 46, 66, 68, 167, 174-75, 192, 215
White, Paul W., 146
White, Stanford, 189
White, Ted, 144, 146, 154
Whitney, Richard, 189
Wilde, Oscar, 70, 256, 285-86
Wilkins, John, 67
Wilson Quarterly, 245
Wimer, Arthur, 22, 144
Winners & Sinners, 185
Wire copy, 32, 34, 46-47
Wolfe, Tom, 286
Word, The, 130, 163
Wordiness, 163-64, 223
Words to avoid
  accessorize, 24
  accord, 17
  actually, 20, 153, 216
  approximately, 25
  arguably, 24, 188, 189
  byzantine, 23
  commence, 25
  controversial, 24, 184-85, 274
  details, 13
  draconian, 23
  evanescent, 23
  flatly, 20
  gratis, 26
  gubernatorial, 23
  here, 45-46
  however, 27, 232
  icon, 24
  implement, 25
  infrastructure, 23

initialize, 179
initiate, 25
interactive, 24
interface, 24
involved, 24
literally, 20
meaningful, 24
meanwhile, 21
methodology, 24
miraculously, 20
Ms., 186-89
near miss, mid-air collision, near-panic, near-riot, 204
nevertheless, 27
no, not in leads, 13-14
notwithstanding, 27
our, 45
out, 46
parameters, 24
parenting, 24
personally, 20, 273
per, 26
pled, 25
print news terms, 15-17
prioritize, 24
pro-active, 24
probe, 249
quote, unquote, end of quotation, 145-48, 279-80
really, 20
rush, 20
scenario, 24, 213
situation, 23
slay, 17
spectacular, 31, 210
stemwinder, 149

supportive, 24
swanky, 219
therefore, 27
unusual, 5
utilize, 25
vagaries, 23
via, 26
viable, 24
youth, 17
Words into Type, 171
"WordWatching," 128, 186
Workbook for Radio and TV News Editing and Writing, 22, 144
Write Clearly—Speak Effectively, 134
Writer's Art, The, 140
Writer's Digest School, 131-32
Writer's Hotline Handbook, 270
Writing News for Broadcast, 143, 147, 153
Writing with Precision, 134-35
Writing and Reporting Broadcast News, 143, 146
Writing with Style, 133, 151
Written Word, The, 168
Wulfemeyer, K. Tim, 135, 145, 147

Y

Yeltsin, President Boris, 222
Yesterday, 12-13, 155
Yoakam, Richard D., 56
Young, Steve, 146, 154
Youngman, Henny, 166

Z

Zousmer, Steven, 145